IMAGES
of America

FARMINGTON WILTON, KINGFIELD, AND SUGARLOAF

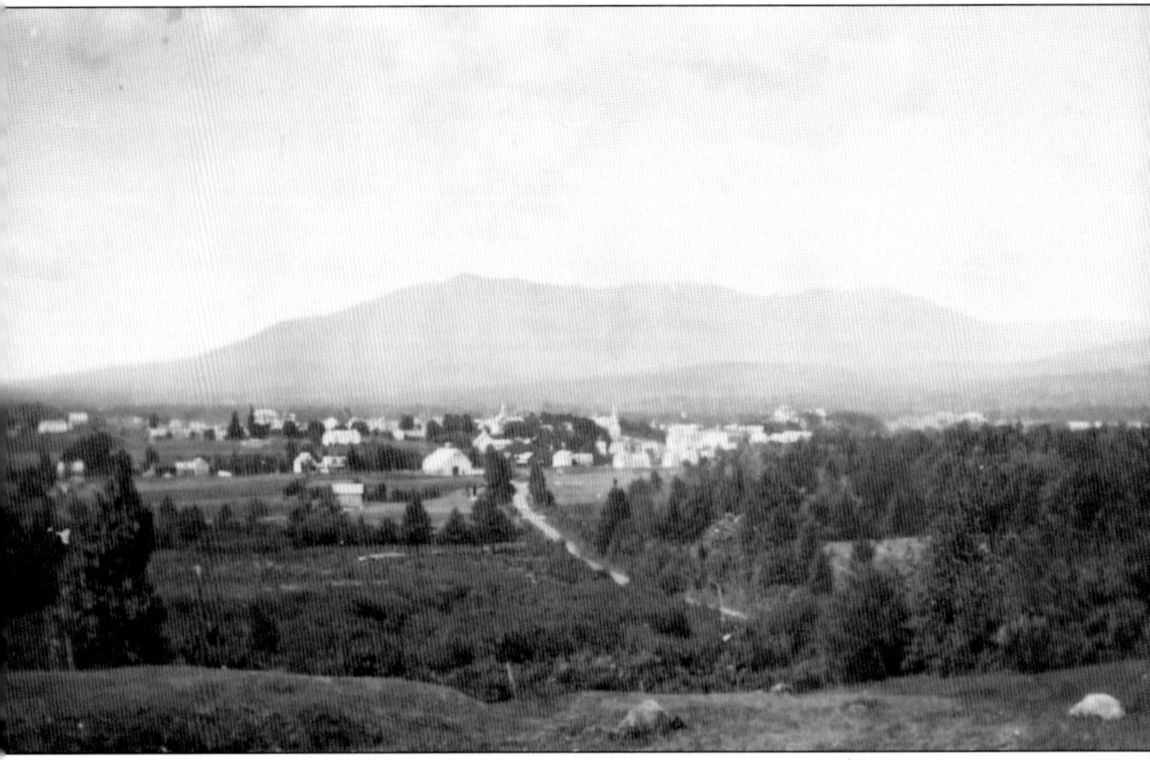

View of Kingfield from a postcard with Mr. Abram in the background, *c.* early 1900s. It gives some idea of this entire area's scenic beauty.

IMAGES
of America

FARMINGTON WILTON, KINGFIELD, AND SUGARLOAF

Frank H. Sleeper
From the Maine Historic Preservation Commission and Others

ARCADIA
PUBLISHING

ISBN 978-0-7385-6396-1

Published by Arcadia Publishing
Charleston, South Carolina

Printed in the United States of America

Library of Congress Catalog Card Number: 2008938740

For all general information contact Arcadia Publishing at:
Telephone 843-853-2070
Fax 843-853-0044
E-mail sales@arcadiapublishing.com
For customer service and orders:
Toll-Free 1-888-313-2665

Visit us on the Internet at www.arcadiapublishing.com

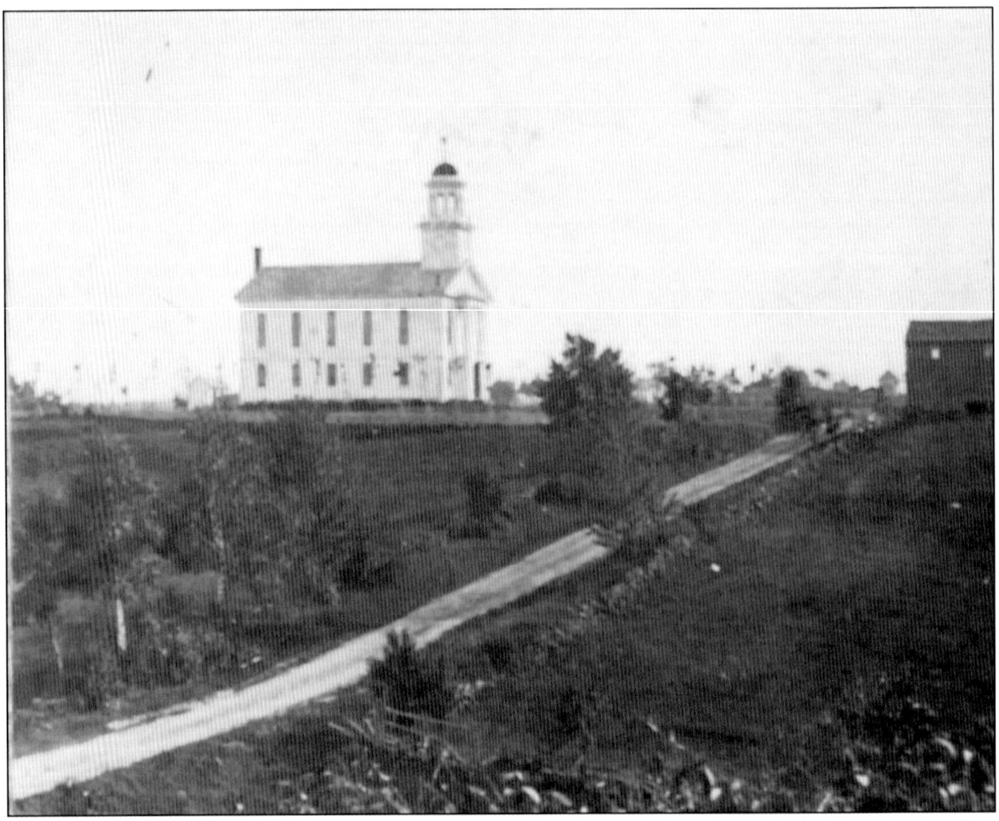

Wilton Academy, *c.* 1880s. The academy had a disastrous fire in May 1980, but was restored as a brick building and is now an elementary school.

Contents

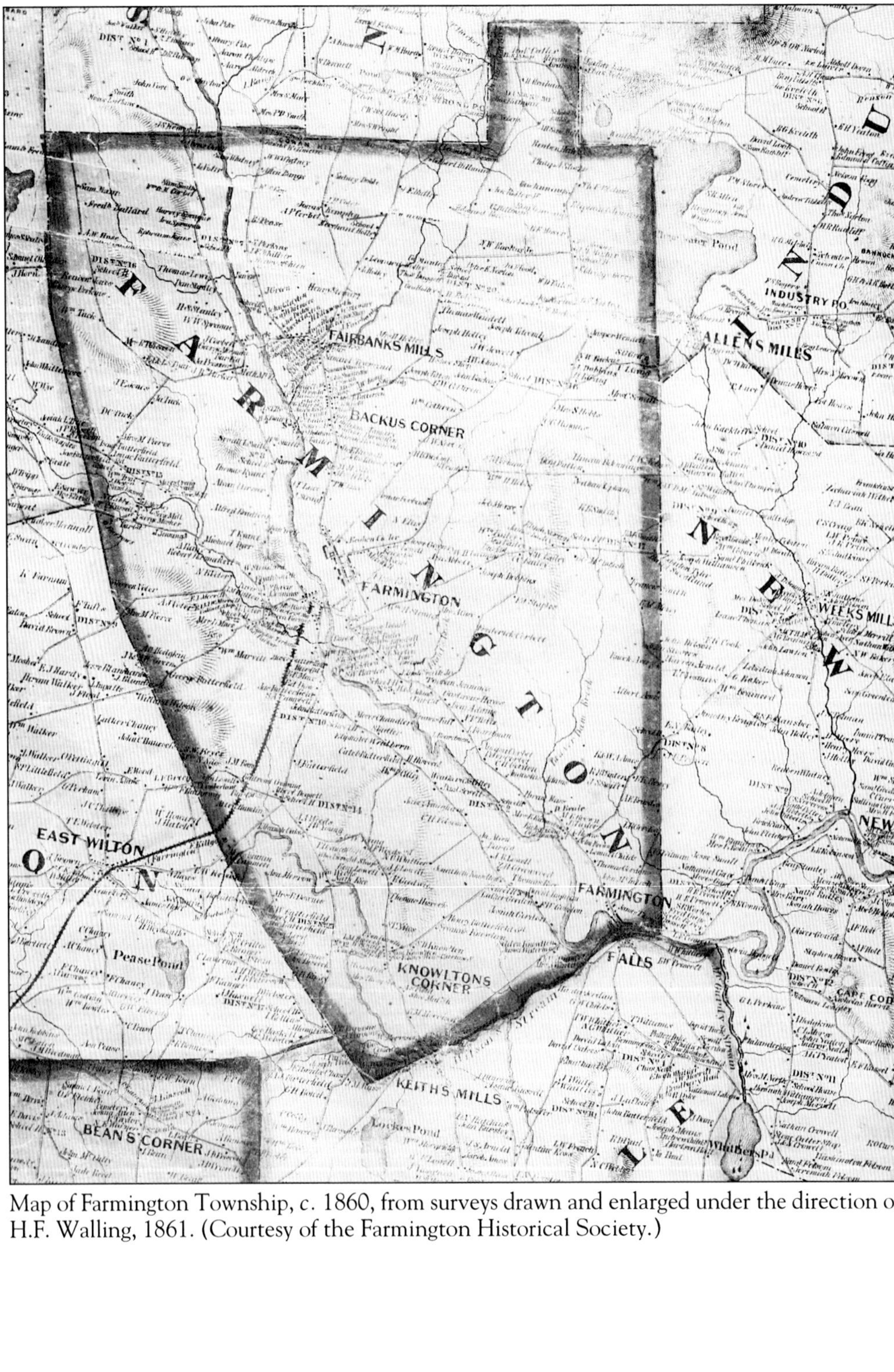

Map of Farmington Township, c. 1860, from surveys drawn and enlarged under the direction of H.F. Walling, 1861. (Courtesy of the Farmington Historical Society.)

Introduction

When one looks at the Farmington-Wilton-Kingfield-Sugarloaf region now, there appears a nice balance. Farmington is the county seat of Franklin County, and political, educational, and cultural effects occur as a result when combined with the University of Maine at Farmington (which my mother attended when it was Farmington State Normal School).

Wilton has been and remains the industrial side of the balance. G.H. Bass & Company sends its shoes, boots, and moccasins all over the world. The days of woolen manufacture in Wilton appear past but it had some wonderful times before ending in the late 1950s and '60s. The town used to have greater retail sales bounce than it now does. The retail strip in Farmington gets much business from Wilton at the present time.

Kingfield-Sugarloaf is a great recreational-tourist area now. It always had great potential and even now not all that potential has been realized. In the past, Kingfield was largely oriented toward manufacturing wood products.

Scenic beauty abounds. Some of the photographs here show that. The unspoiled scenic beauty was perhaps even greater at the turn and into the twentieth century. But plenty of it remains.

This is my ninth book in the Images of America series, eight of them about Maine communities. Based on that experience in Maine and my over thirty-seven years of reporting experience with the Portland newspapers, I'd say the strength of the family still remains stronger in Maine than in many other states, especially those which are urbanized. Maine's Franco-Americans, Irish, and old line first settlers all have many strong families. To illustrate this I have picked out three families, one from each community, to concentrate upon.

The Millses of Farmington have now served that community, others around it, and the entire state for years and three generations. That service has often been political but it's an outgrowth of three generations of Farmington town meeting moderators. It's another example of the old axiom that all politics is basically local.

The Basses in Wilton personify a type of capitalism that is on the wane. Here the family owning the biggest industry in town melded into many phases of that community's life. It was much the same pattern that the S.D. Warren Company followed for years in Westbrook. However, the Wilton example was much more family-based. Five generations of Basses were involved from the mid-1800s to 1978. It was enlightened capitalism at its best.

Finally, we have the Winters of Kingfield and Sugarloaf. Amos Winter Jr. became a legend in his own lifetime. Amos Winter Sr., his father, didn't become a legend but left a legacy, including one of the most beautiful, if not the most beautiful, houses in Kingfield, now the Inn at Winter's Hill. And he also left his son the gift of business acumen, which was needed to open the area to its great tourist potential.

Each town seems to have grown up quite self-sufficient. This was the story for most Maine communities through the nineteenth century at least. Now, both Wilton and Kingfield appear dependent on Farmington for much of their retailing. The distances between the three towns are not that great, especially by Maine standards. The region is much more integrated than it was in the nineteenth century.

Men and women of the nineteenth century often did a variety of things well, a trait inherited from their settler ancestors. In this century, Amos Winter Jr. seemed somewhat of a throwback to the men of an earlier day, a man who could ski all day and dance much of the night, a good tennis player, a lover of Chinese food and, with all that, a pretty good businessman. There are still some of those around in Maine but not as many as there used to be.

After dealing extensively with the history of Maine communities, one is tempted to look back at the good old days with nostalgia and even regret that they are gone. However, one must always remember that the majority of photographs were taken during times of prosperity, not when times were tough. As a result, the overall effect is a slanted one.

The integration of this region with Wilton as industry-based, Farmington as retail-political-cultural-based, and Kingfield-Sugarloaf as recreation-based is undoubtedly more efficient than the three relatively self-sufficient towns of the nineteenth century. Of course, the automobile was the great catalyst of this change, eventually bringing the shopping centers and shopping strip of Farmington, and the recreational development of Kingfield-Sugarloaf. That integration may also have increased the region's ability to withstand national and state economic ups and downs through greater diversification.

Many of the Kingfield photographs in this volume focus on Sugarloaf's start and on the Winter family, which had so much to do with that start. The basic reason for this is the pictorial history of the town compiled in 1980 by Beulah Moore and others. I decided not to repeat photos that were used in the fairly recent past. Those photographs contained within this book reveal part of the region's life that was not well covered in the aforementioned history.

Finally, as in all of these books I've done, I dedicate this one to the young people of this region. I hope this will keep them away from their TV sets for an hour or so. And I hope it will awaken in at least some of them an interest in learning more about the history of their area. As for the older folks, I hope you read it and remember, or at least get a kick at looking back at, the Farmington-Wilton-Kingfield-Sugarloaf region in the good old days.

Frank H. Sleeper

One

Farmington

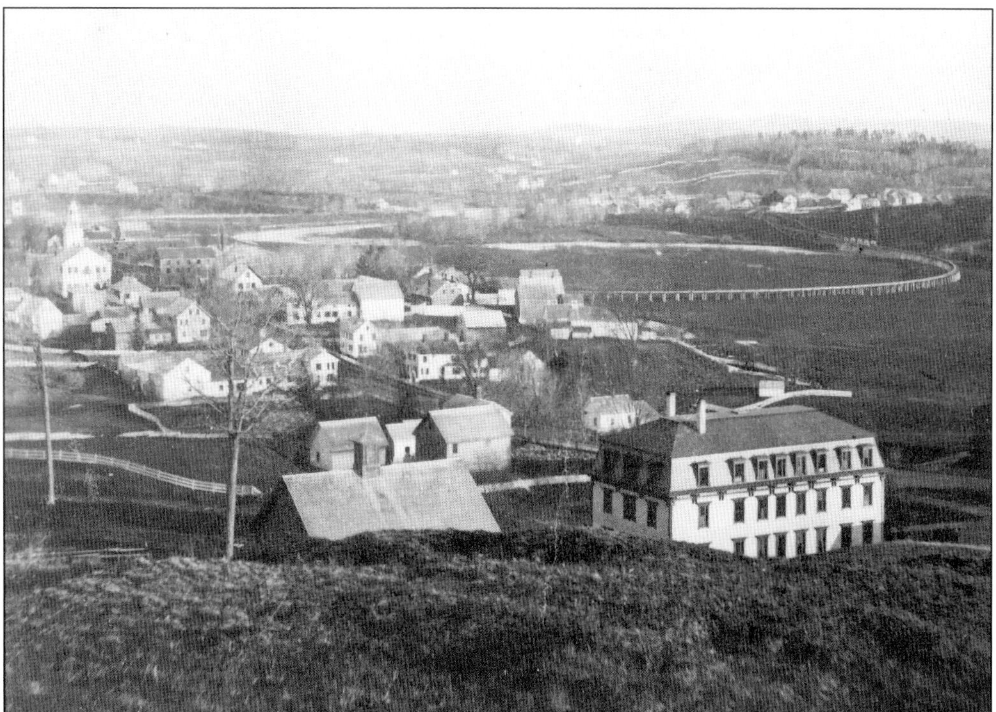

Part of Farmington village with the railroad bridge across the Sandy River in the middle right, c. 1880s. This was taken from Powder House Hill.

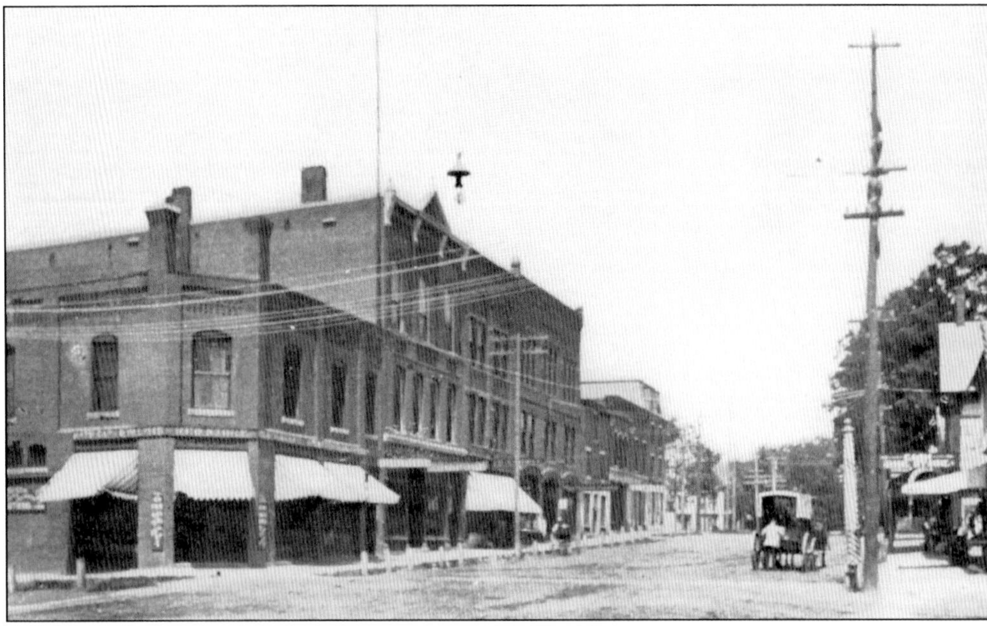

Main Street, Farmington, looking north in the early 1900s.

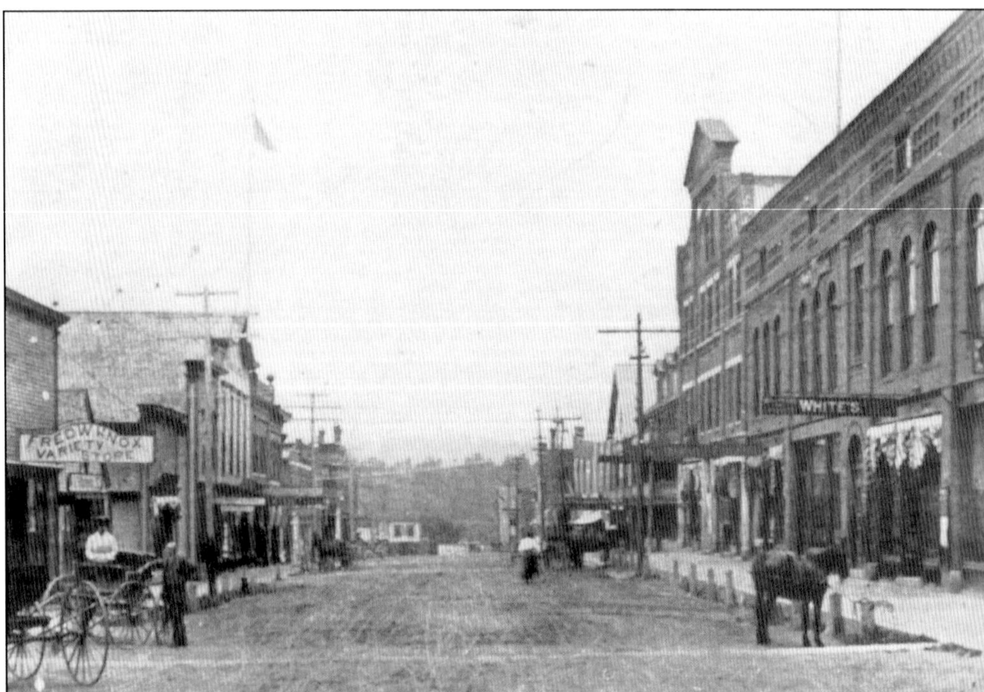

Broadway, Farmington, *c.* 1880s. White's is on the right and Fred W. Knox's Variety Store is on the left. There appears to be no pavement and only horses are visible for transportation.

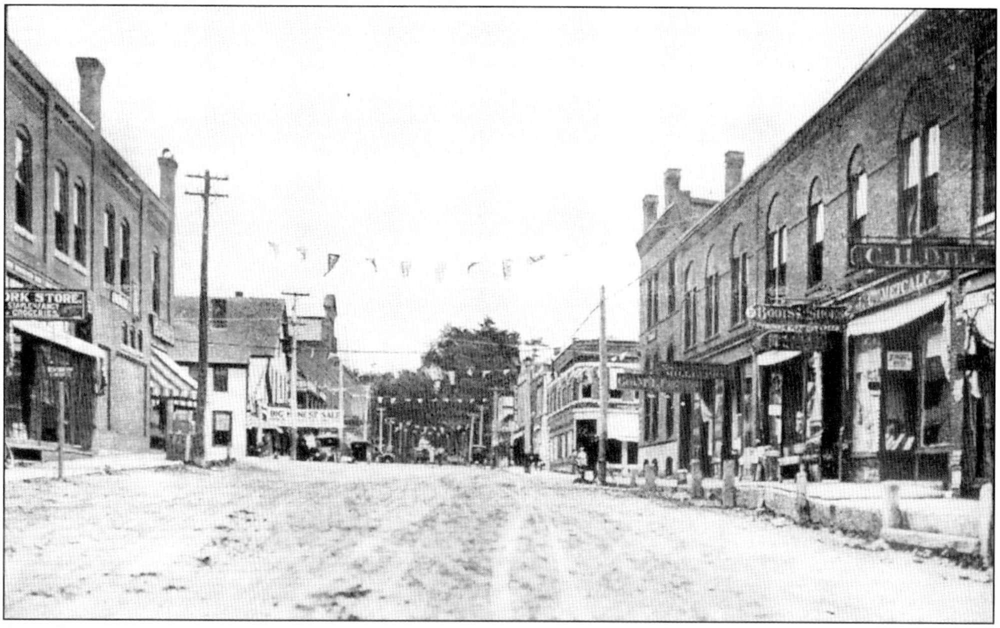

Broadway, Farmington, in the late 1910s or early 1920s. The horseless carriage had arrived, though the hitching posts for horses remained. Stores visible on the right are C.H. Dill, J.C. Mitchell and a millinery shop, while on the left is the ? York Store for groceries. Farther on the left is a sign for a "Big Maine St. Sale."

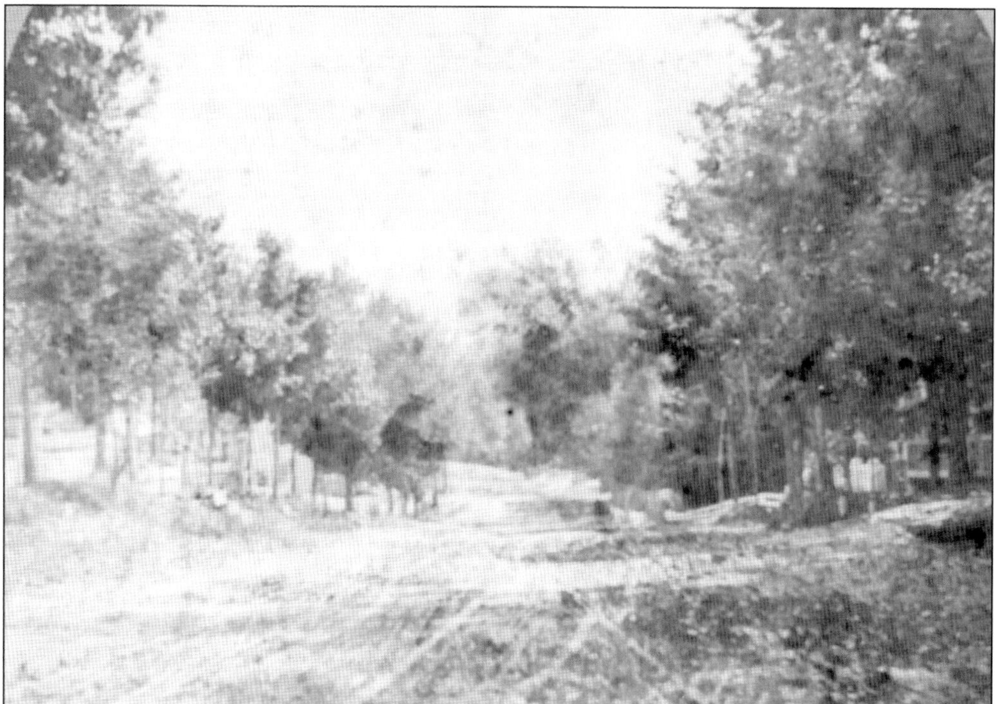

Main Street, Farmington, from South Street, looking south, *c.* early 1870s. Note the wonderful trees, the rutted road, and the scarcity of houses.

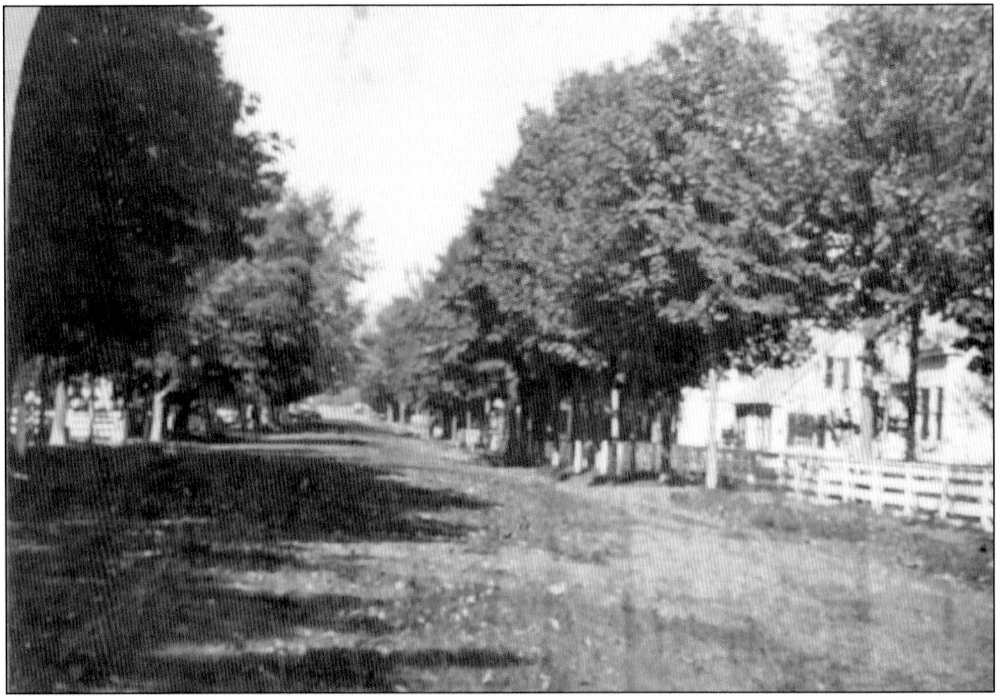

Main Street, Farmington, from South Street, looking north, early 1870s. Once again, note the shade trees and the unpaved road.

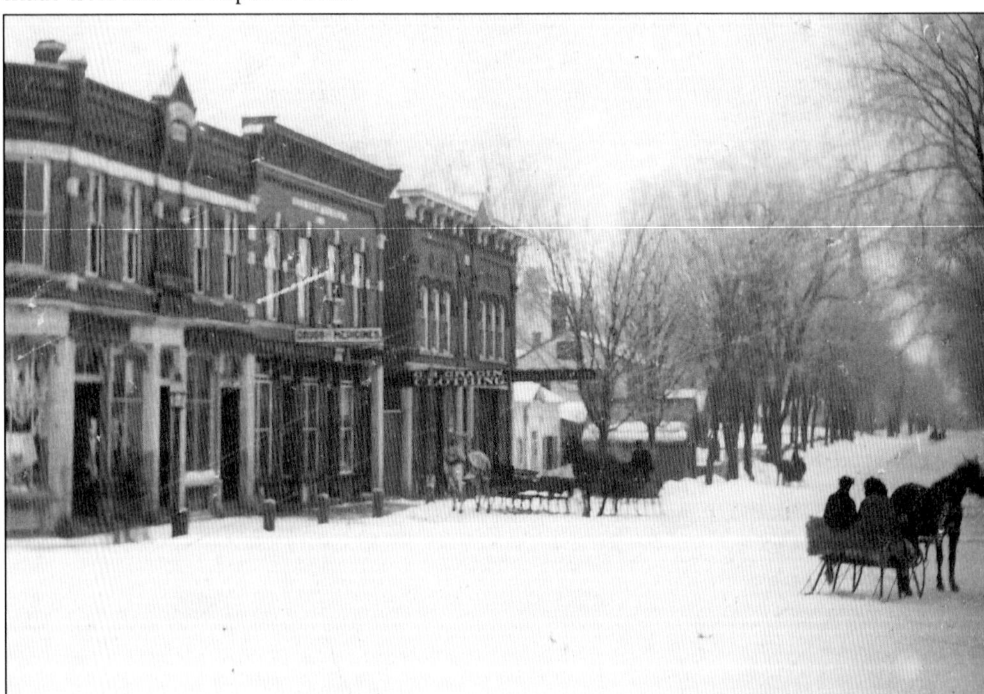

Yes, there was snow in Farmington in the late 1870s. This is Main Street from Broadway. Note the horses and sleighs riding on packed-down snow.

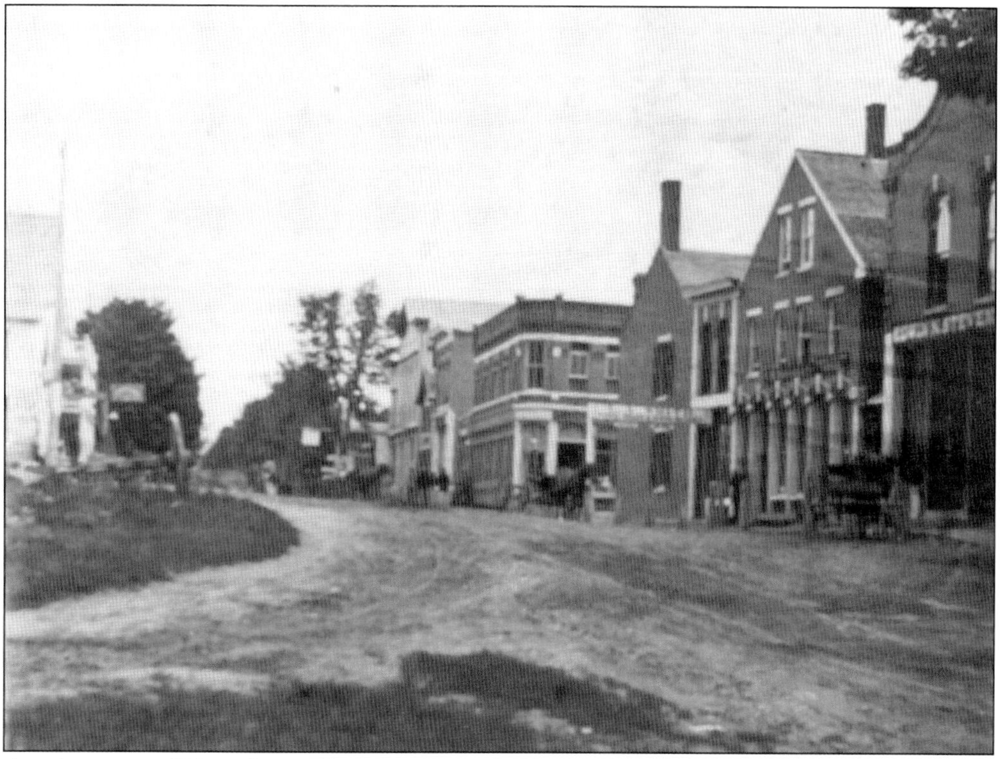

Another view of Main Street, Farmington, in the late 1870s. The Edwin M. Stevens business is in the right foreground.

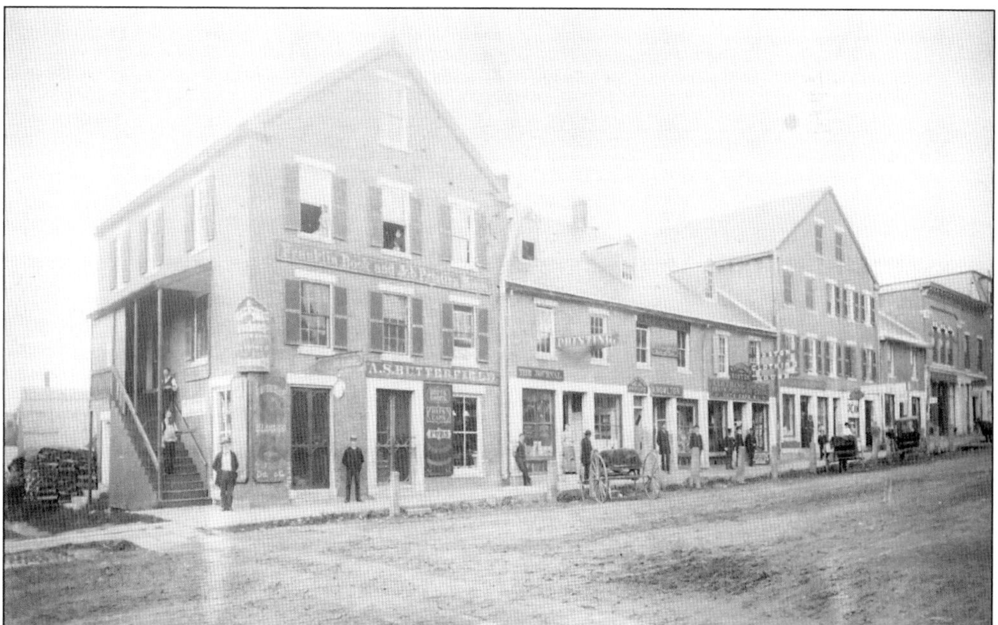

Main Street, Farmington, before the Great Fire of 1886. Visible are A.S. Butterfield, furs, boots and shoes, and hats and caps; the Franklin Book and Job Printing House; A. Purington; The Journal, printing; Knowlton's; and the Boston Clothing House.

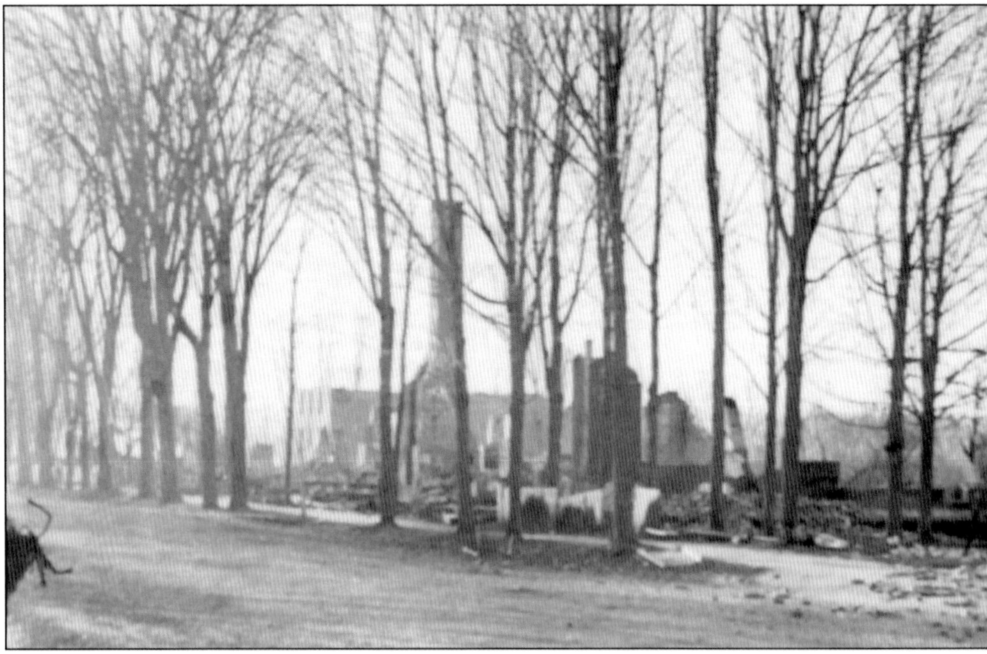

Ruins of Farmington after the Great Fire, the night of October 22, 1886, with loss estimated at $500,000. This was Main Street.

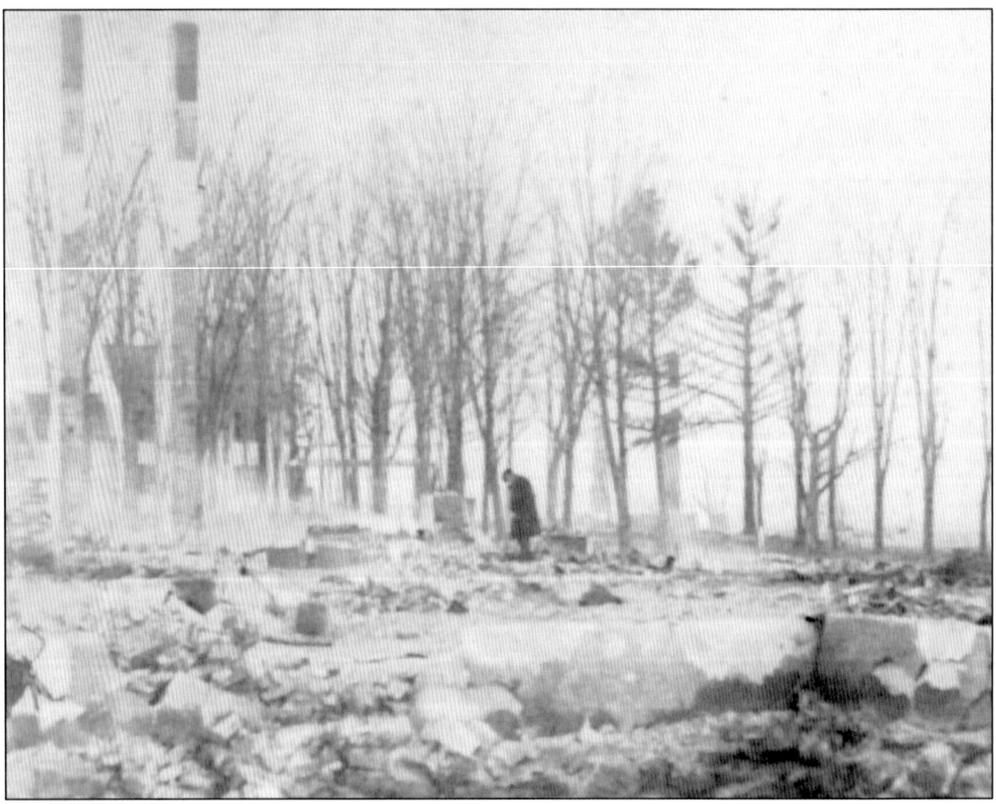

Farmington Common after the Great Fire.

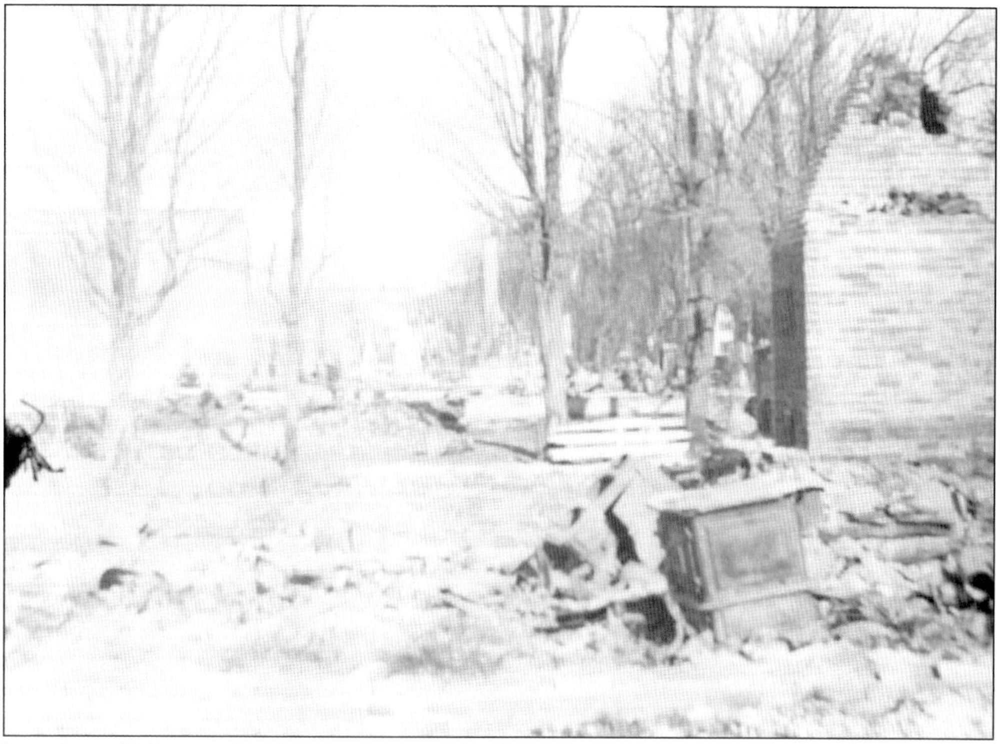

Isaac Russell's house after the Great Fire. In the blaze, thirty-two houses and forty-two businesses were destroyed. The Lewiston Fire Department played a great role in extinguishing the blaze.

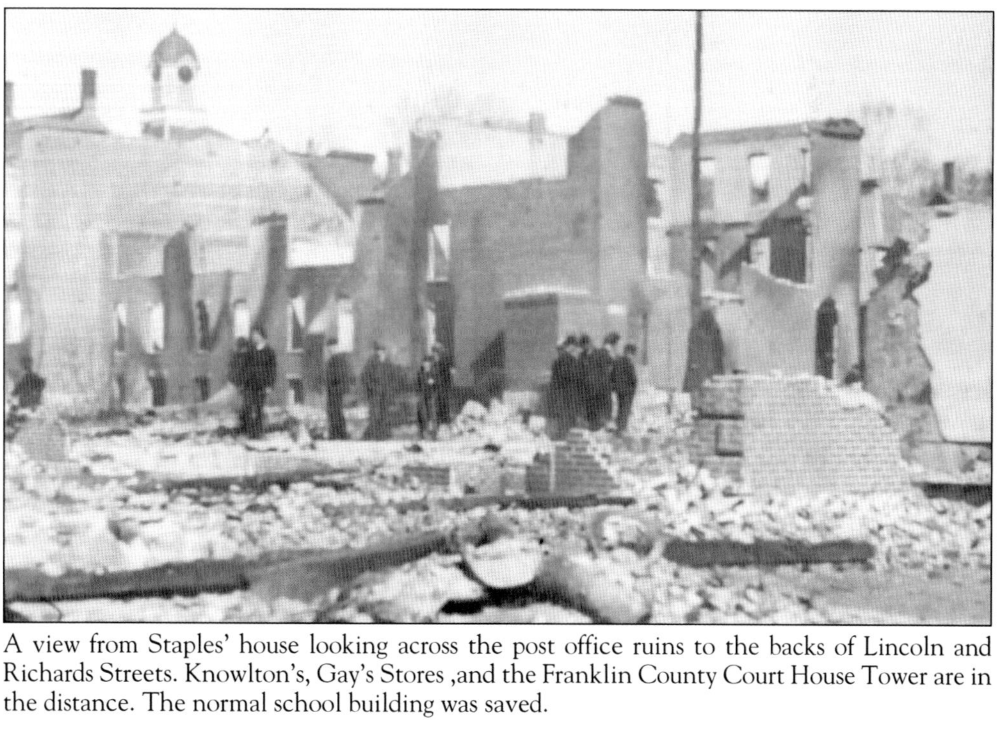

A view from Staples' house looking across the post office ruins to the backs of Lincoln and Richards Streets. Knowlton's, Gay's Stores ,and the Franklin County Court House Tower are in the distance. The normal school building was saved.

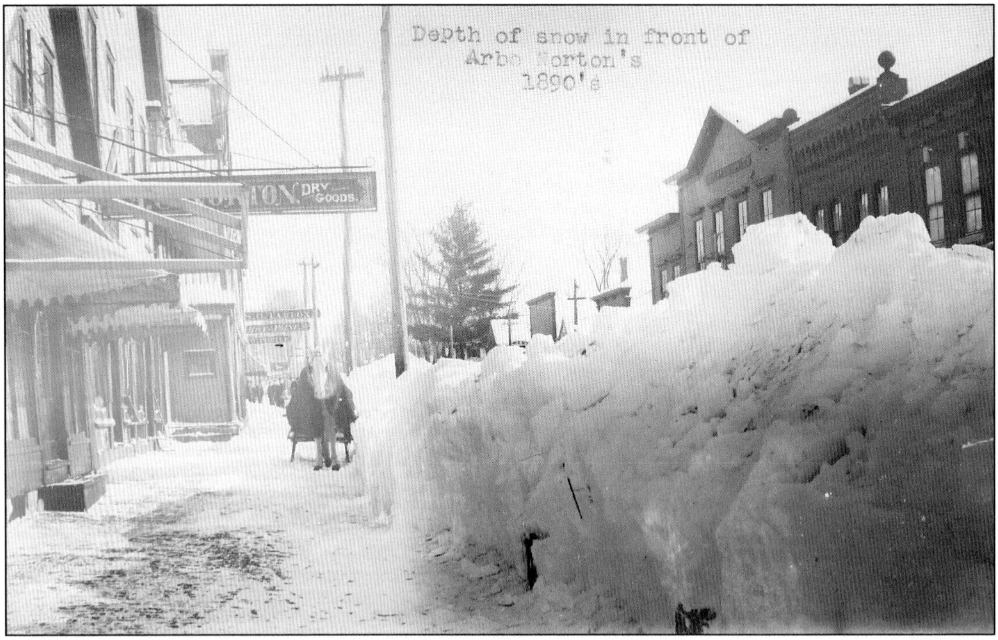

Let's go from one extreme to another—from fire to snow. Farmington and the whole area are close to or in the mountains and get added snow as a result. Look at the snow depth in front of Arbo Norton's Dairy Goods Store in the 1890s.

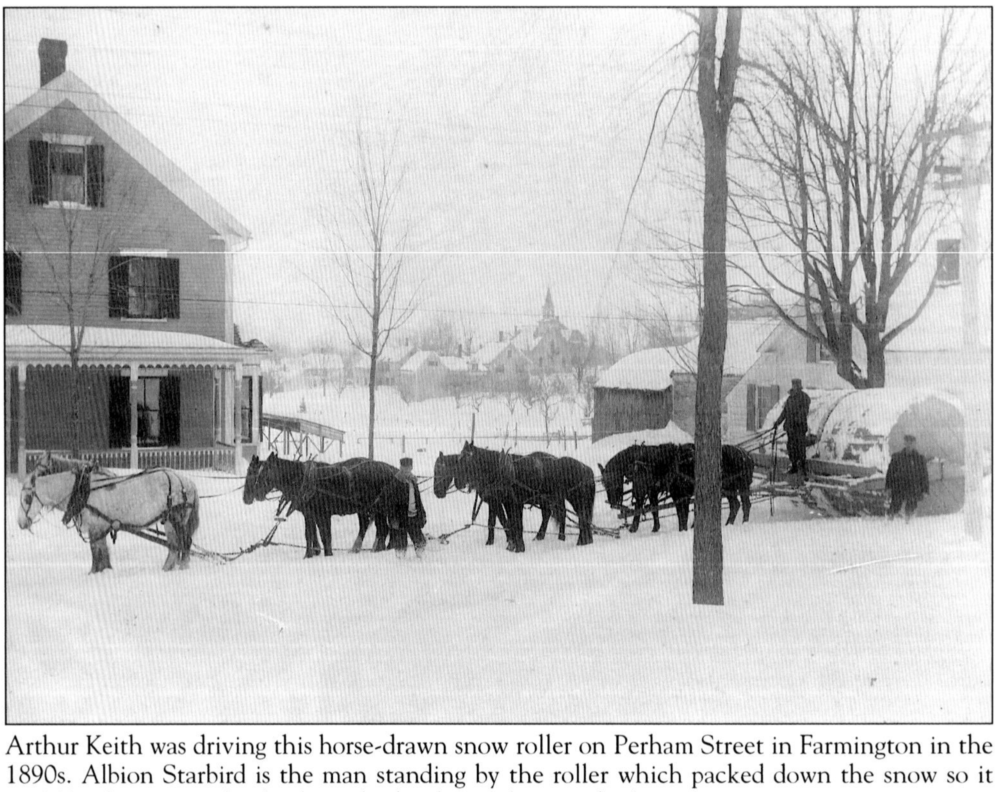

Arthur Keith was driving this horse-drawn snow roller on Perham Street in Farmington in the 1890s. Albion Starbird is the man standing by the roller which packed down the snow so it could be driven over by sleighs and other horse-drawn vehicles.

Here is Perham Chambers with snow in the 1930s.

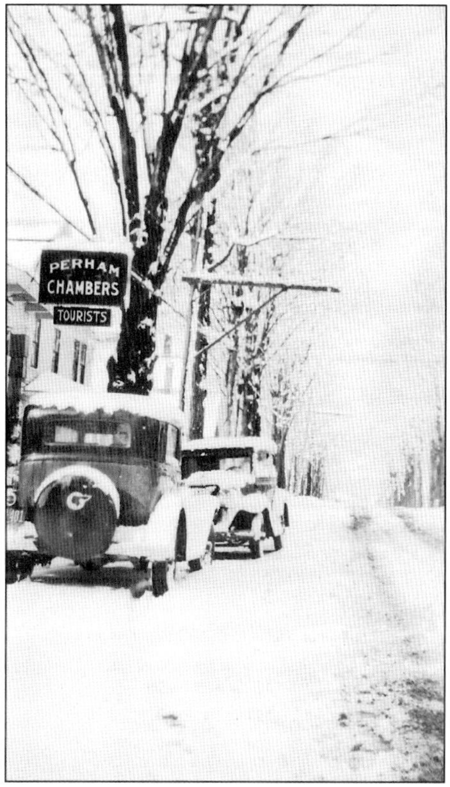

Move in closer to Farmington in the past. This is lower Broadway in the 1880s. E.G. Blake is the name of the clothing store. Cigar in hand, the apparently oldest man in the photo gets a shoe shine.

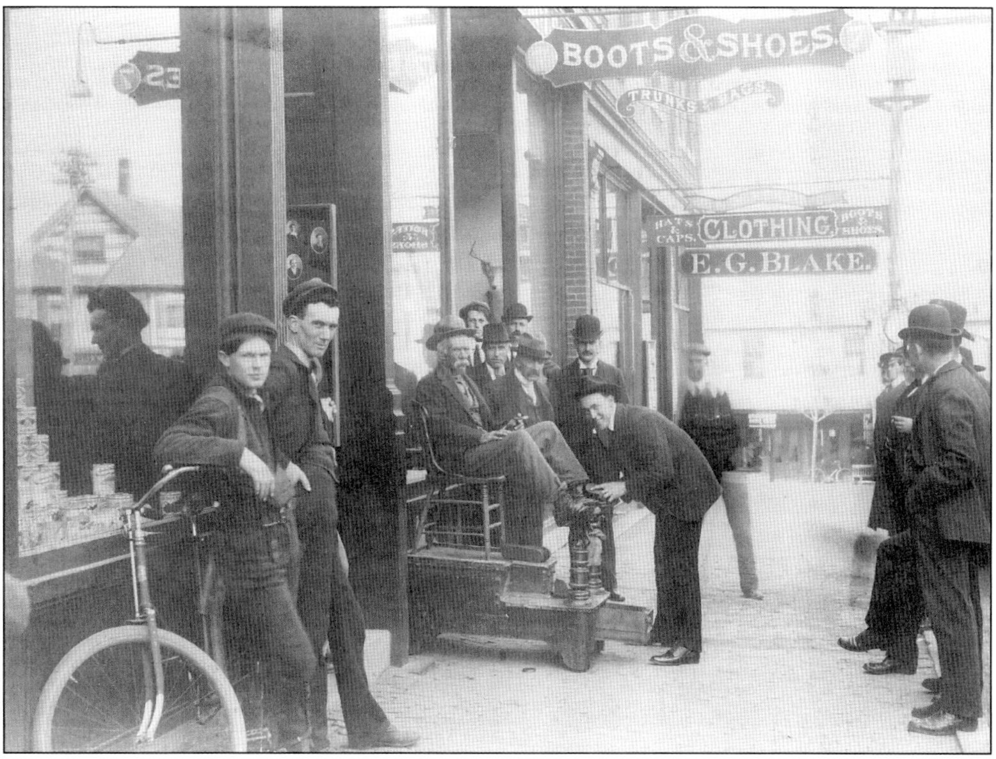

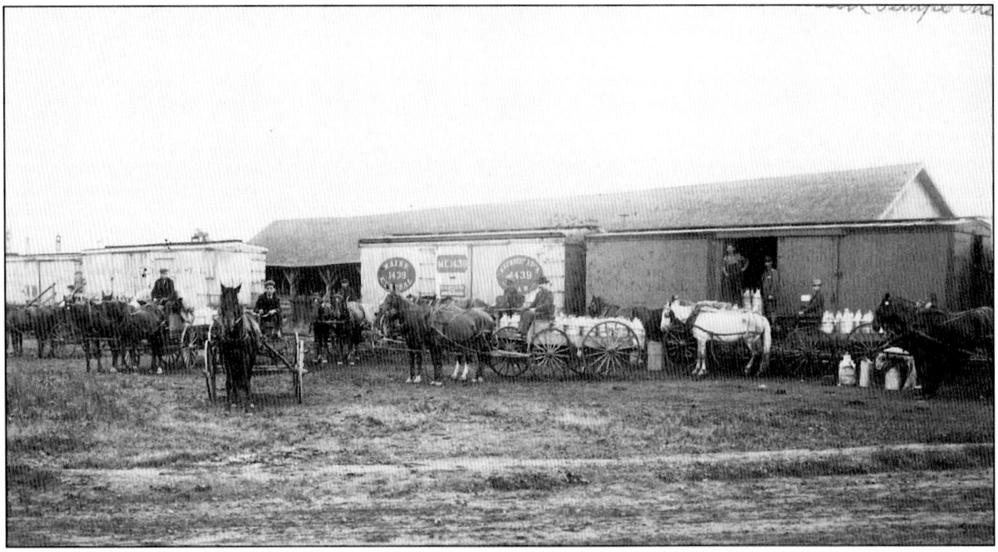

At 5:30 am on a May day in 1902 in West Farmington, Dana E. Hamlin unloaded cream from forty-five farms in Temple (near Farmington), Wilton, and Farmington into Maine Central Railroad cars. The cream went to the Turner Center Creamery in Auburn. Hamlin, whose own team (the gray horses) can be seen here in front of the car door, hauled cream and milk for sixty years.

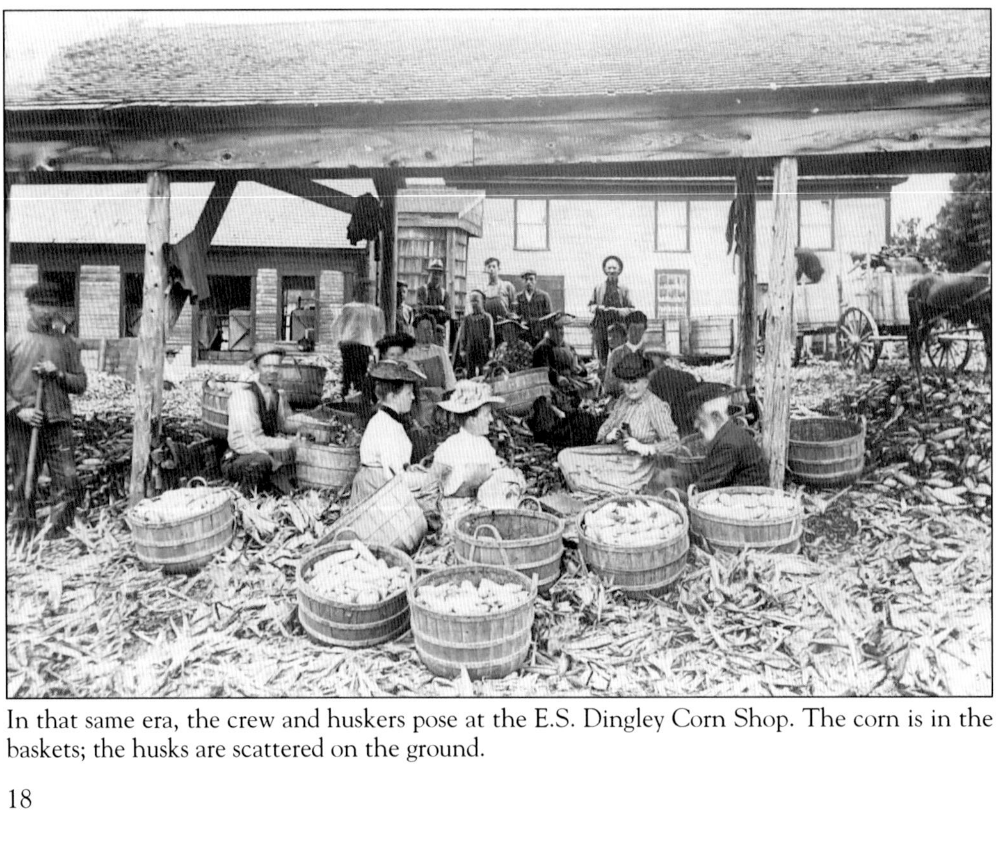

In that same era, the crew and huskers pose at the E.S. Dingley Corn Shop. The corn is in the baskets; the husks are scattered on the ground.

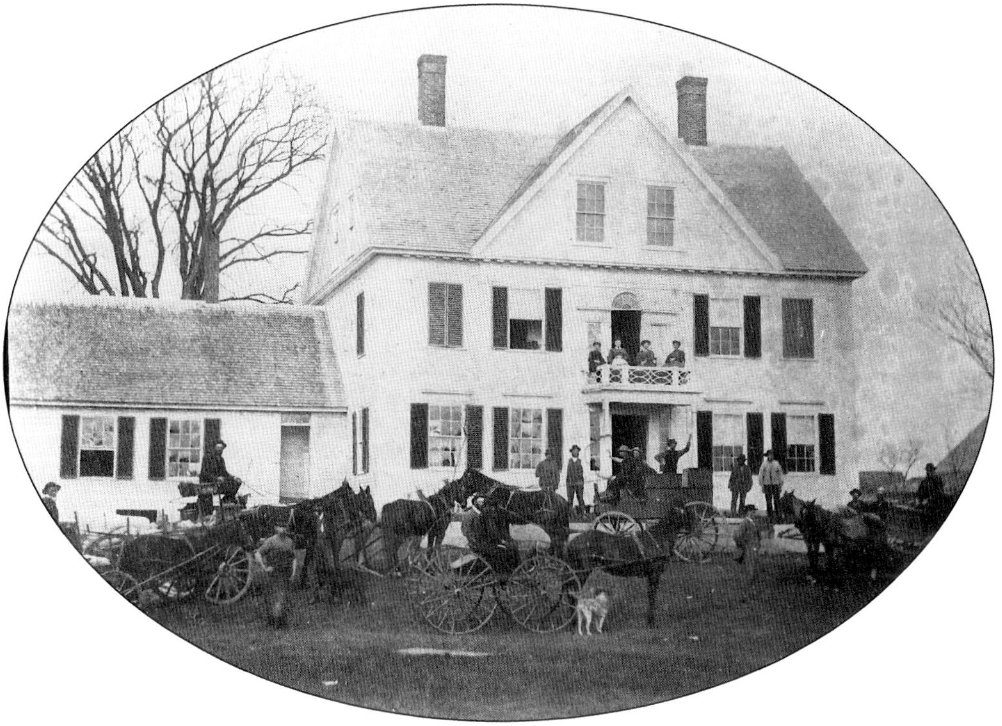

Much earlier, in front of an old Farmington tavern which burned in 1873, stands the New Sharon stagecoach. On the left is Walter Jordan with the horses; Dana Maddox poses with the dog; Leonard Lovejoy; George Davis is in the buggy; and Charles Davis is on the porch. On the right are Irving Gilman and his brother, Gus; Mr. Cutler; and an unidentified man, with Deacon Mansen Woodman in the center. The women on the balcony are Julia E. Gilman, Mary Knowlton, Clara Gilman, and Rose Allen.

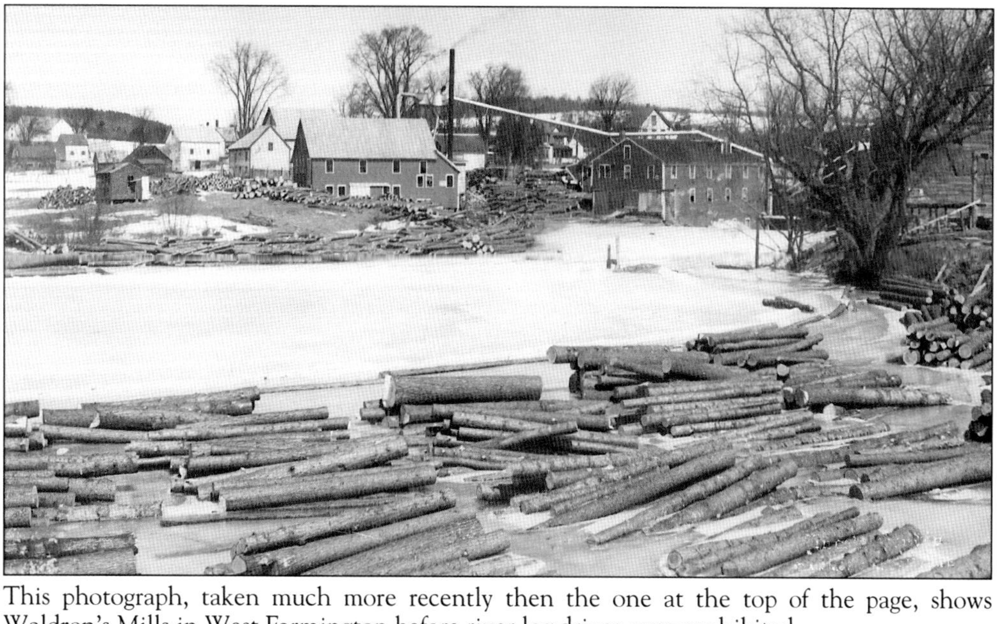

This photograph, taken much more recently then the one at the top of the page, shows Waldron's Mills in West Farmington before river log drives were prohibited.

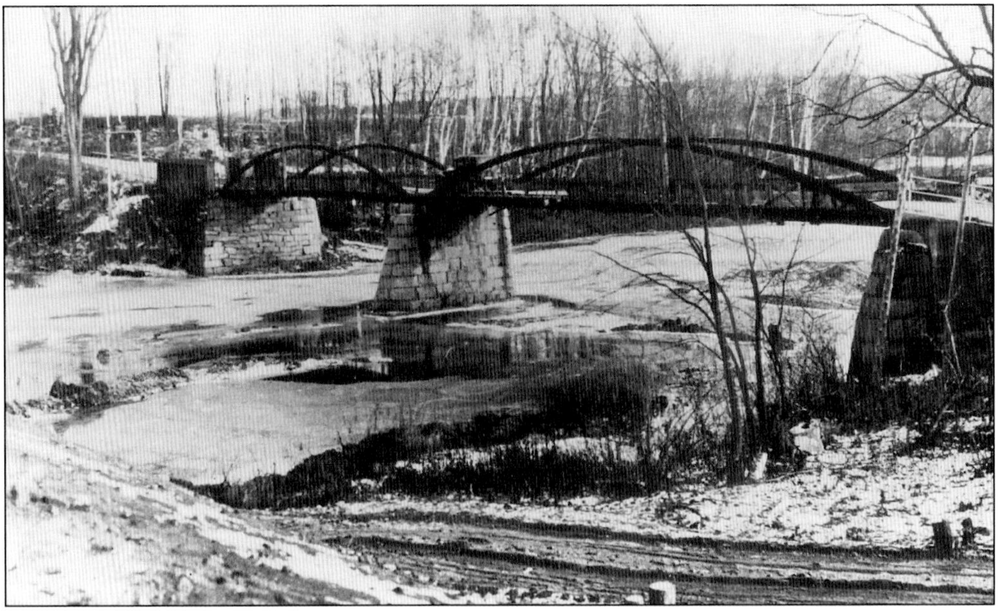

And, in 1929, we see the Fairbanks bridge in Farmington with a background of leafless trees and half-formed ice, almost as bleak as the stock market crash of that year which helped bring the Depression.

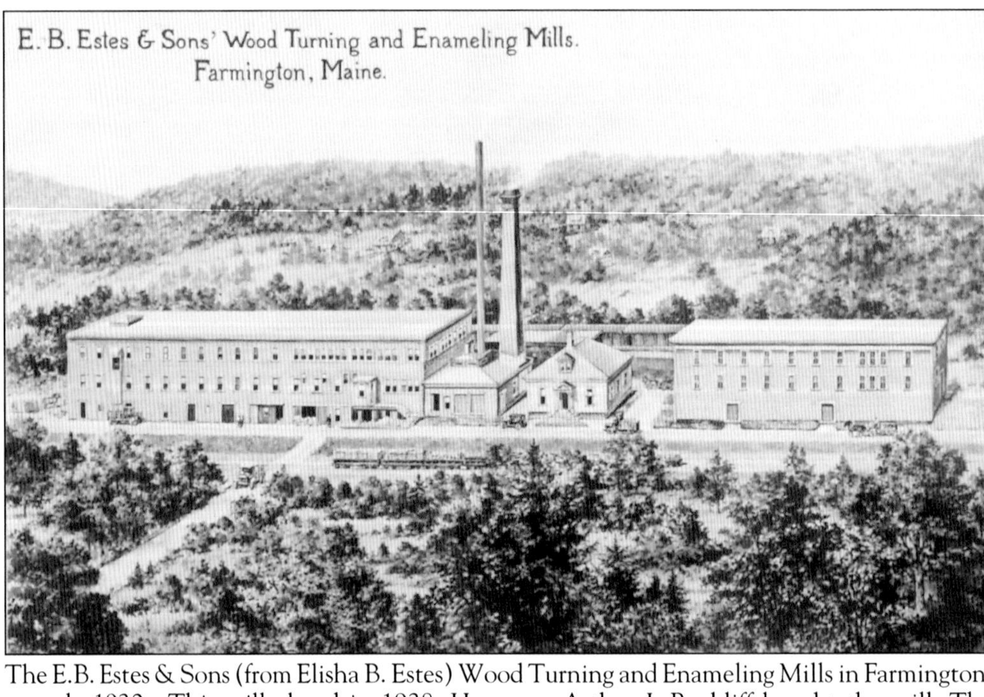

The E.B. Estes & Sons (from Elisha B. Estes) Wood Turning and Enameling Mills in Farmington, c. early 1920s. This mill closed in 1928. However, Arthur I. Rackliff bought the mill. The Depression was slow in coming to Farmington. Thus, the area suffered less than many and revived with World War II.

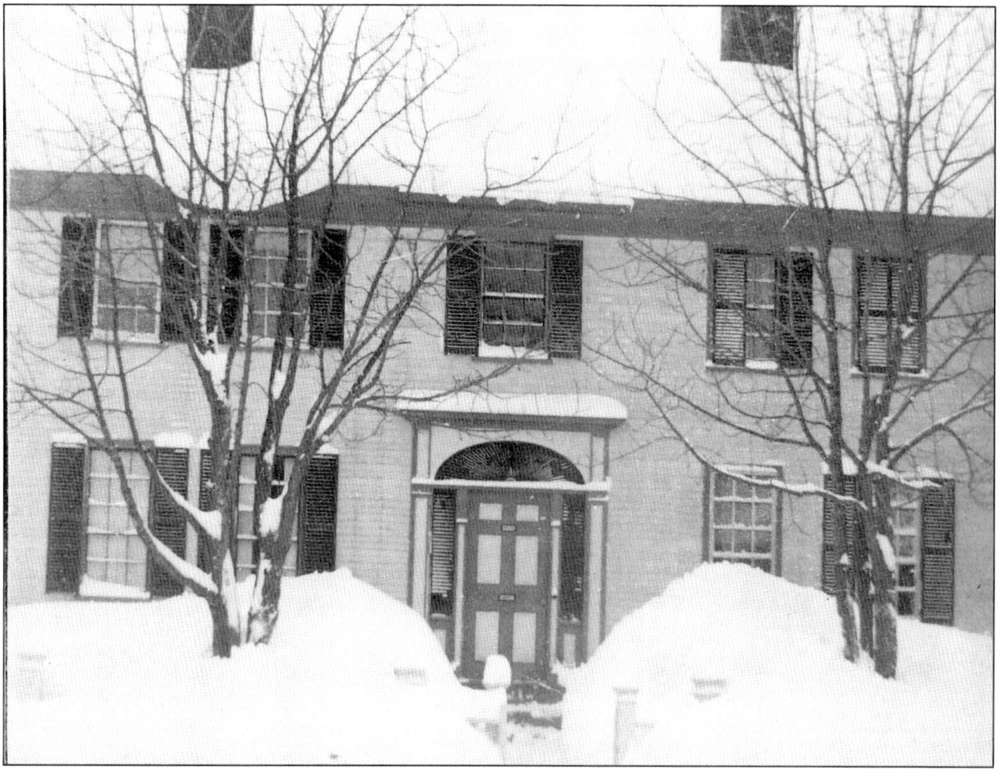

But, long before the Depression, fine homes had been built in Farmington. This was the residence of Joseph A. Linscott, in a photograph taken on March 3, 1869. Linscott, a lawyer, was cashier of the Sandy River Bank (the town's first bank), and straightened out legal problems it faced. He was, with his law partner Eben Pillsbury, editor of the *Franklin Patriot* from 1860 to 1864, treasurer of the Androscoggin Railroad, and auditor of the Maine Central Railroad.

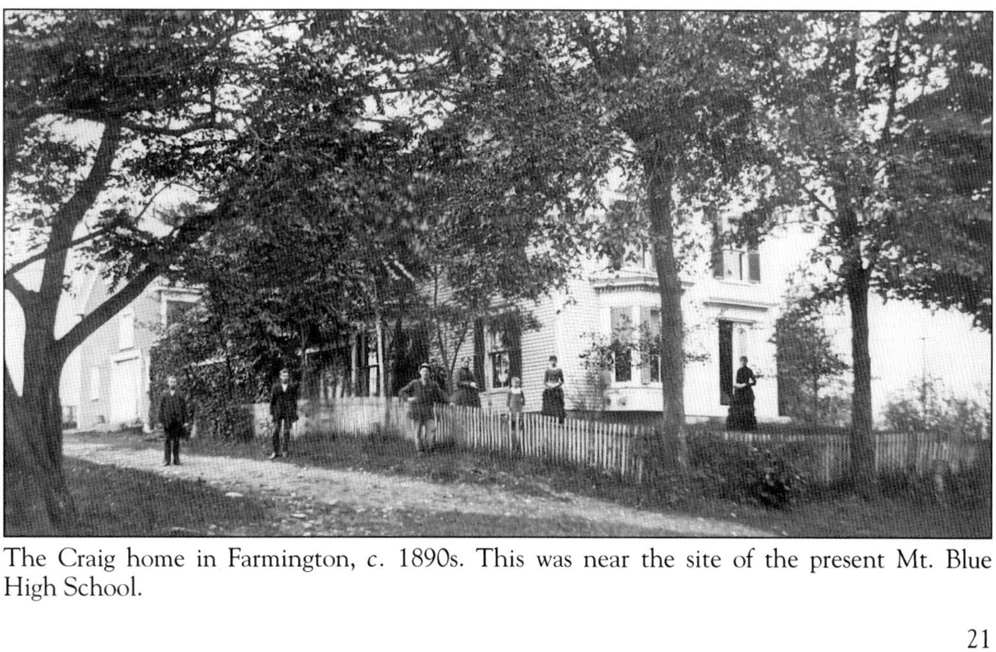

The Craig home in Farmington, *c.* 1890s. This was near the site of the present Mt. Blue High School.

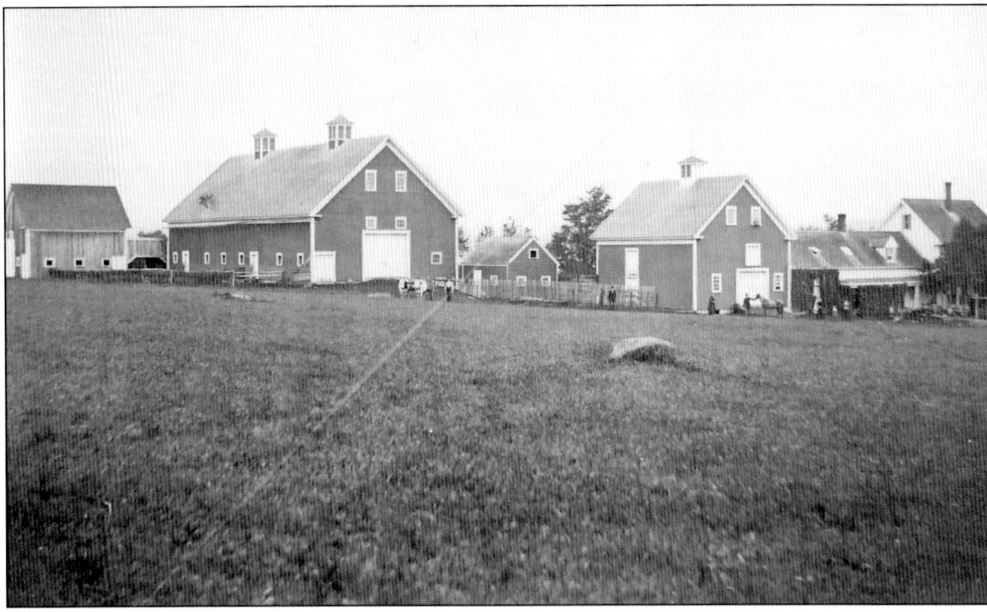

And there were beautiful farms. This is the Craigin Farm (later the Blanchard Farm) where Mt. Blue High School now stands.

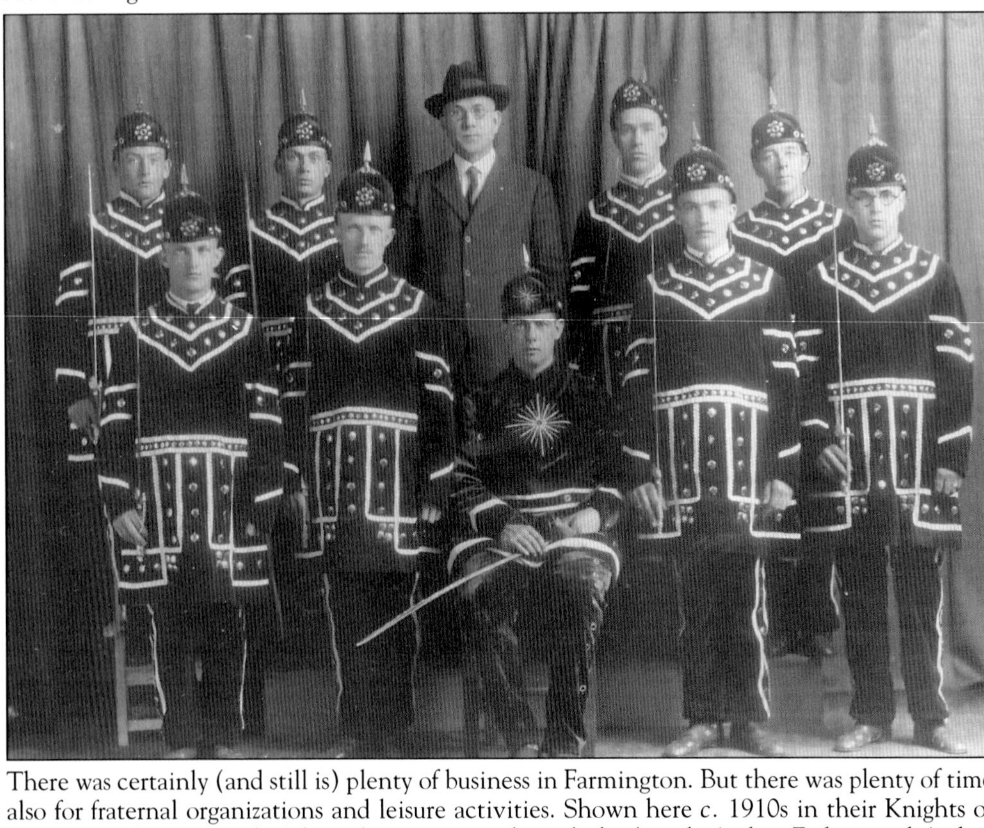

There was certainly (and still is) plenty of business in Farmington. But there was plenty of time also for fraternal organizations and leisure activities. Shown here *c.* 1910s in their Knights of Pythias regalia are Frank Adams (center in civilian clothes) with Arthur Fickett and Arthur Corbett to his right and John Carville in the front row on the left. Carl Berry is seated.

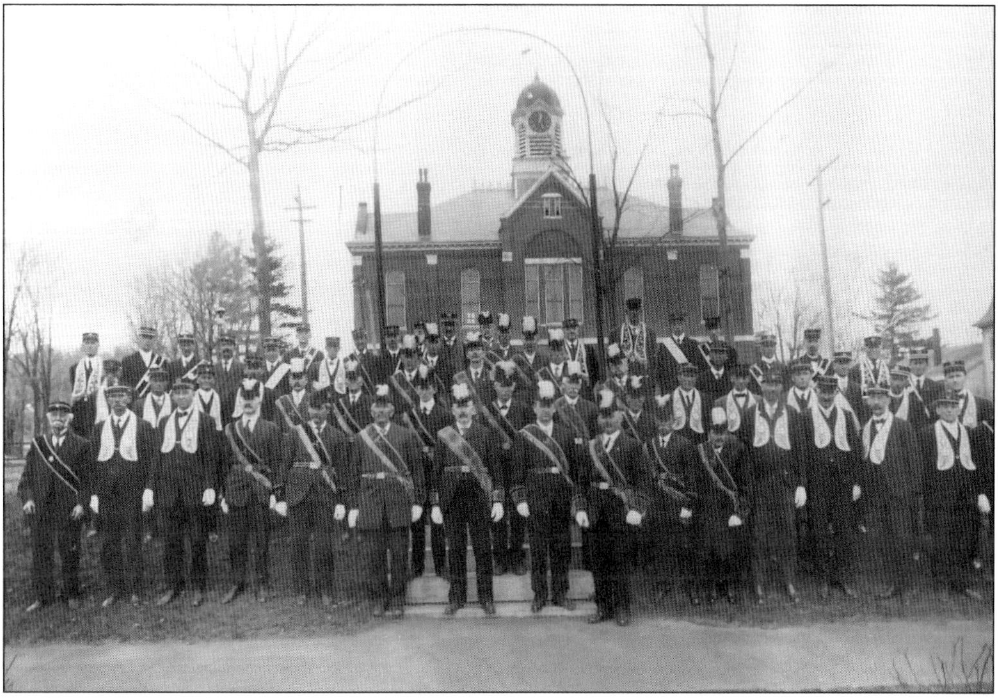

And here are members of Franklin Lodge Number 58, Independent Order of Odd Fellows at 12:25 pm, again in full regalia. This would appear to be at the turn of the century. Some of the men have been identified as follows: (front row) O.P. Dudley, second left; Daniel Locke, third left; John Linscott, fifth from left; Arbo Norton, sixth from right; and Floramund E. Voter, eighth from right; (second row) John Morton, fifth from right; E.I. Merrill, eighth from right; and Hanley Smith, eighth from left; (third row) C.H. Pierce, eighth from left; (back row) Newell Knowlton, twelfth from left.

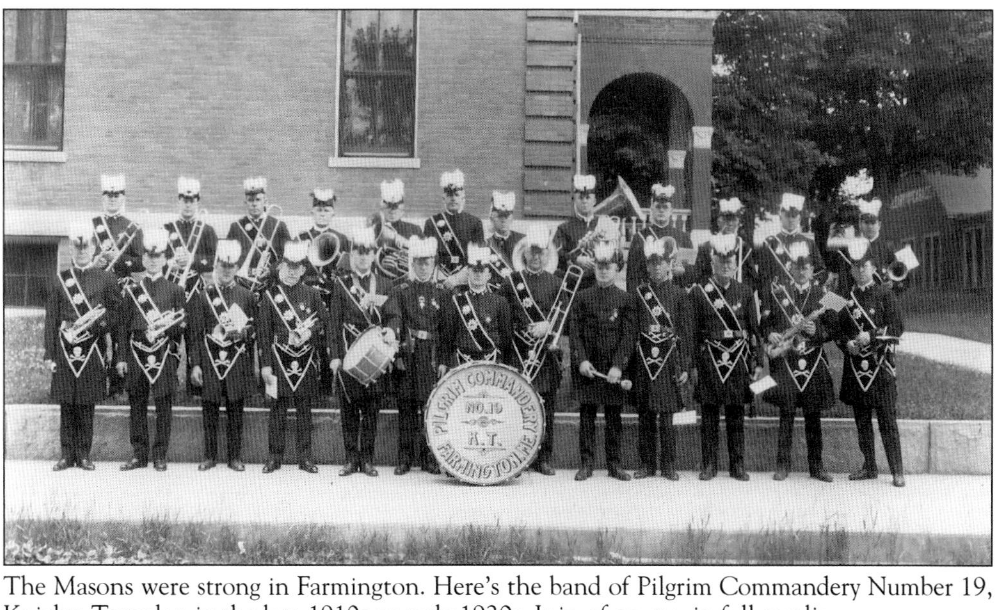

The Masons were strong in Farmington. Here's the band of Pilgrim Commandery Number 19, Knights Templar, in the late 1910s or early 1920s. It is, of course, in full regalia.

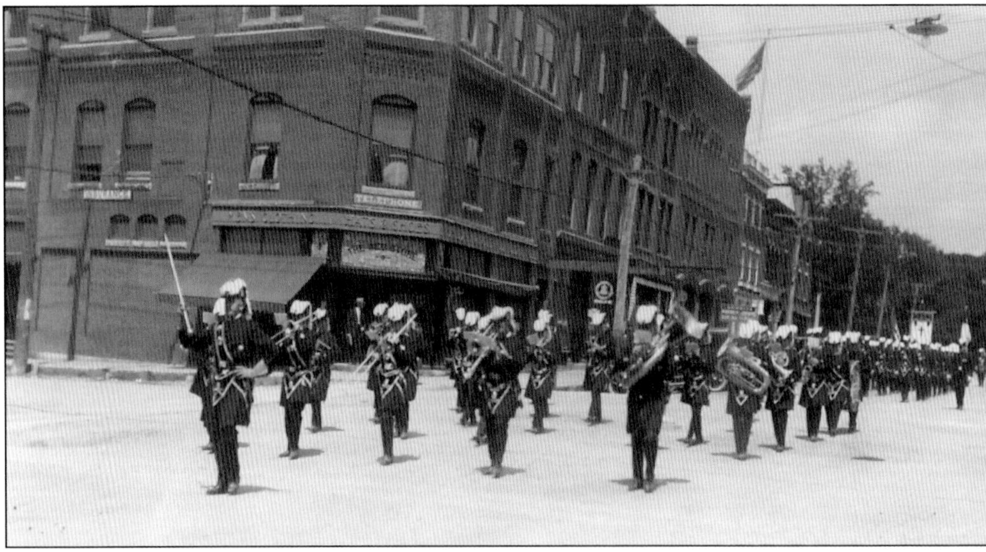

That same band is marching in the same time span, right down Main Street. It's going past the Red Store and Main Street Market.

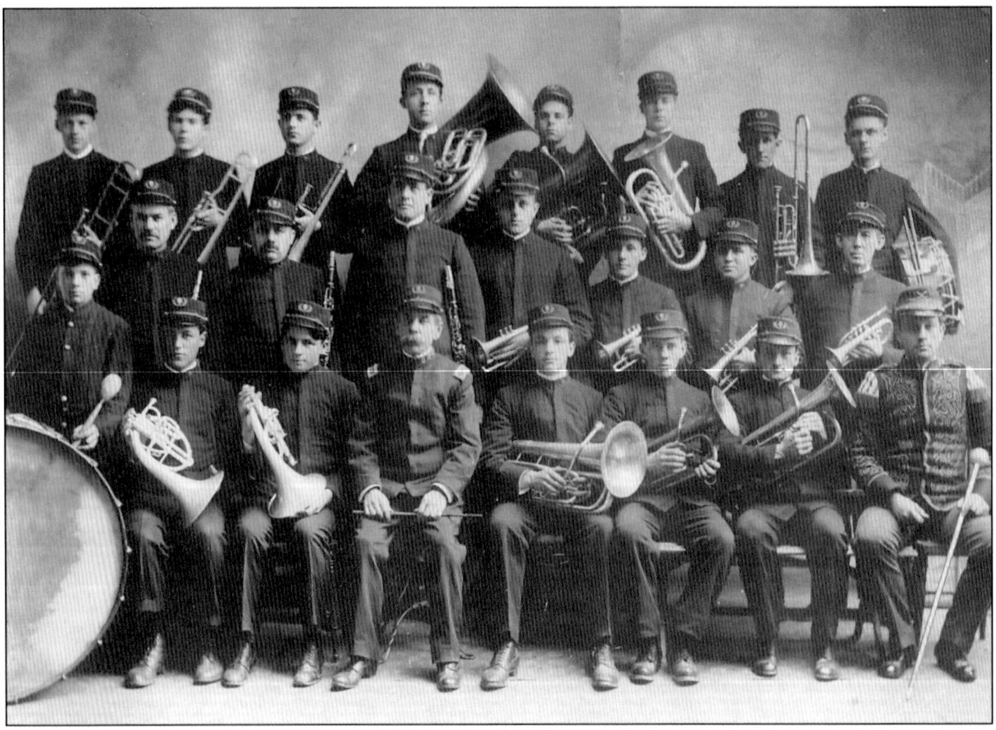

Speaking of bands, here is Farmington's Wheeler's Band in 1909. The following men have been identified: (front row) Hector Roderick, third from left; Charles Wheeler, the leader, fourth from left; Eddie Besaw, seventh from left; and the drum-major on the right; (middle row) Henry Knapp, left; Charles Lake?, third from left; Ray Davis, fourth from left; and Ken Rollins, right; (back row) Ray Small, left; Fred Moulton, second from left; Vic Huart, third from left; John Gilkey, fourth from left; and Rob McLeary ?, sixth from left. Started around the turn of the century, Wheeler's Band played at varied functions in the Farmington area for years.

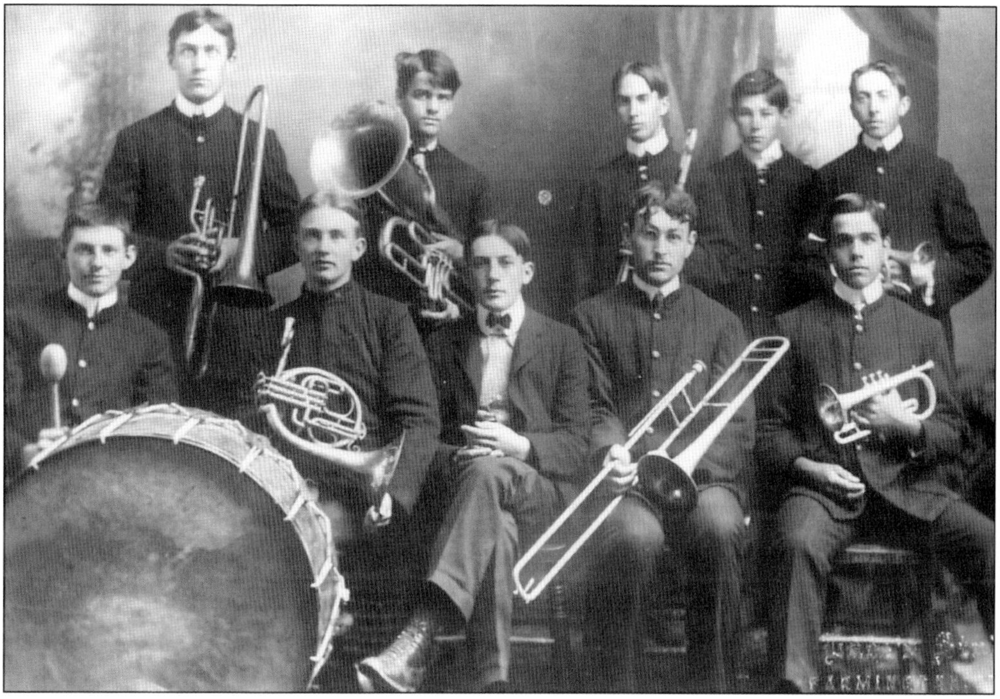

This is probably Ray Davis' band, *c.* early 1900s. From left to right are as follows: (front row) unknown, Wally Gould, Arthur McDonald, Ray Davis and Lester ?; (back row) Leon Marr, Don ?, Ken Rollins, Dean R., and Allie Davis.

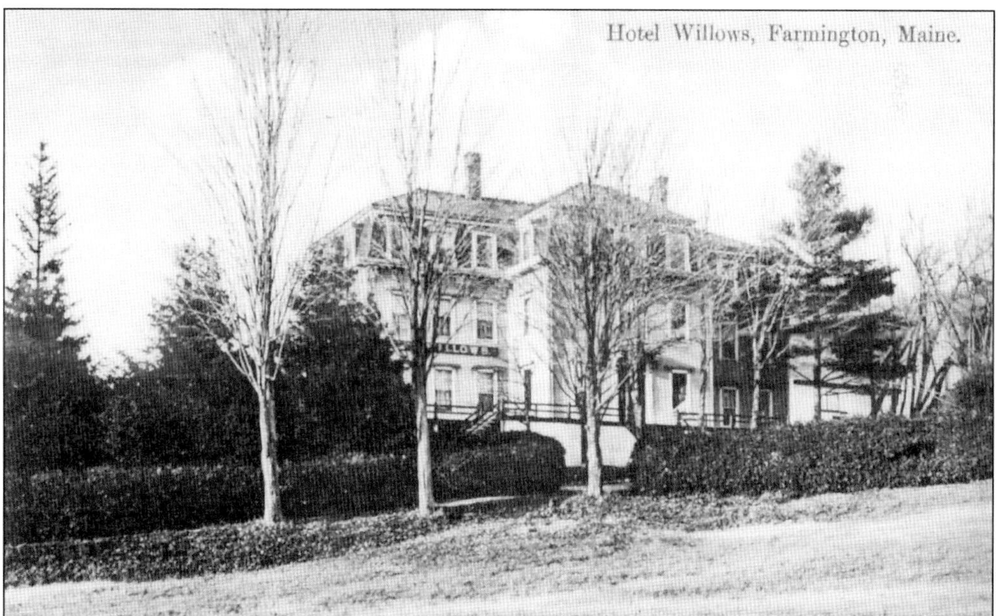

A part of the leisure time scene in Farmington was the Willows Hotel, razed about 1930. Here's the way it looked in 1910.

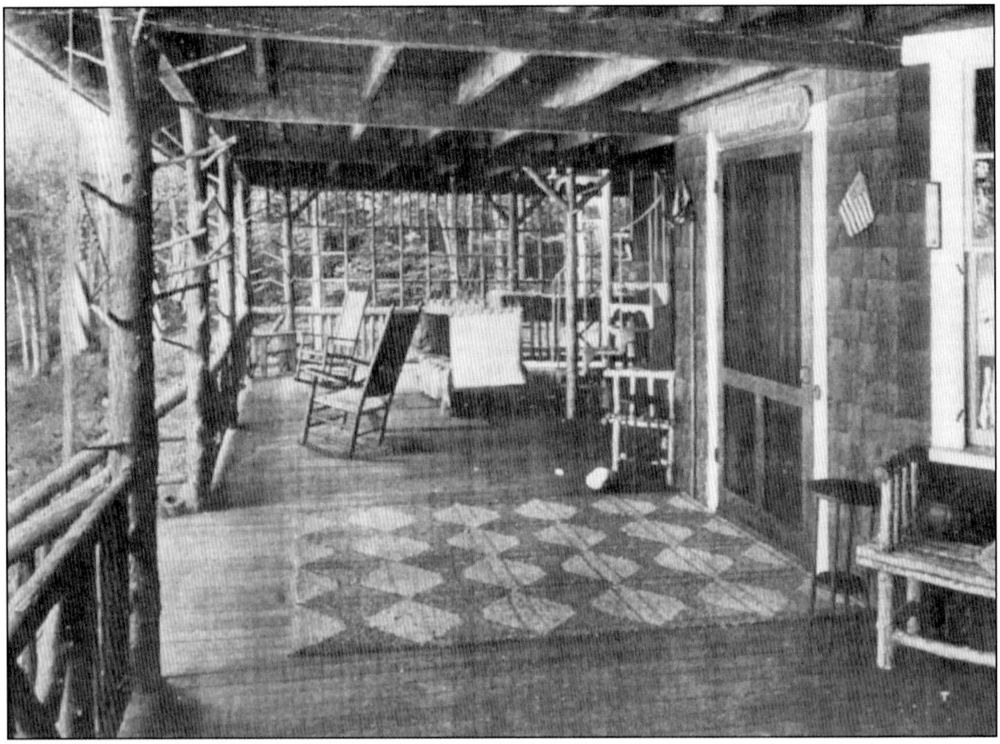

Camp Liberty on Clearwater Pond, right on the town line between Farmington and New Sharon, *c.* 1910s.

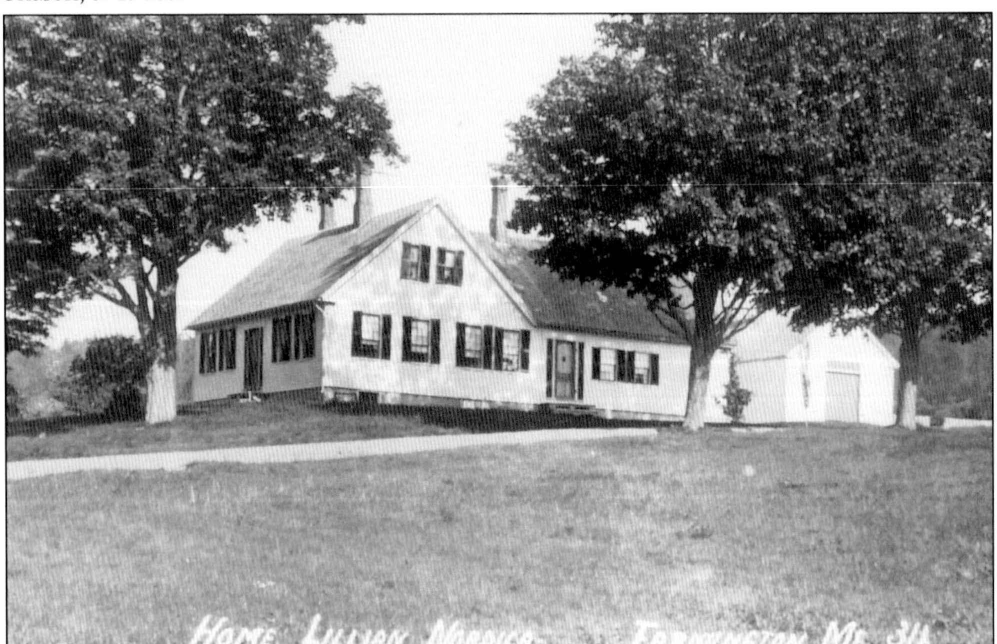

The home of famed opera singer Lillian Nordica in Farmington. Her real last name was Norton and she left the town while still young—but always kept in touch. Nordica gave three concerts in her home town, in 1878, 1883, and 1911. Each was a great success.

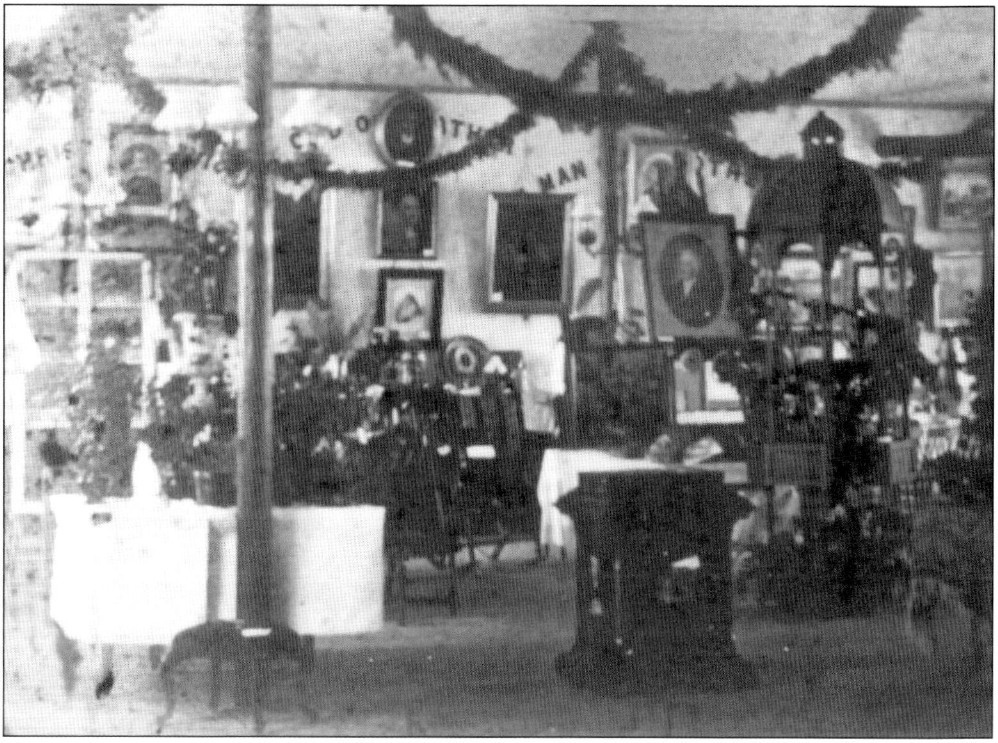

The Methodist Art Gallery, Farmington, April 1, 1879. Churches in the town have always played a large part in cultural and leisure time activities.

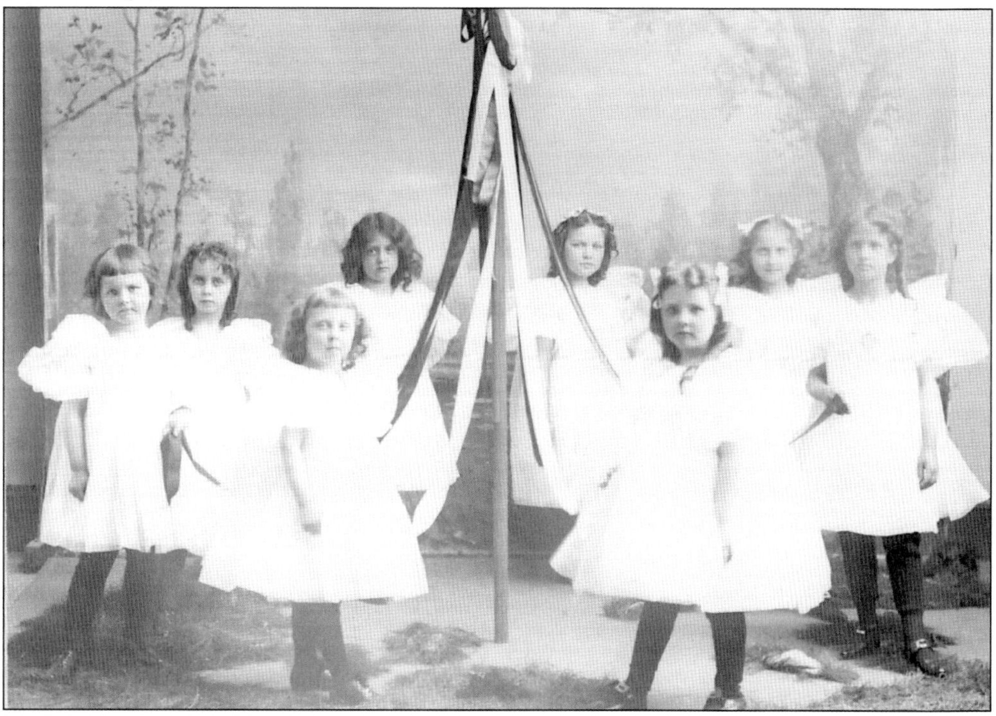

May Day at the Unitarian Church in Farmington, *c.* early 1900s.

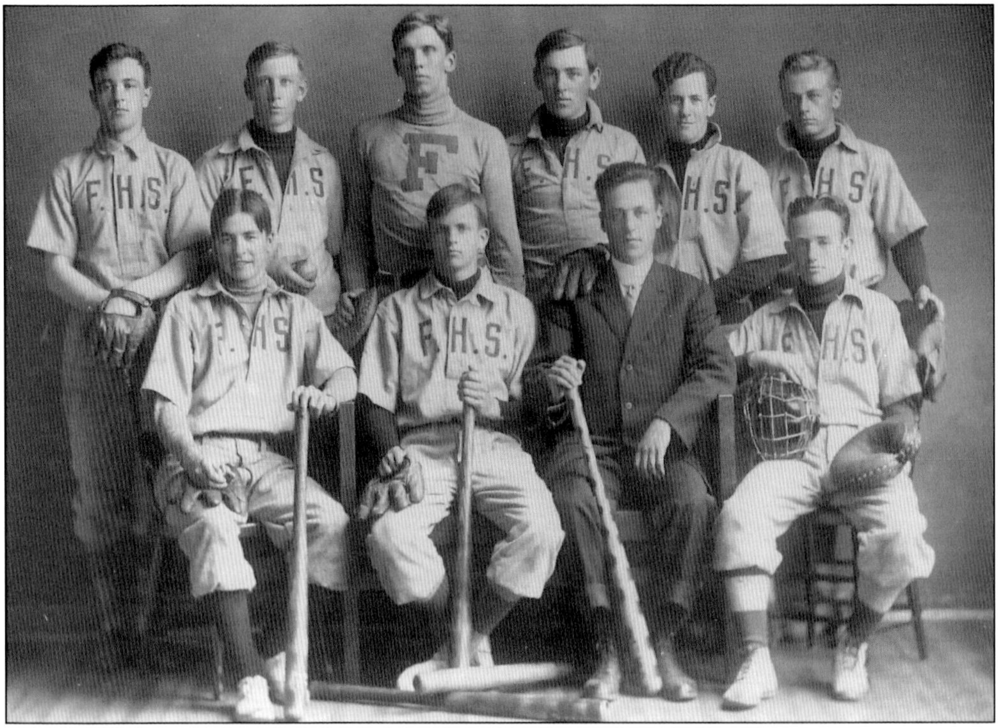

The Farmington High School baseball team, probably of 1910. Baseball was extremely popular in the area, which sported such teams as the Farmington Flyers. Some of those shown here have been identified from left to right as follows: (front row) Thaddeus Roderick, Phil Marsh, unknown, and Schuyler Tardy; (back row) unknown, Richard Dingley, unknown, unknown, Dan Adams, and Harold Trask.

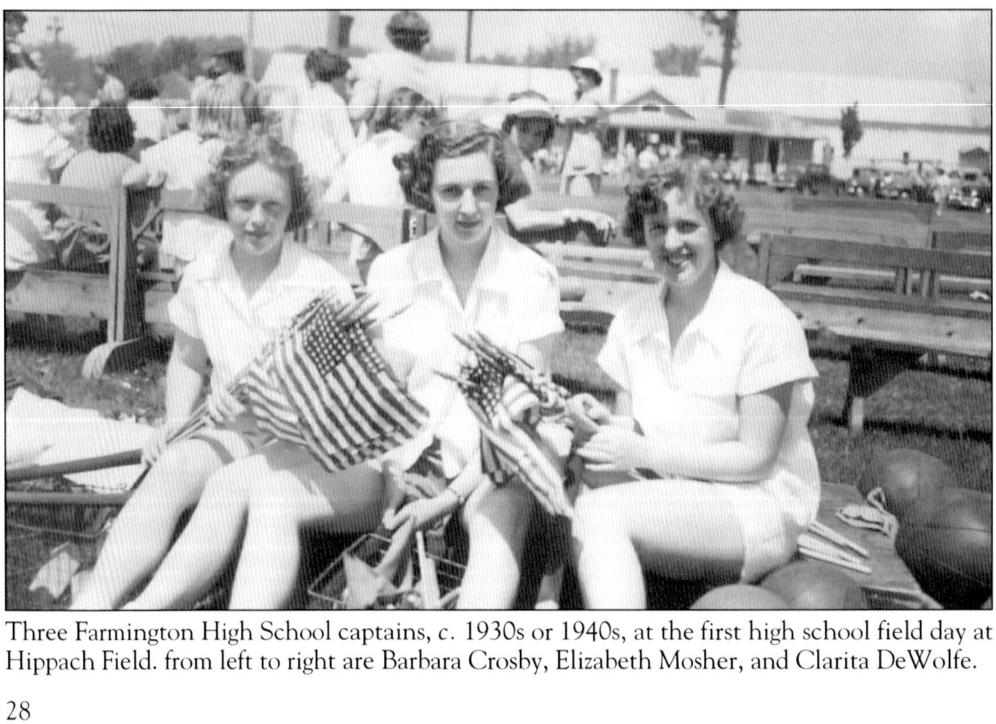

Three Farmington High School captains, *c.* 1930s or 1940s, at the first high school field day at Hippach Field. from left to right are Barbara Crosby, Elizabeth Mosher, and Clarita DeWolfe.

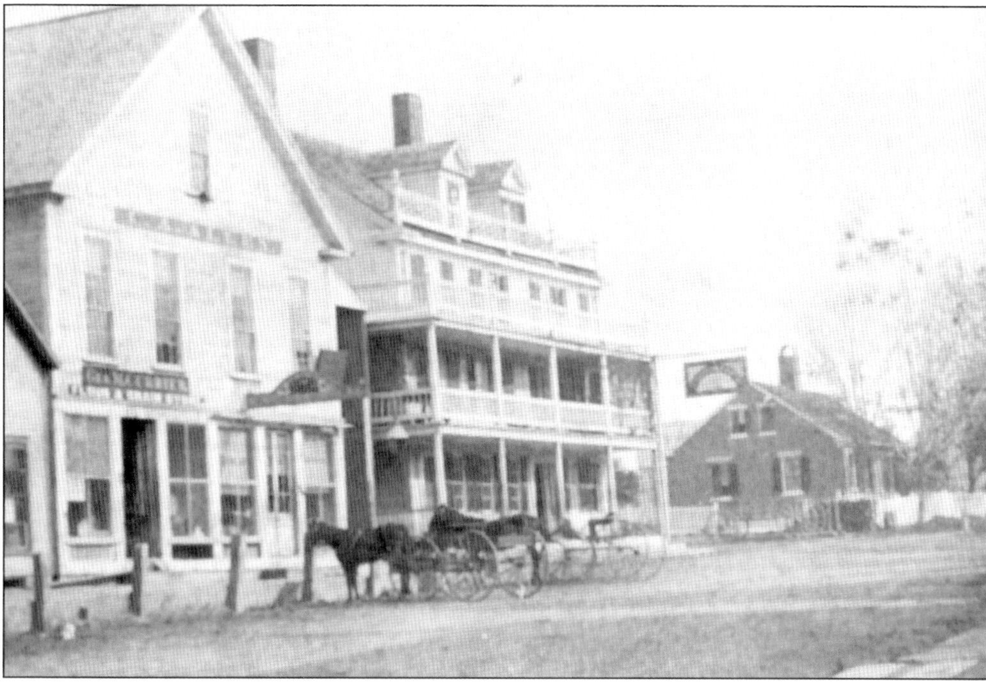

Another Farmington hotel, the Stoddard House in the center with the three porches, stands next to George McCarter's flour and grain store and L.A. Allen in this *c.* 1880s photograph. The hotel opened on February 8, 1849, with Samuel F. Stoddard as owner. It stayed open until the 1940s.

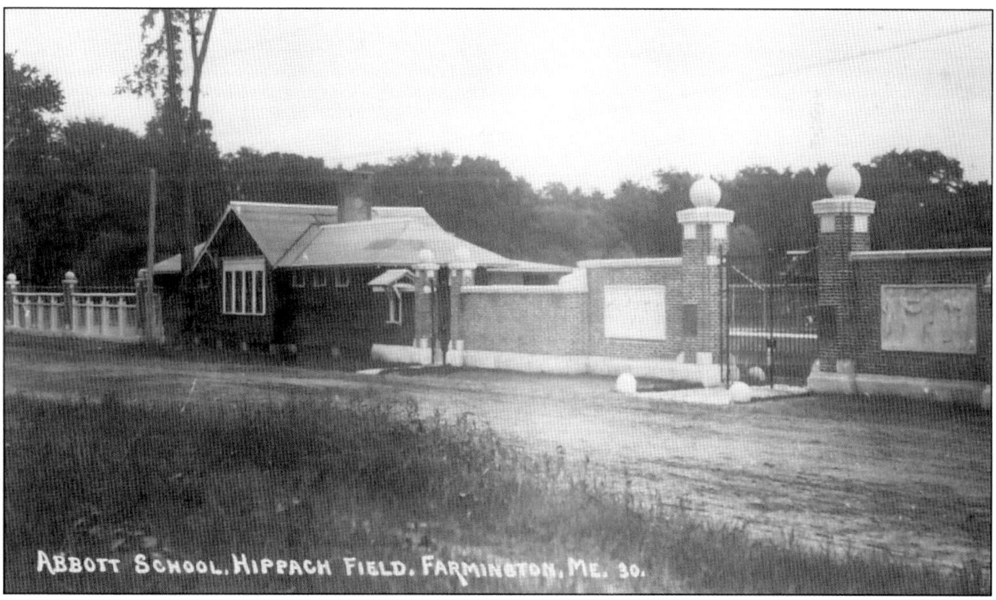

Howard Hippach Memorial Field was part of the Abbott School when this postcard was issued. The first game on this field was played on October 2, 1915. The field was used for various other schools' and organizations' contests in the 1920s and by varied schools and groups after Abbott School closed in the 1930s. The Farmington Flyers, the high school, and Farmington State Normal School used it. Happach Field burned in 1996.

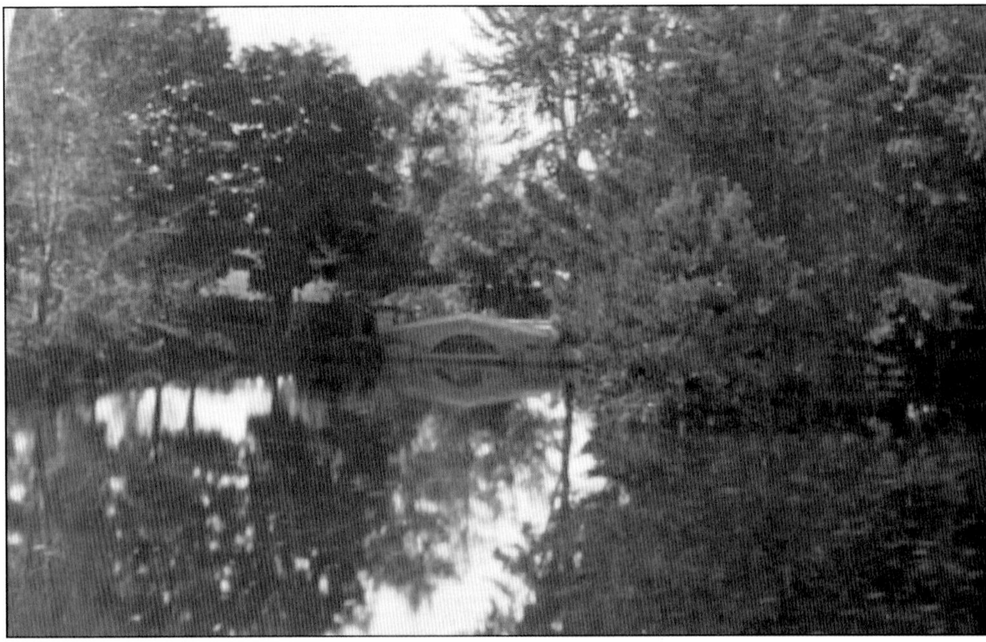

Some of the beautiful grounds of the Abbott School for Boys which took youths from all over this country and from foreign nations, *c.* 1870s. Started in 1844, the school was open into the 1930s. The area was called Little Blue.

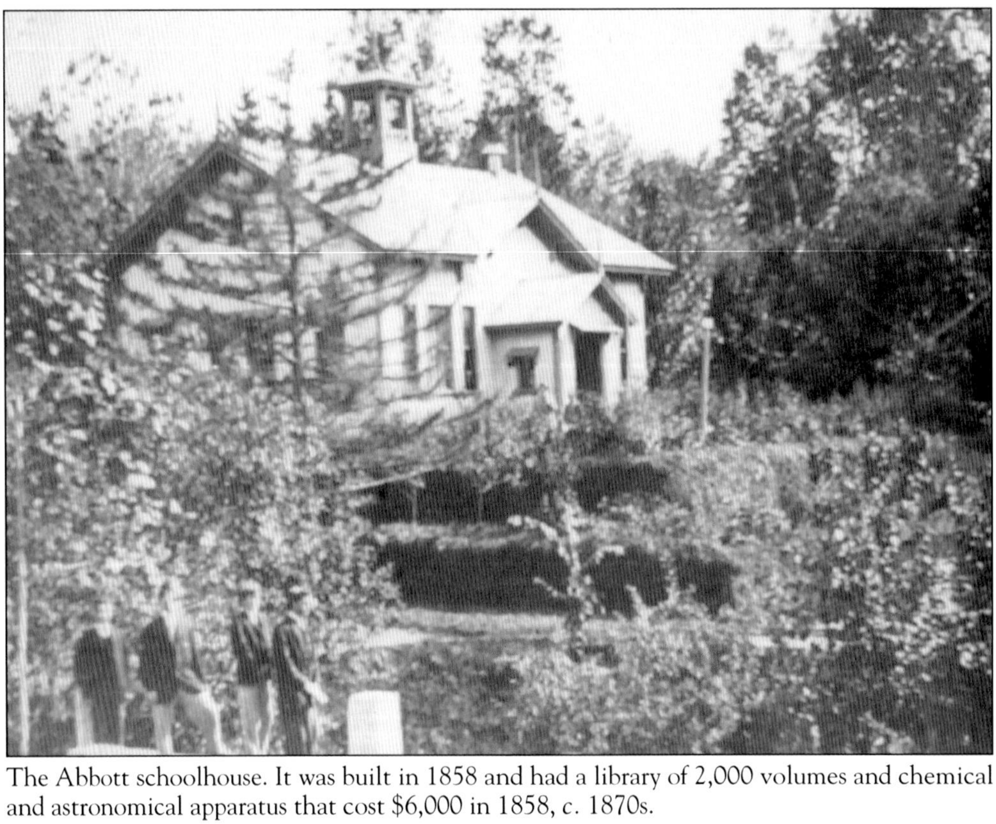

The Abbott schoolhouse. It was built in 1858 and had a library of 2,000 volumes and chemical and astronomical apparatus that cost $6,000 in 1858, *c.* 1870s.

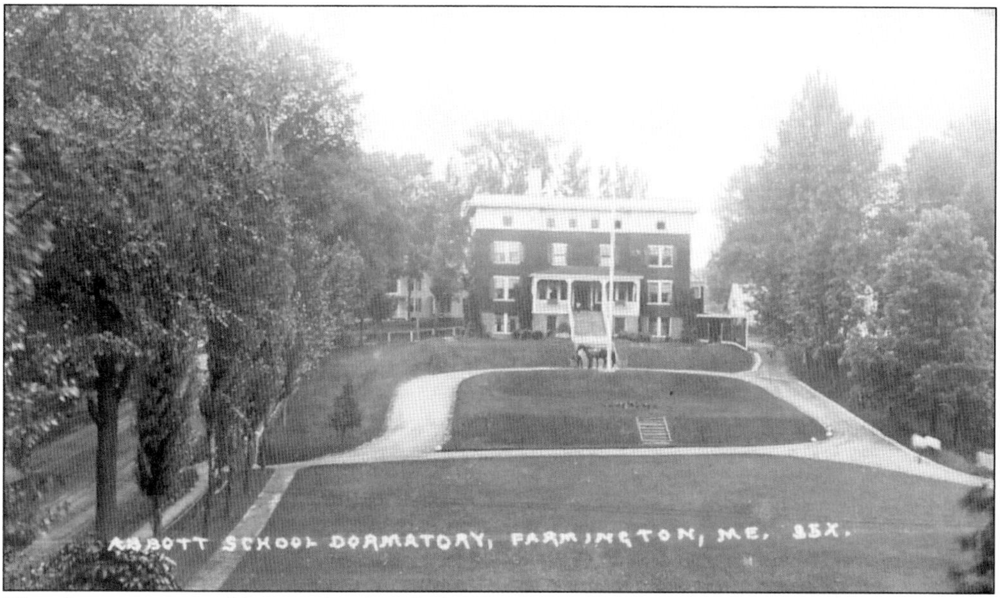

The dormitory at Abbott School called a "mansion" by G.D. Merrill of Farmington, its photographer. It accommodated about sixty students. The Little Blue complex covered about 20 acres.

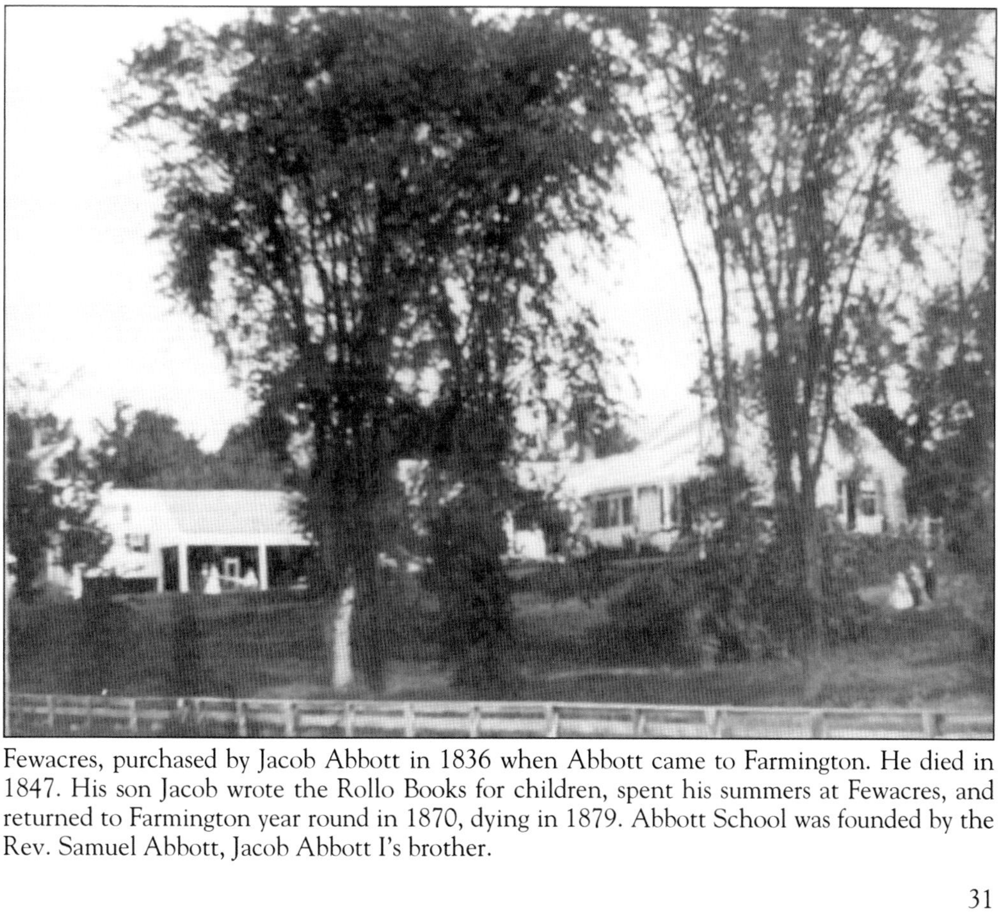

Fewacres, purchased by Jacob Abbott in 1836 when Abbott came to Farmington. He died in 1847. His son Jacob wrote the Rollo Books for children, spent his summers at Fewacres, and returned to Farmington year round in 1870, dying in 1879. Abbott School was founded by the Rev. Samuel Abbott, Jacob Abbott I's brother.

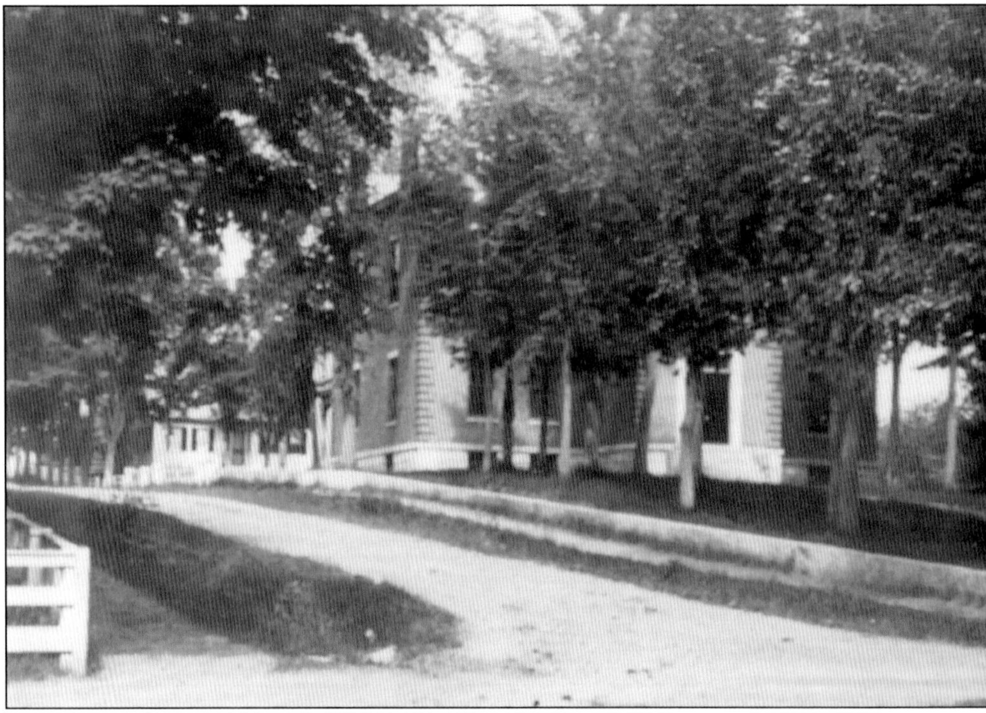

The leading educational facility in Farmington in the long run was Farmington State Normal School (now the University of Maine at Farmington, UMF). This is that school, *c.* 1890s. It was an outgrowth of Farmington Academy, which conveyed all its property to the state. First classes at the normal school were held on August 24, 1864.

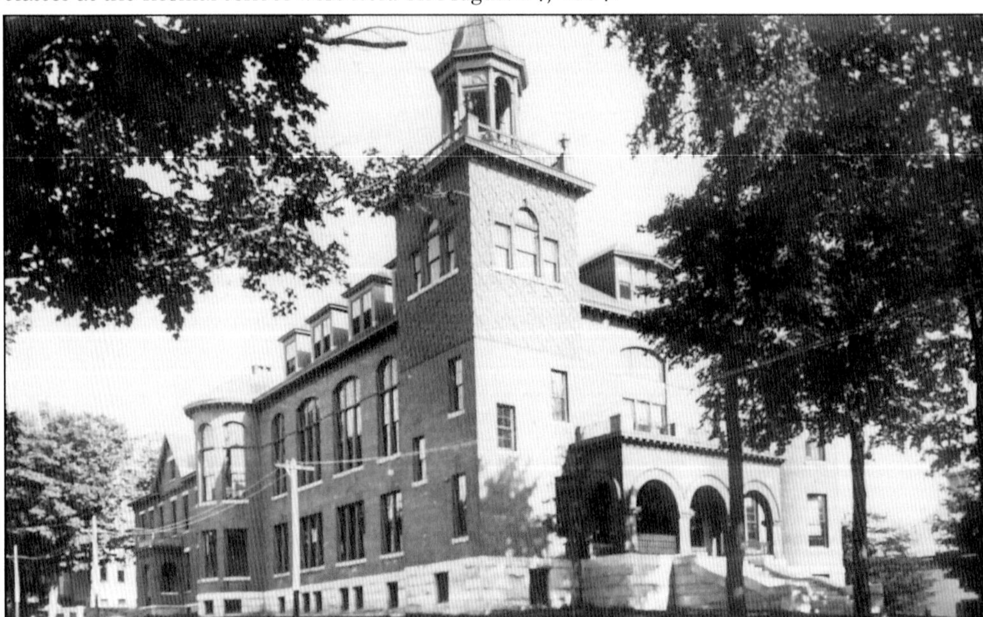

Another view of the normal school, *c.* 1920s or 1930s. The name was changed to Farmington State Teachers' College on July 19, 1945. Later, it became the University of Maine at Farmington.

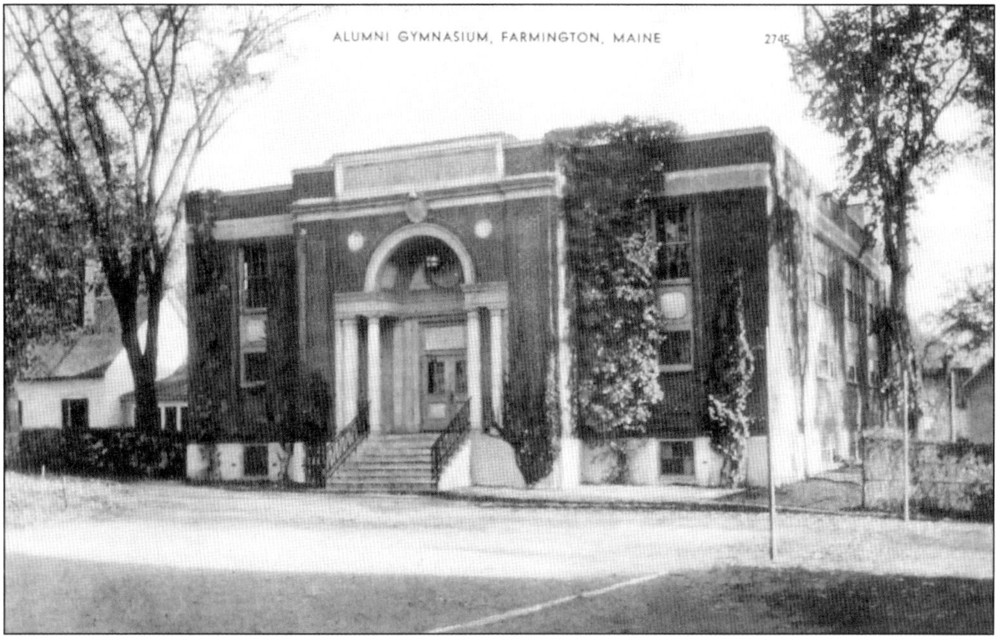

Alumni Gymnasium at the normal school, *c.* 1961. It was built in 1931 and was used by teams from other Farmington schools at times.

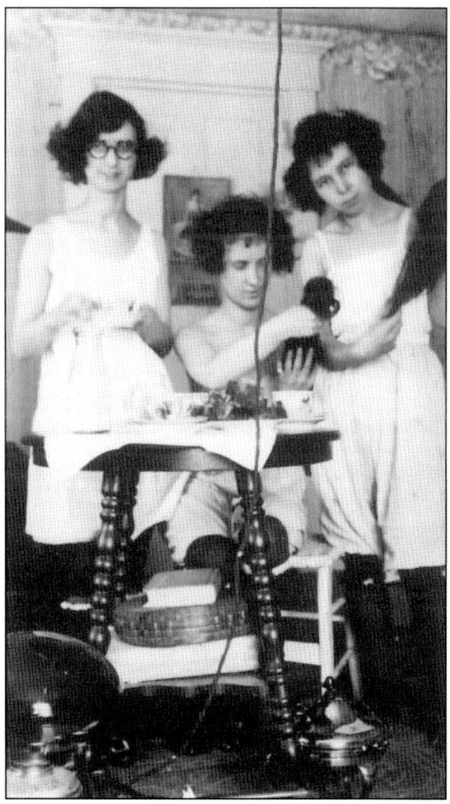

The girls at Farmington State Normal School had good times. My mother, then Ruth Putnam, is on the left at this 1919 tea party.

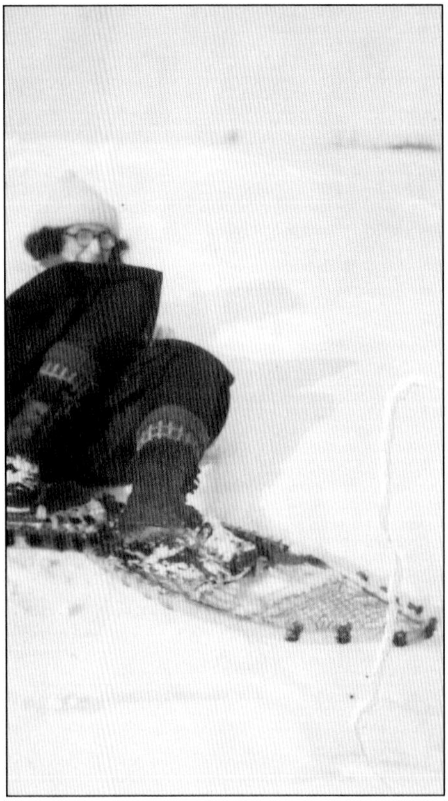

My mother had her ups and downs at Farmington Normal. This was one of the downs.

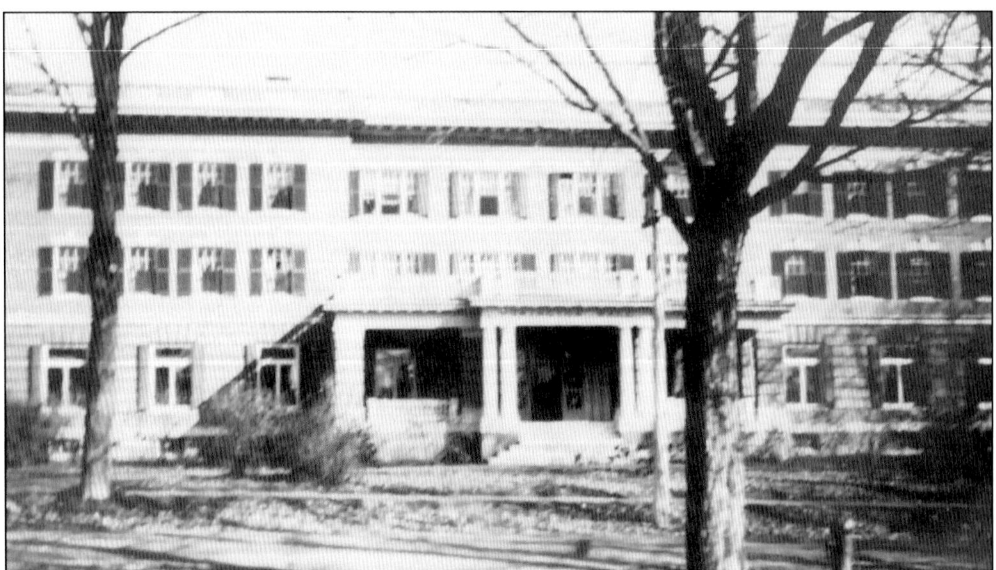

The FSNS dormitory, Purington Hall, in which my mother stayed, *c*. 1919–20.

Ruth Putnam (right) is back on her feet again with her snowshoes.

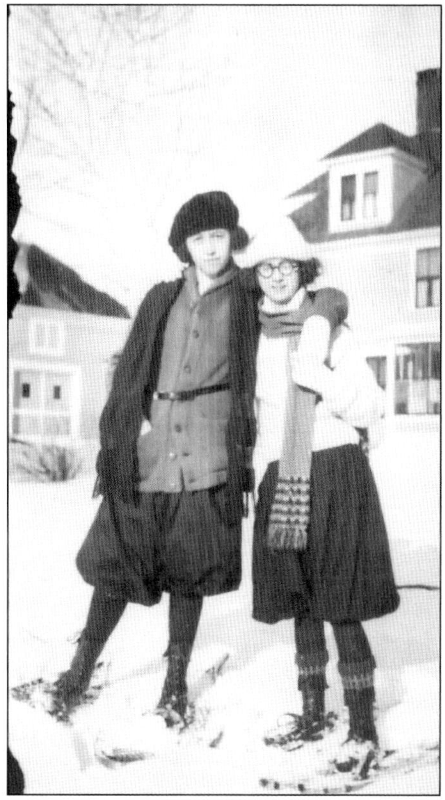

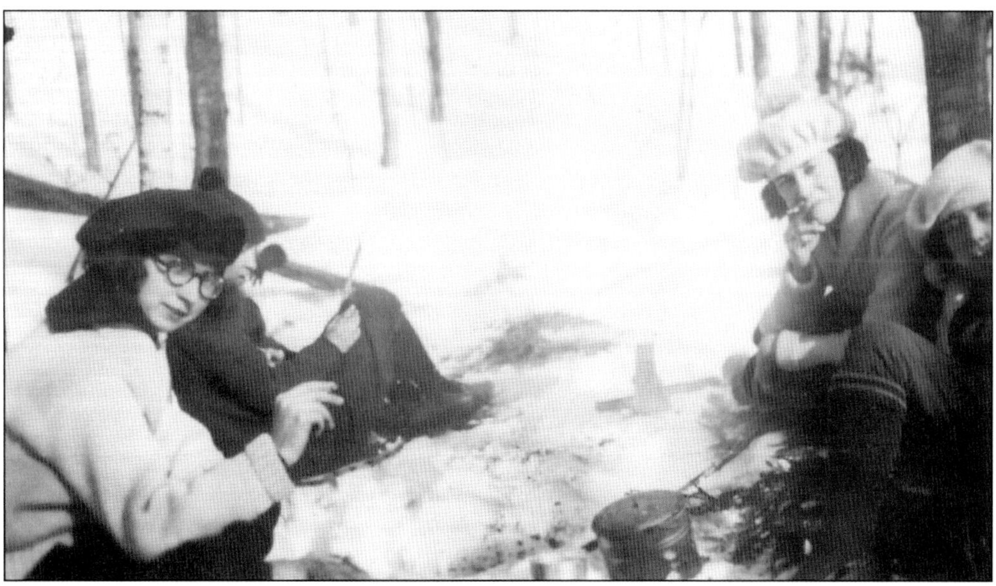

This photograph was not taken during an anti-cigarette era. The flapper age was just beginning.

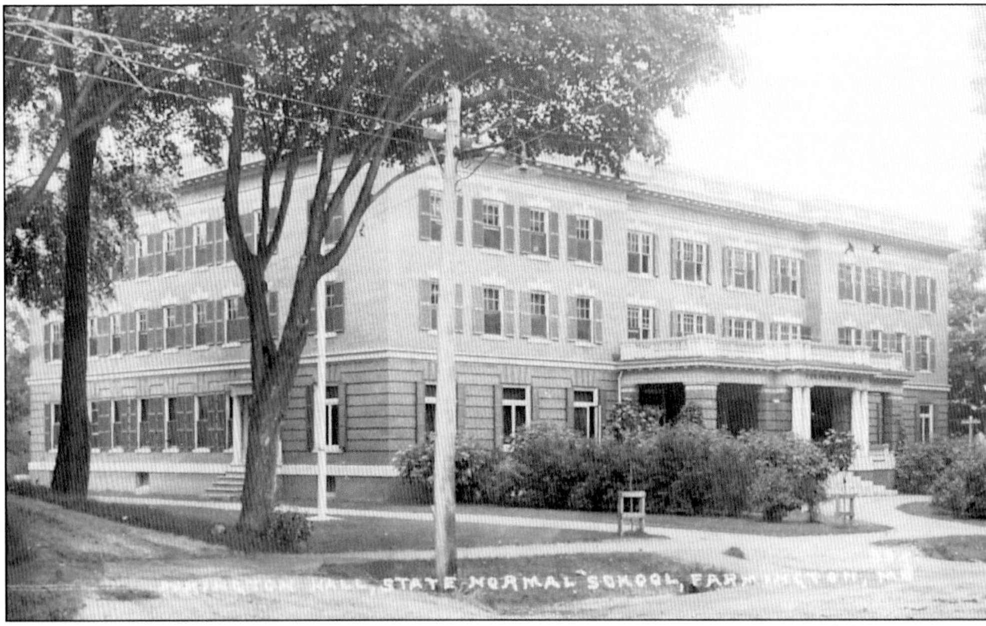

Another view of Purington Hall at FSNS, *c.* early 1920s. The hall was named for George C. Purington, FSNS principal from 1883 to 1909.

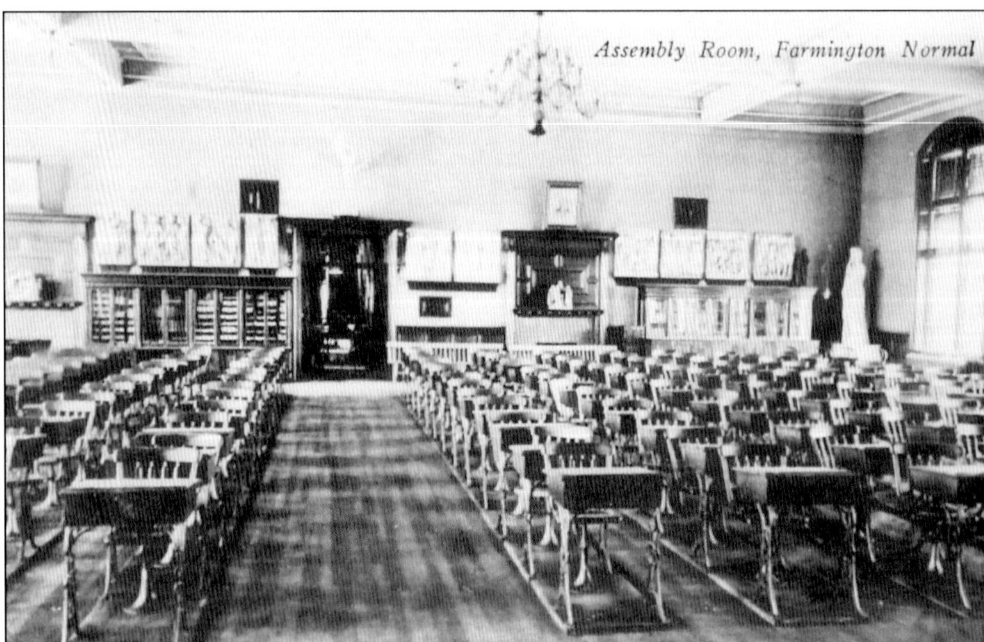

The assembly room at Farmington State Normal School, *c.* 1920s.

Two

The Millses: Political Savvy

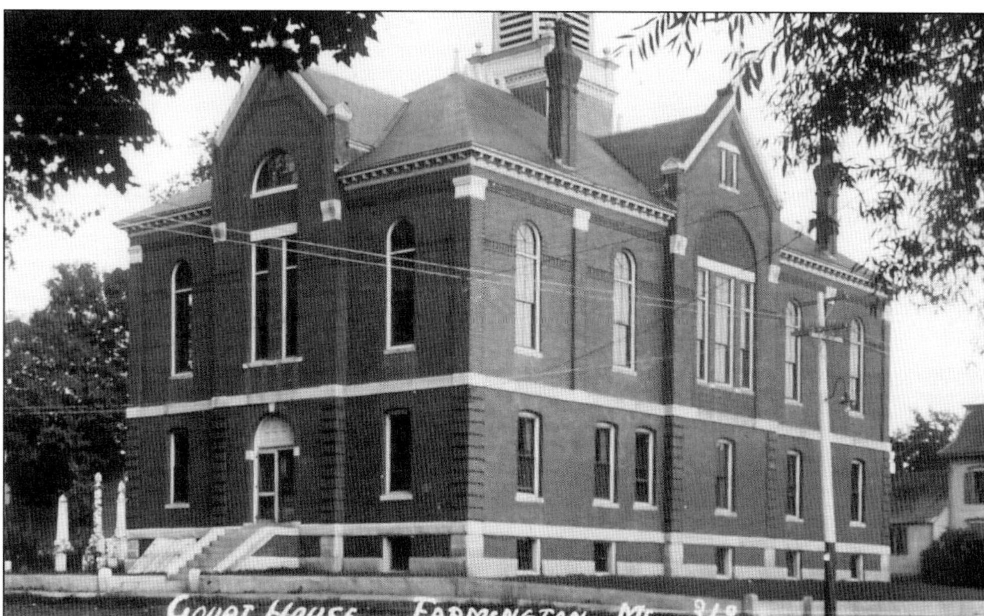

The Franklin County Court House in Farmington. As the county seat, Farmington has added political clout.

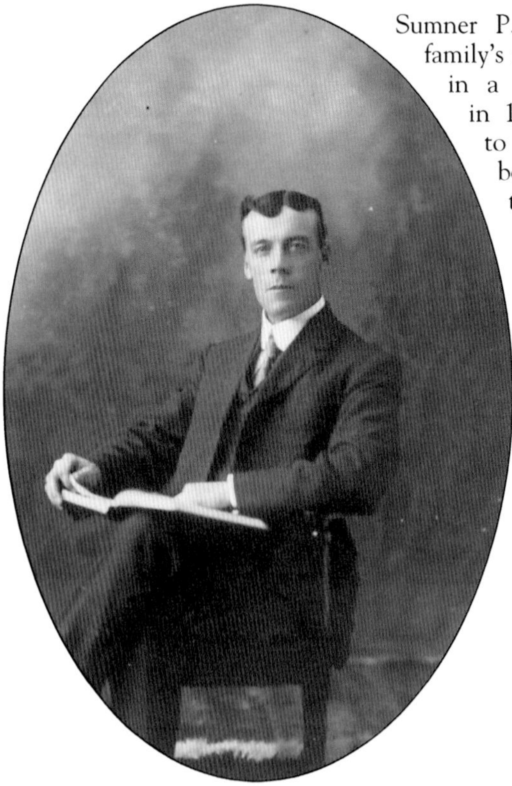

Sumner P. Mills, 1874–1956, founder of the Mills family's record of service in Farmington and beyond, in a photograph taken in Stonington, Maine, in 1907. Mills, already a state senator, moved to Farmington on May 17, 1911, basically because his wife, Flora Pearson, came from that town. On May 30, 1912, Sumner Mills was a speaker during Farmington Memorial Day ceremonies.

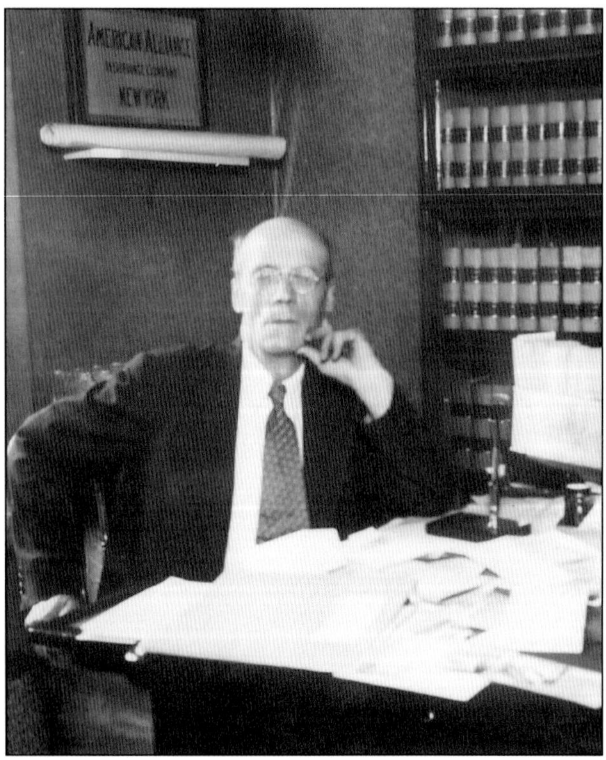

Sumner P. Mills in his office about 1940. In 1919, he succeeded Currier C. Holman as judge of the Farmington Municipal Court, a post he held twelve years. Mills was one of the presidents of the Farmington Chamber of Commerce. He started what became a tradition in his family, serving as moderator of the Farmington town meeting from 1916 to 1946, when he was succeeded by his son Peter. Peter Mills served in that post a number of years. In the early 1980s, after a non-Mills interval, Paul Mills, Peter's son, became the moderator and has held that post since.

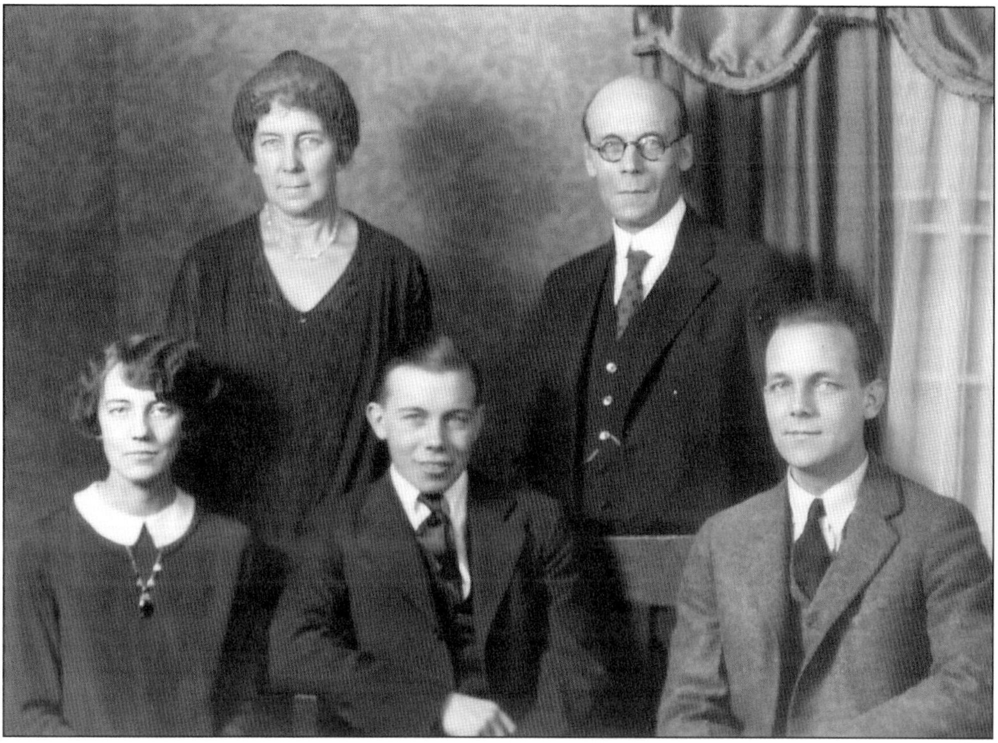

The Mills family in 1933. On the left in the front row is Virginia Mills (1909–1983), who taught English in several Maine schools and, then, for thirty years, was an English teacher at Springfield (Mass.) Classical High. In the center front is Peter Mills (1911–?), former U.S. attorney for Maine, and to the right in the front row is William Mills, a Bowdoin graduate who served as a clerk at the U.S. District Court in Portland from 1934 to 1942, as a lieutenant commander in the U.S. Navy, as vice president of the St. Joe Paper Co., Jacksonville, Fla., and as president of the Florida National Bank, Jacksonville. In the back row are Flora Mills (1875–1964) and Sumner P. Mills. The family was living on High Street, Farmington.

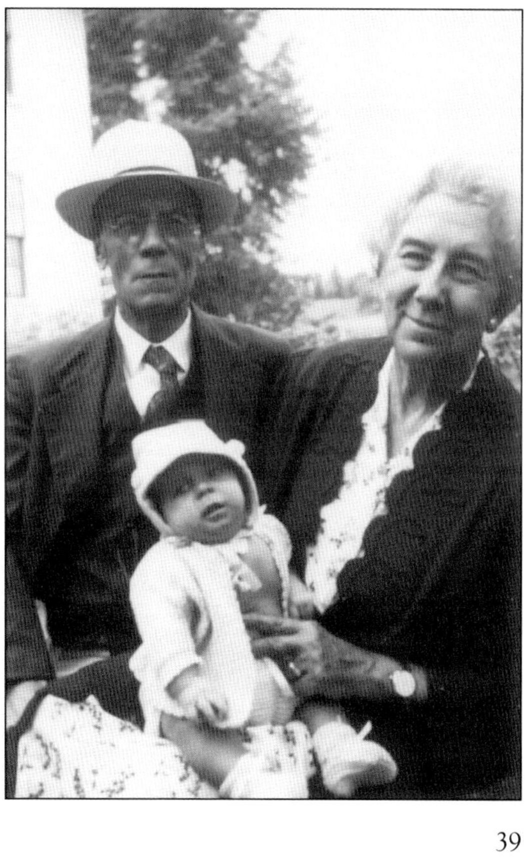

Mr. and Mrs. Sumner P. Mills with their grandchild, S. Peter Mills III, in 1943.

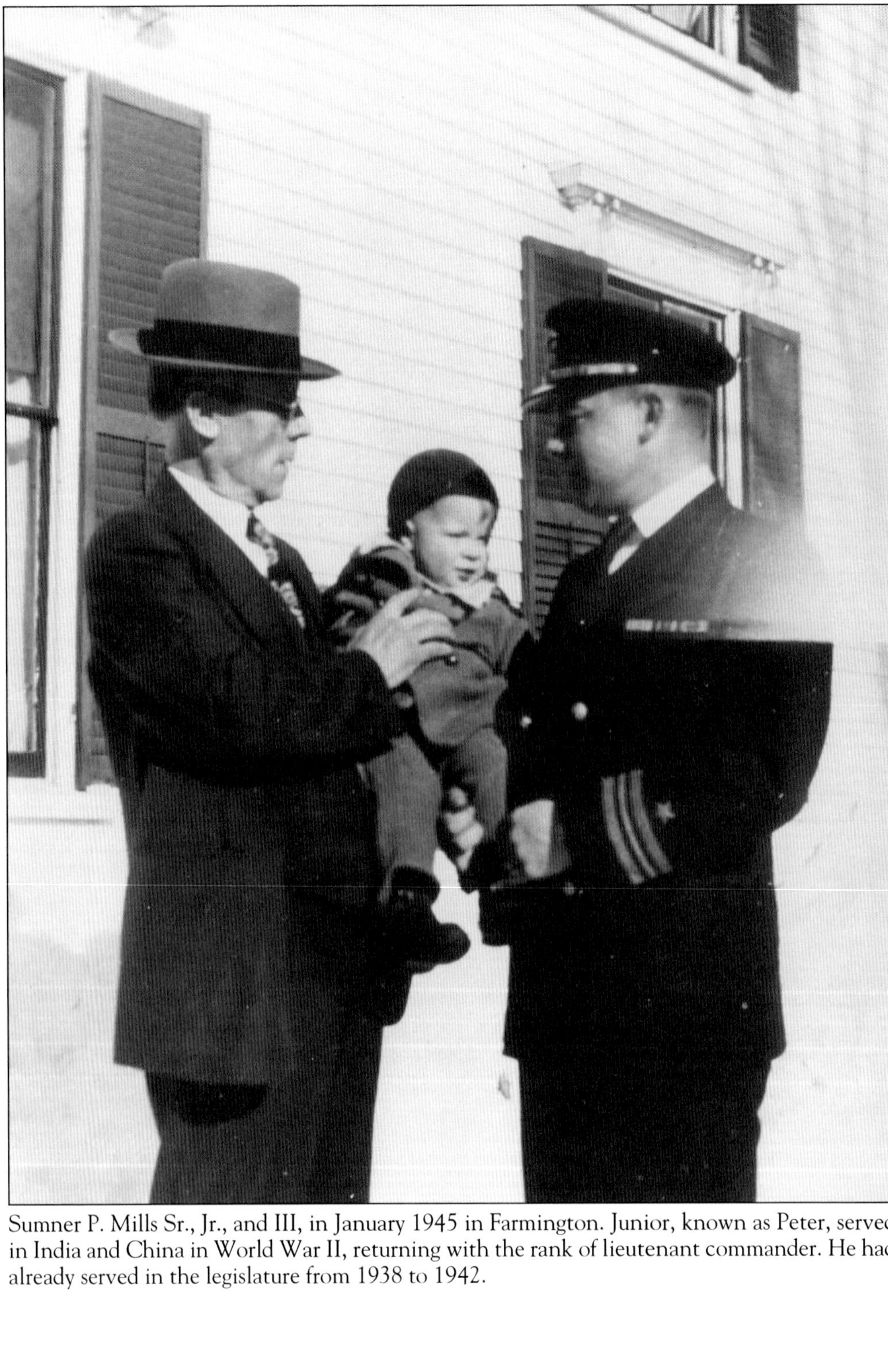

Sumner P. Mills Sr., Jr., and III, in January 1945 in Farmington. Junior, known as Peter, served in India and China in World War II, returning with the rank of lieutenant commander. He had already served in the legislature from 1938 to 1942.

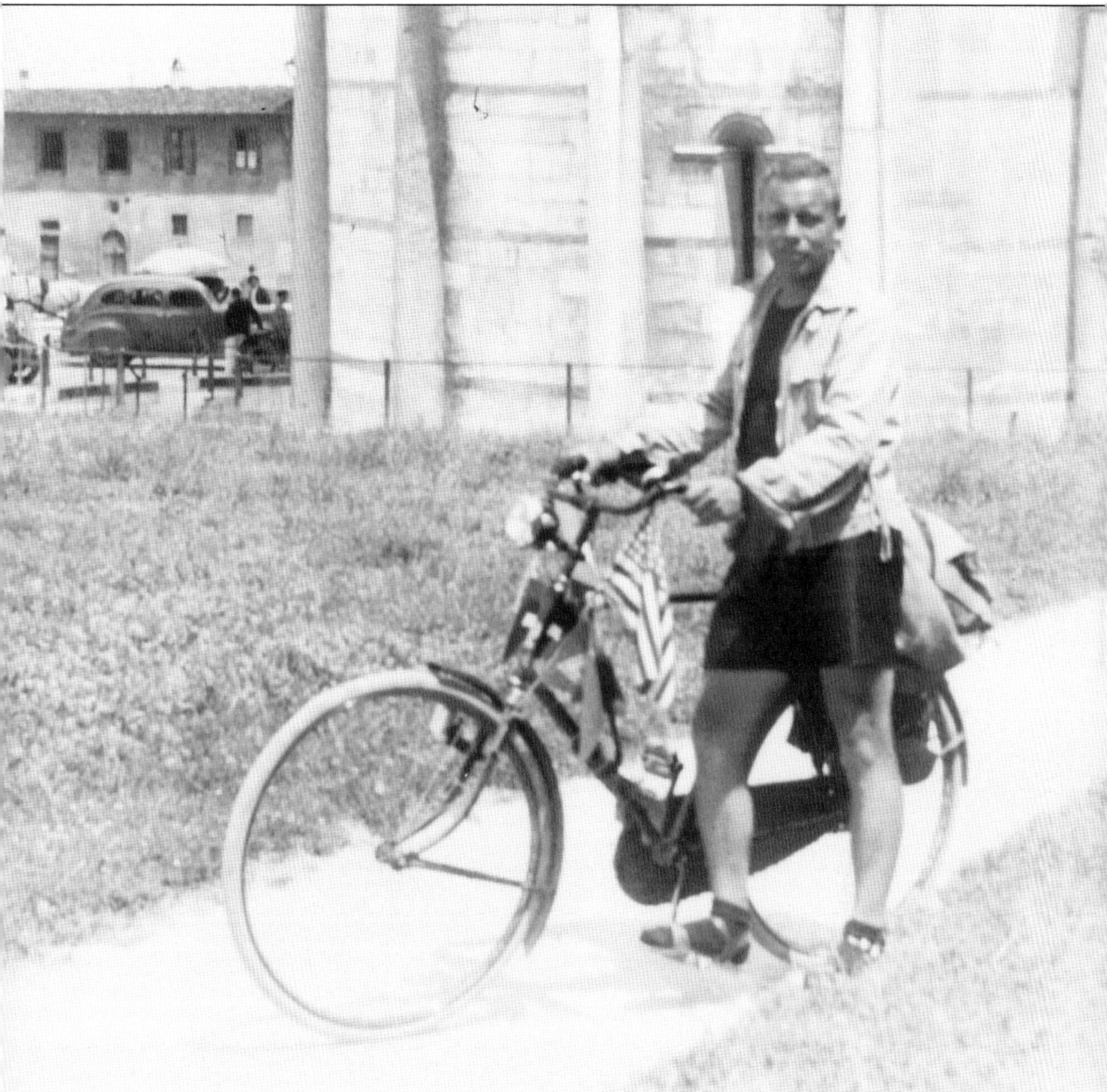

Peter Mills in Italy in 1937. He pedaled almost 3,000 miles through Europe, then earned his passage on the ship *Excalibur* by working in its laundry. Once back home, he gave about 110 talks in Franklin County about his travels. There are those who say he did so with his eye on a run for the legislature.

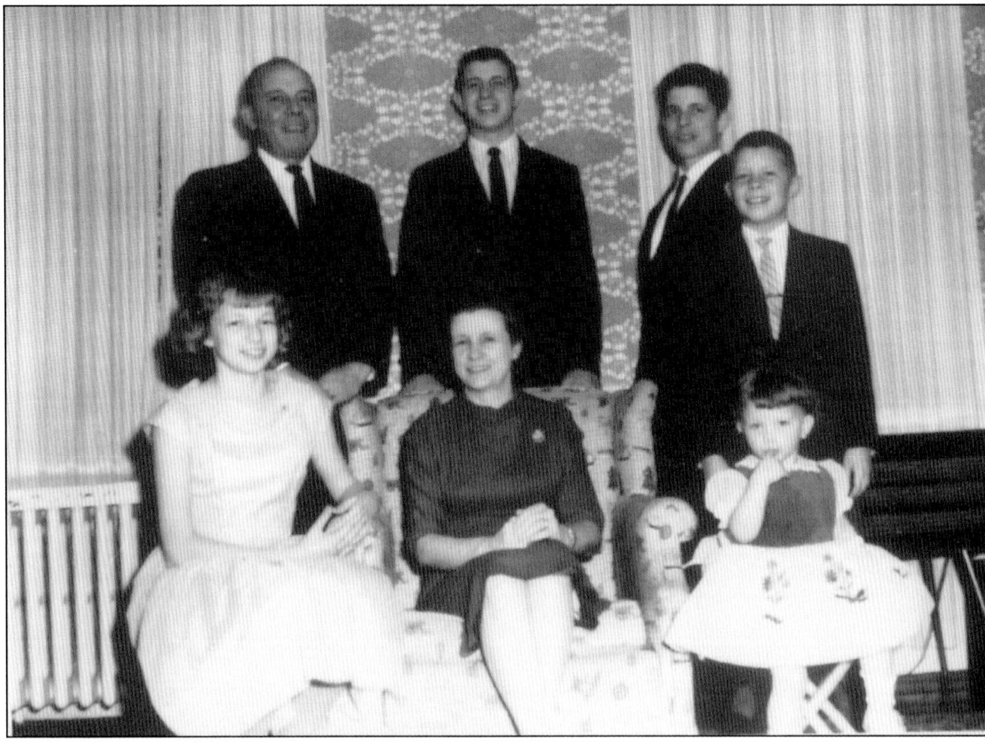

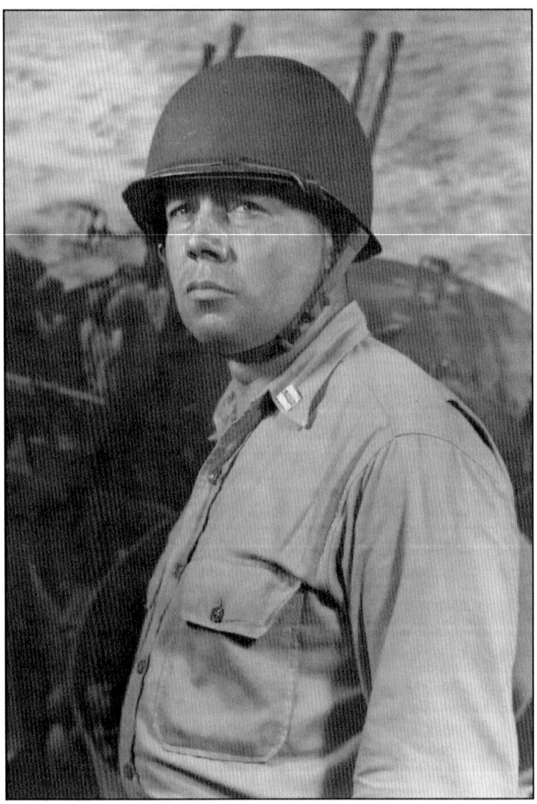

The Peter Mills family in 1961. From left to right are as follows: (front row) Janet, Katherine (Mrs. Peter Mills), and Dora; (back row) Peter, S. Peter Mills III, David, and Paul. S. Peter III, an attorney, is a Republican state senator from Skowhegan now. Janet, an attorney, was district attorney for Androscoggin, Franklin, and Oxford Counties from 1980 to 1994. Paul, an attorney, is a free-lance political analyst and town meeting moderator in Farmington; and David is an antique car buff and free-lance worker on such cars.

Peter Mills in battle dress during World War II with a landing craft in the background. Mills served two stretches as U.S. attorney for Maine during the Eisenhower and Nixon-Ford administrations, a total of sixteen years, a Maine record for length of service in that federal post. In between his two U.S. attorney stints, he served in the Maine State Senate.

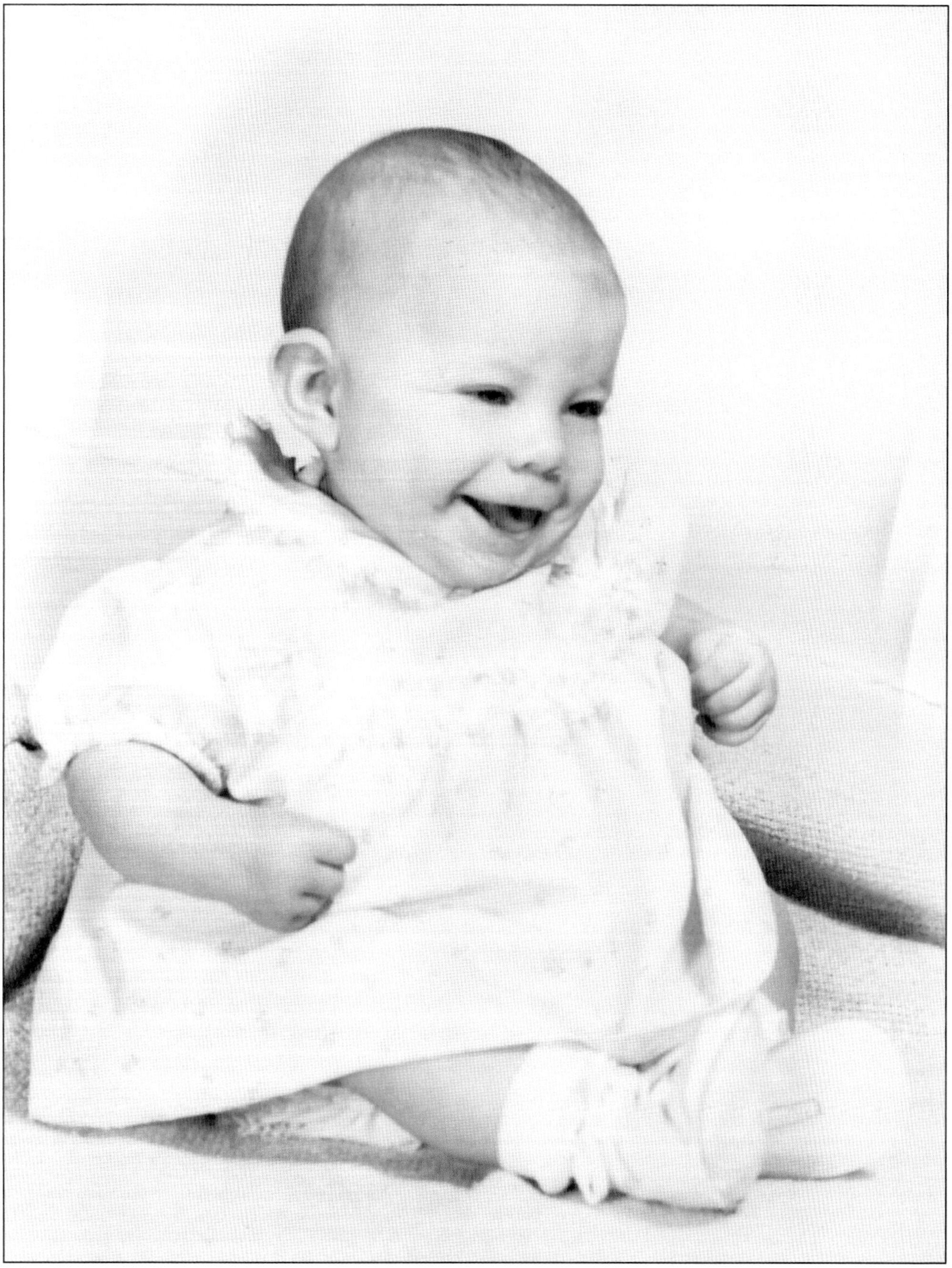

This healthy baby, six months old in 1960, is now Dr. Dora Anne Mills, director of public health for Maine's Department of Human Services. A pediatrician and graduate of the University of Vermont Medical School, she has been working all over the world to help keep babies healthy. After private practices in California and Wilton, she was elected Democratic National Committeewoman from Maine but resigned that post when appointed to her state position by Governor Angus King. The white shoes above were a gift from U.S. Senator Margaret Chase Smith.

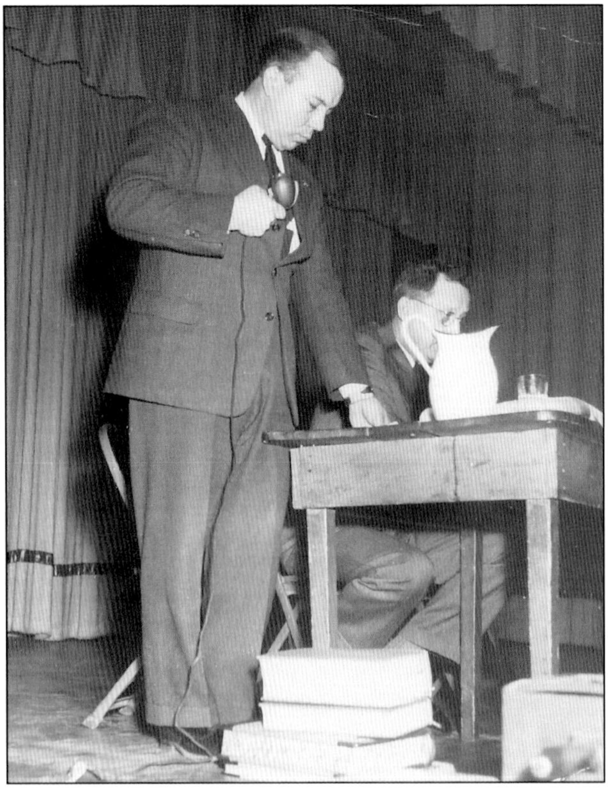

Peter Mills, newly appointed Farmington Municipal Court judge in 1949 by Governor Frederick Payne, is moderator at the first town meeting held in Farmington under the town manager form of government at the Community Center. Seated is Town Clerk Leon R. Goodwin.

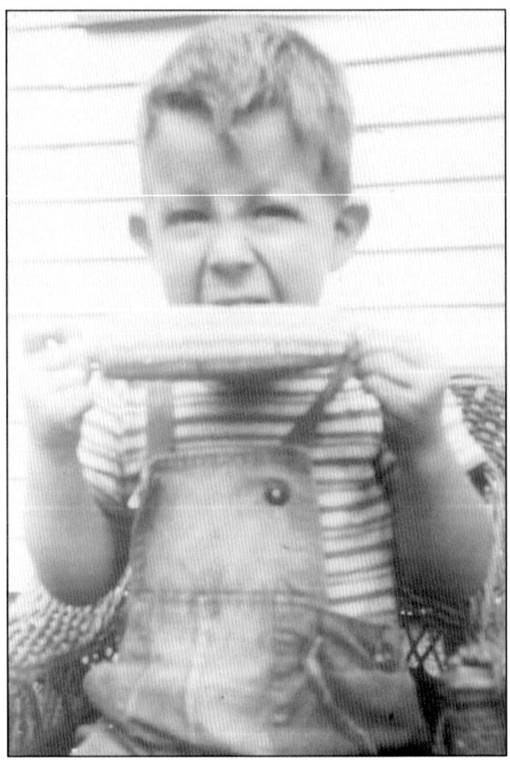

A future Maine state senator is obviously enjoying his corn, c. 1947–48.

Three

Wilton

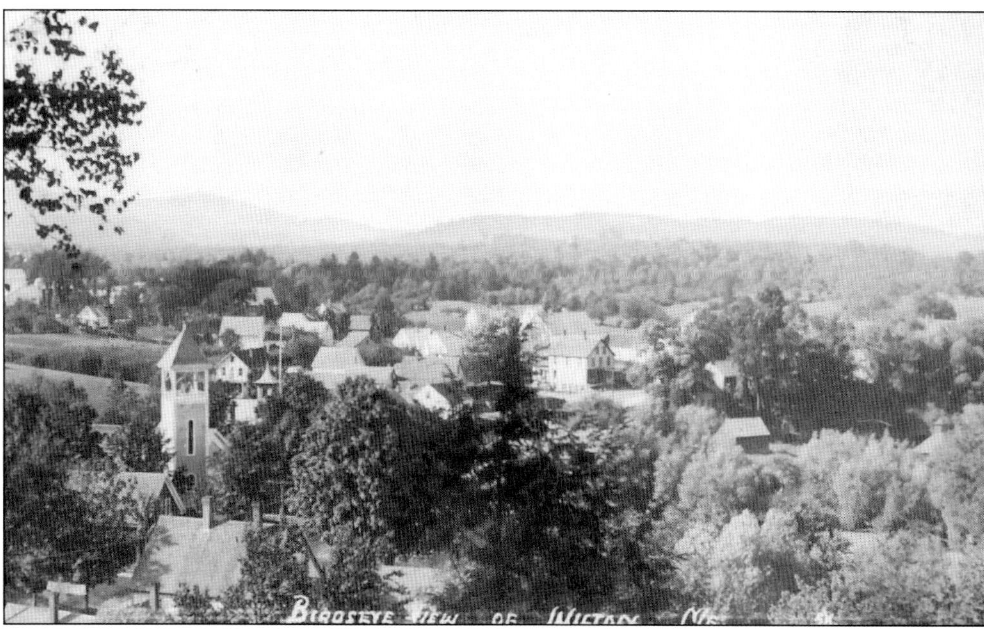

Bird's-eye view of Wilton, *c.* 1900s. The Methodist church is in the left foreground.

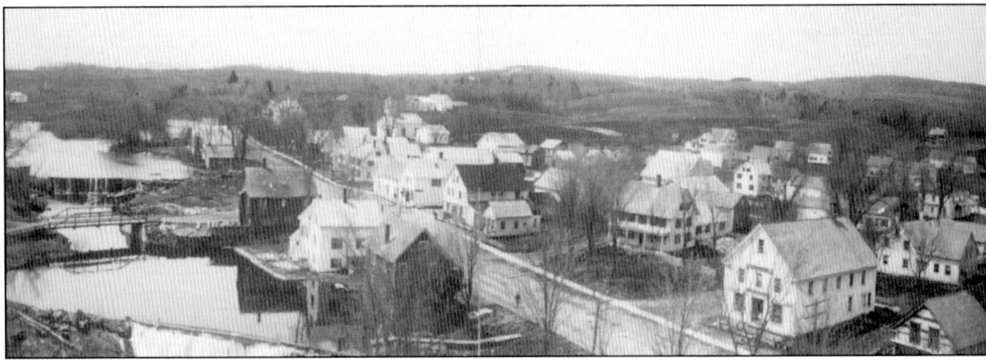

East Wilton Village, pre-1935.

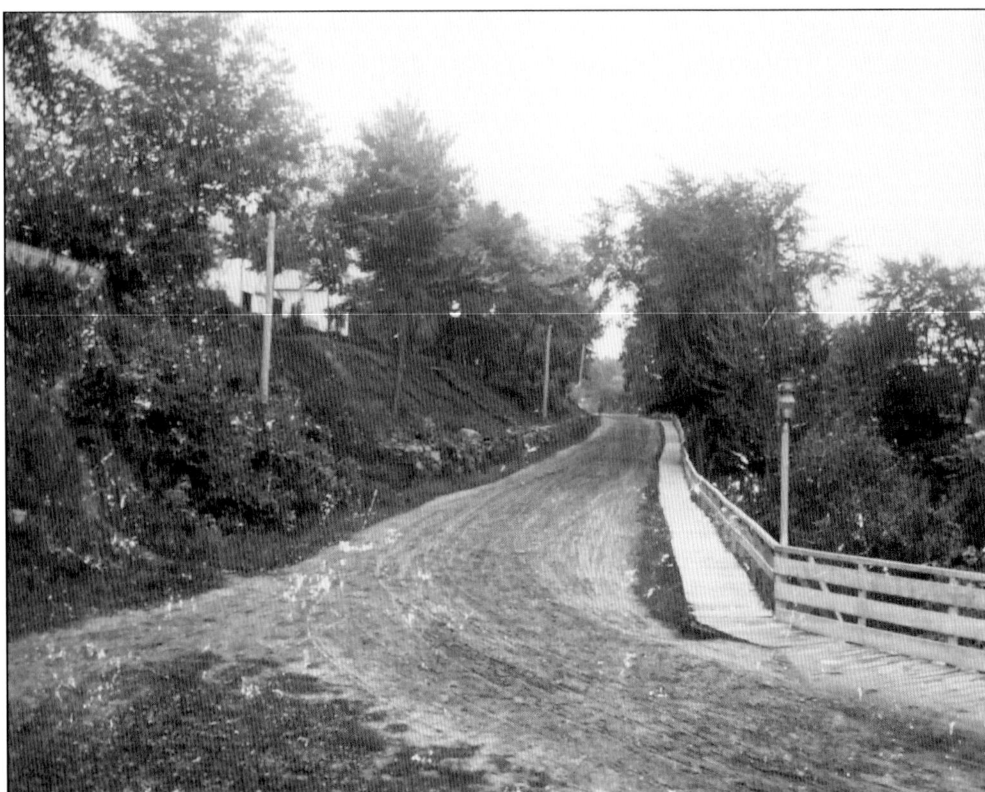

Looking up Dugway in Wilton, before the 1917 bridge was built. It's an example of how roads were at the turn of the century.

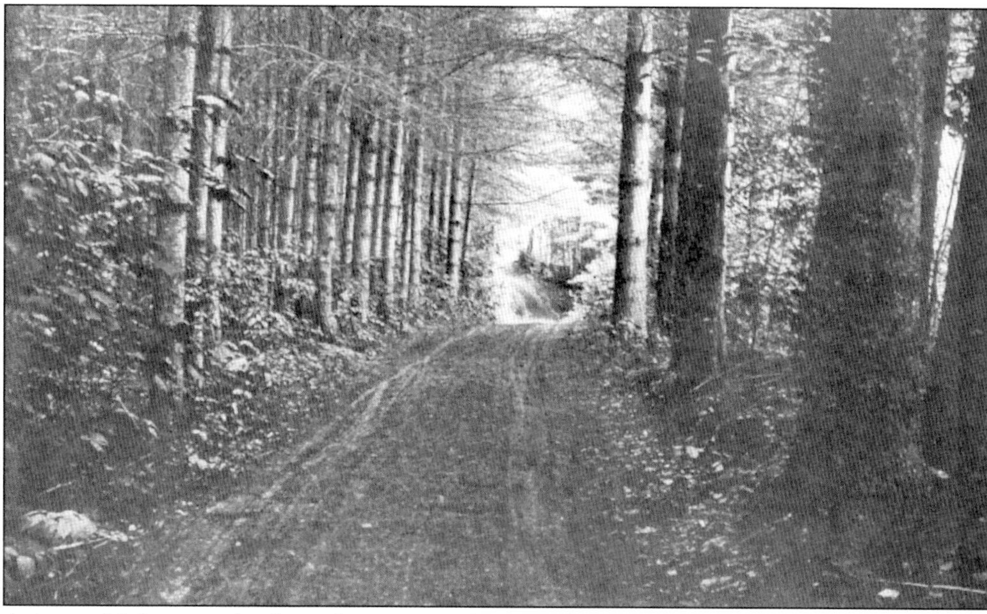

A beautiful buggy ride through pine woods in Wilton, *c.* 1880s. Allen Street is now in this location.

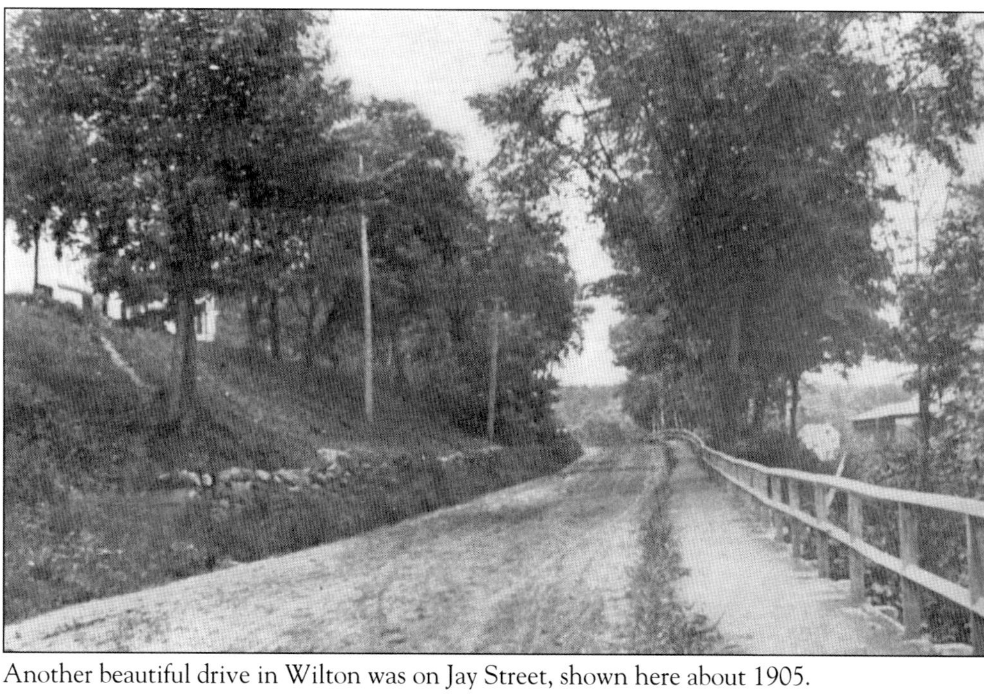

Another beautiful drive in Wilton was on Jay Street, shown here about 1905.

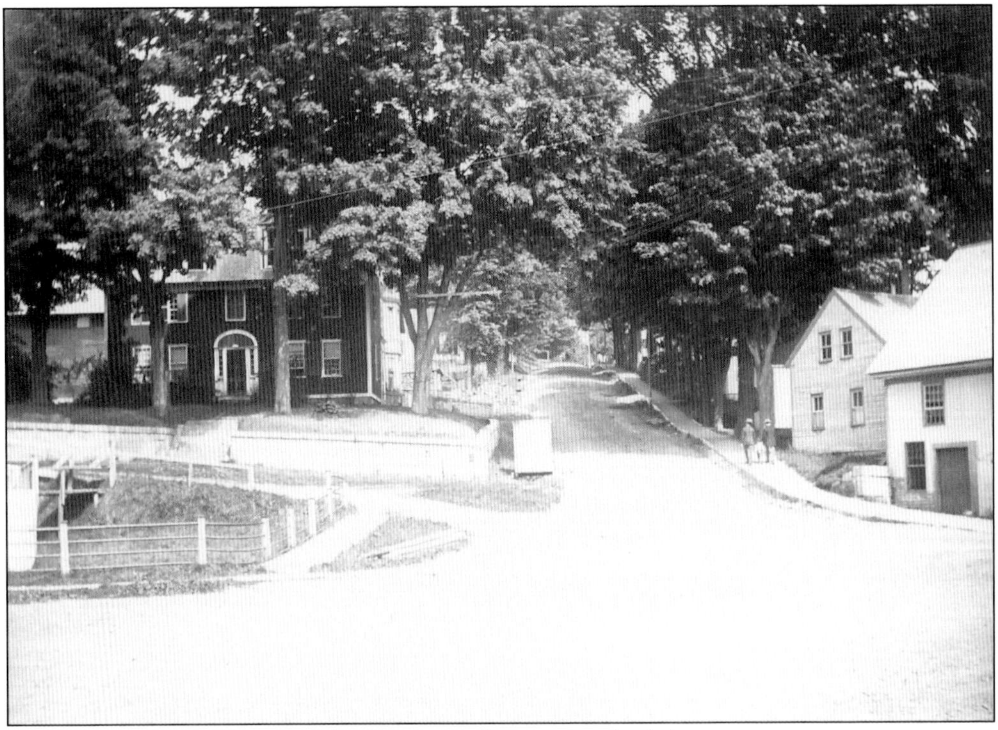

High Street, Wilton, *c.* 1900. The Fenderson house is on the left.

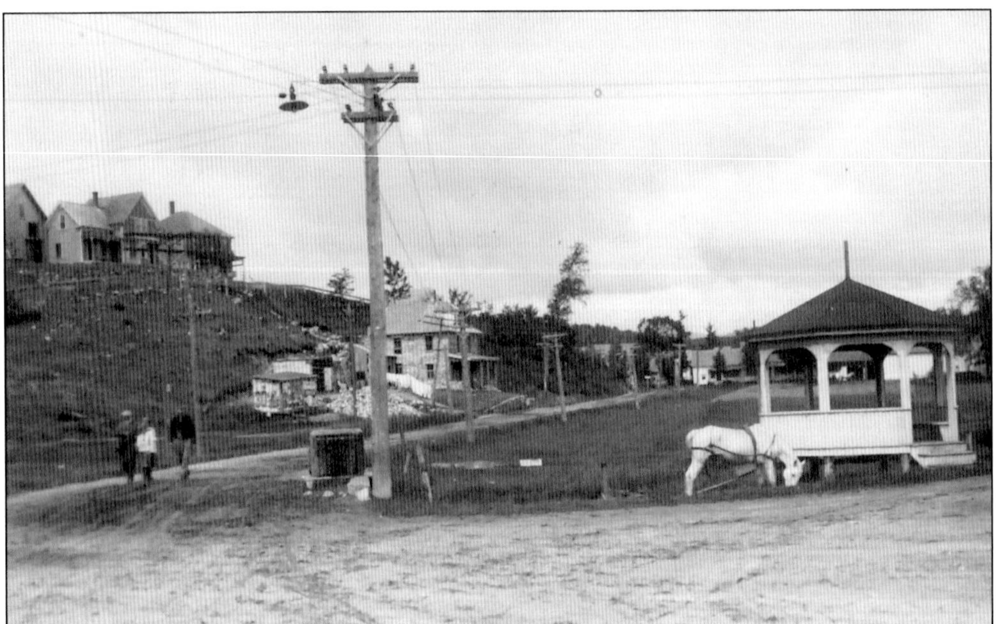

Street view of Dryden, a section of Wilton, *c.* 1910. Note the white horse either feeding or drinking. The parking lot for the railroad station is in the foreground.

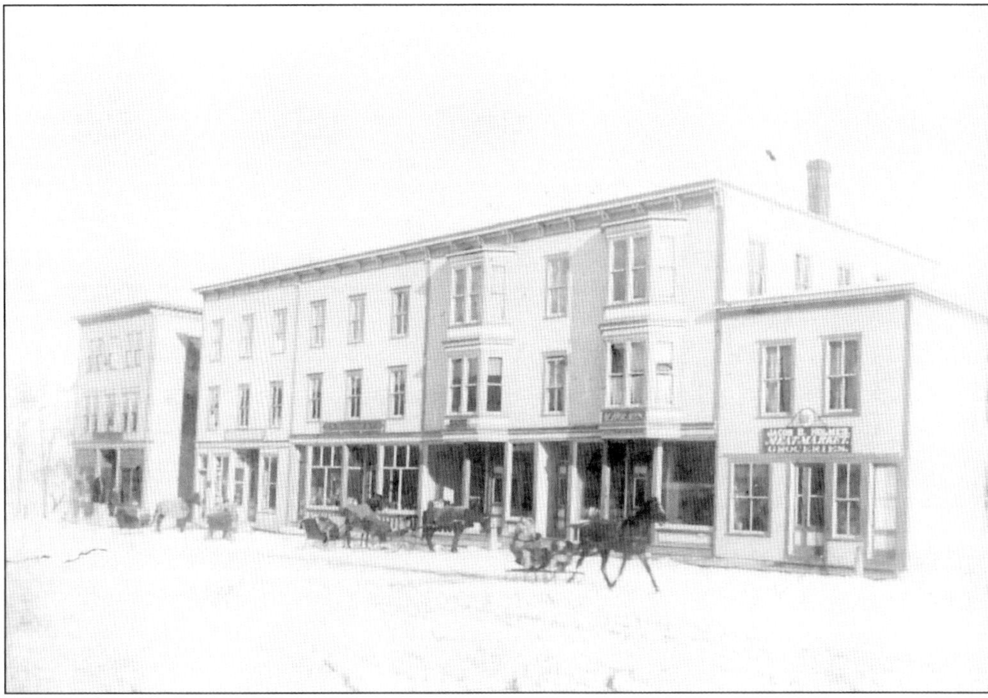

A horse pulls a sled right along on Main Street, Wilton, before the 1893 fire. Other horses are hitched up along the street. Visible businesses include Pike and Mossman, hardware?; H.S. Houghton & Co.; Ora Miller, harnesses; and Jacob B. Holmes, meat and groceries.

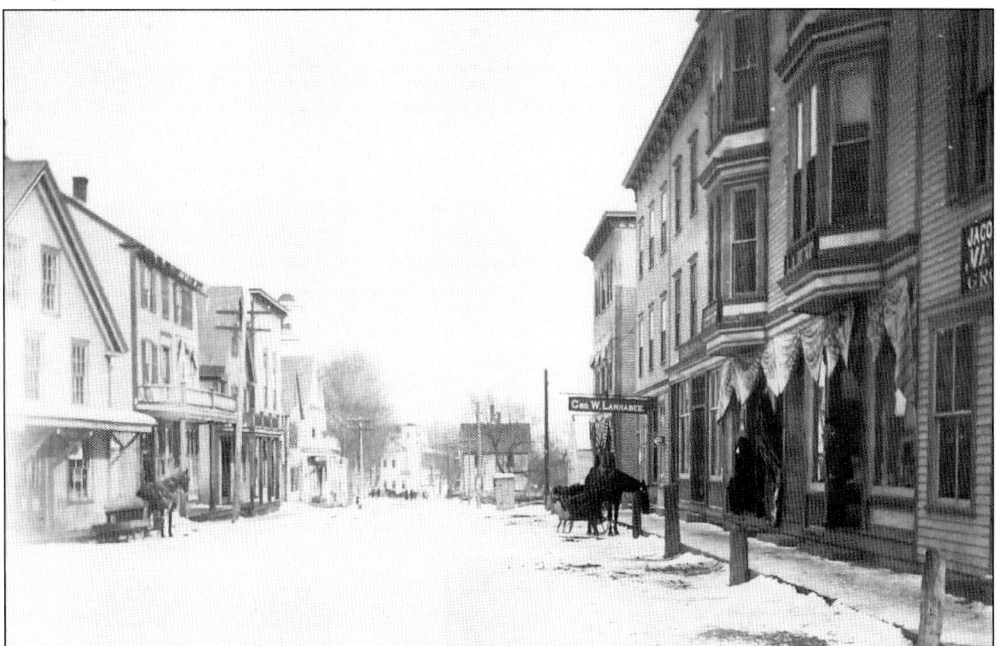

Main Street, Wilton, *c.* 1910. To the right is a horse with a sleigh; to the left is another horse with a sleigh carrier. Jacob Holmes, meat and groceries, is in the right foreground, and the George W. Larrabee sign can also be seen.

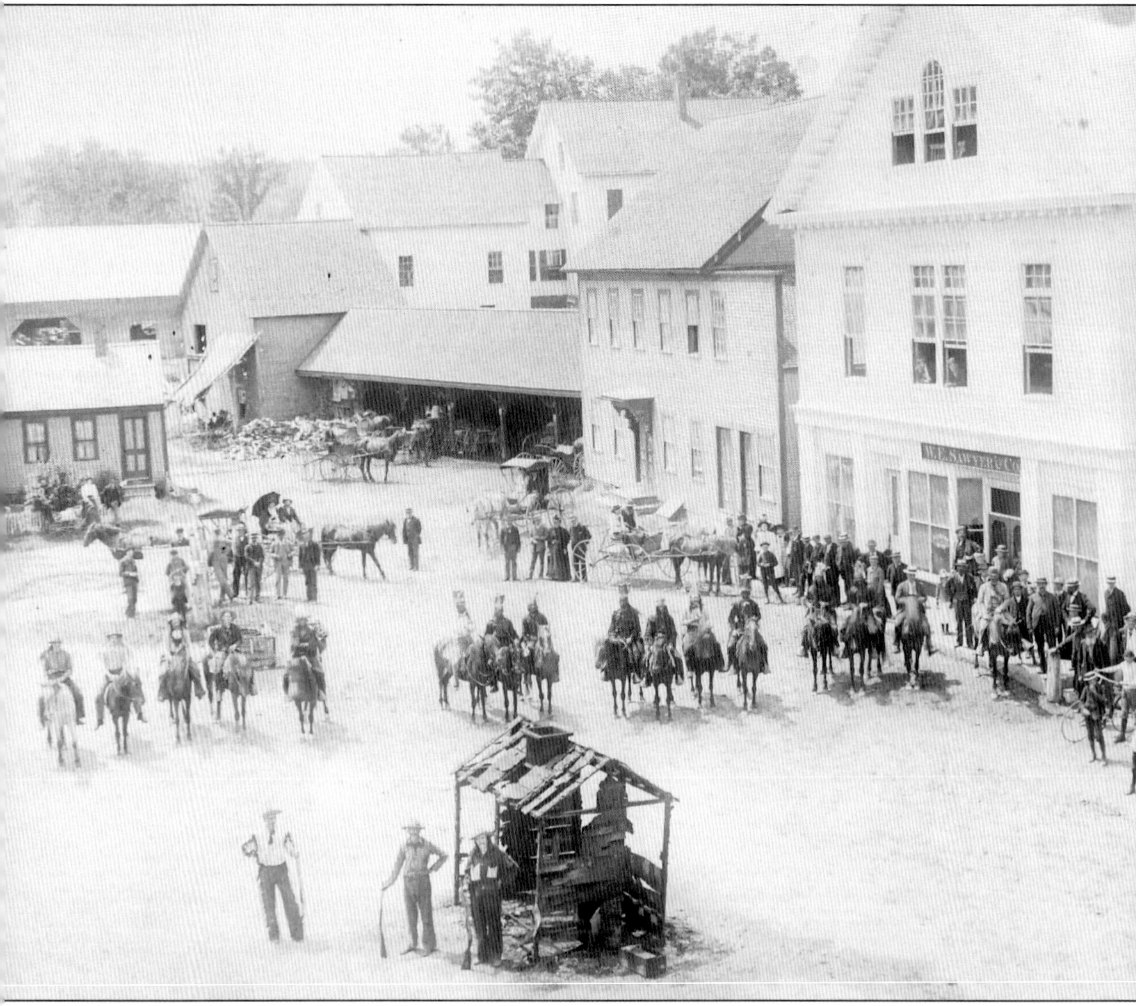

The Wild West comes to Wilton Square, *c.* 1880s. It's not known whether this was a local celebration or a show from outside. The audience doesn't appear to be very large.

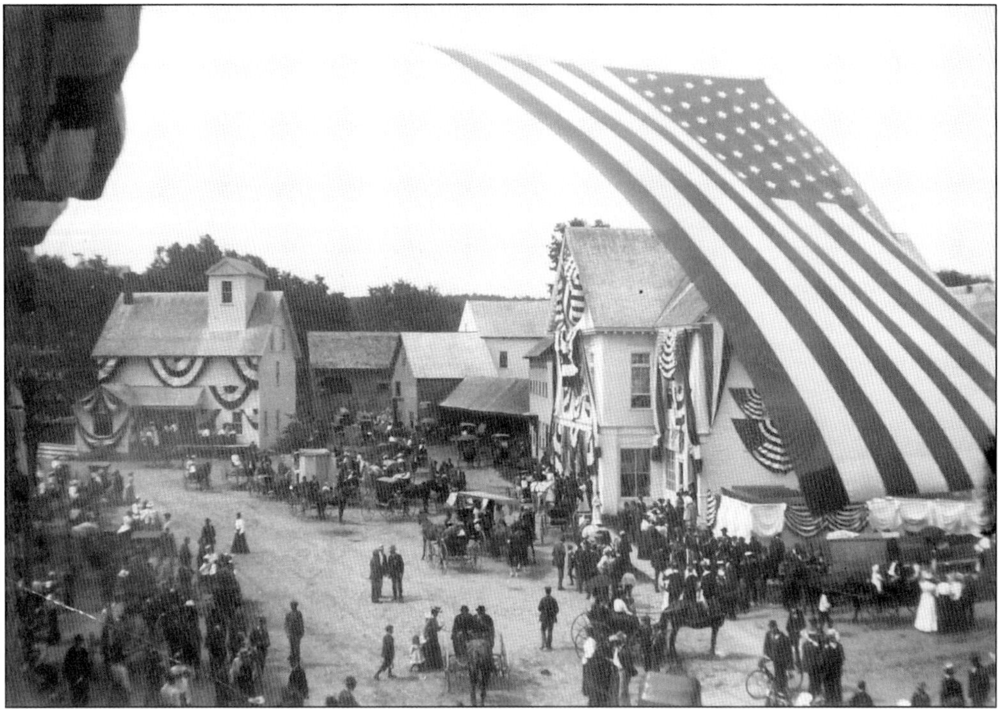

Wilton Square during the 1903 centennial celebration. The American flag flies over everything. It's a busy scene with people on foot, horses, buggies, freight carriers, and bicycles. The gristmill is at the rear left. An old sawmill is next to it.

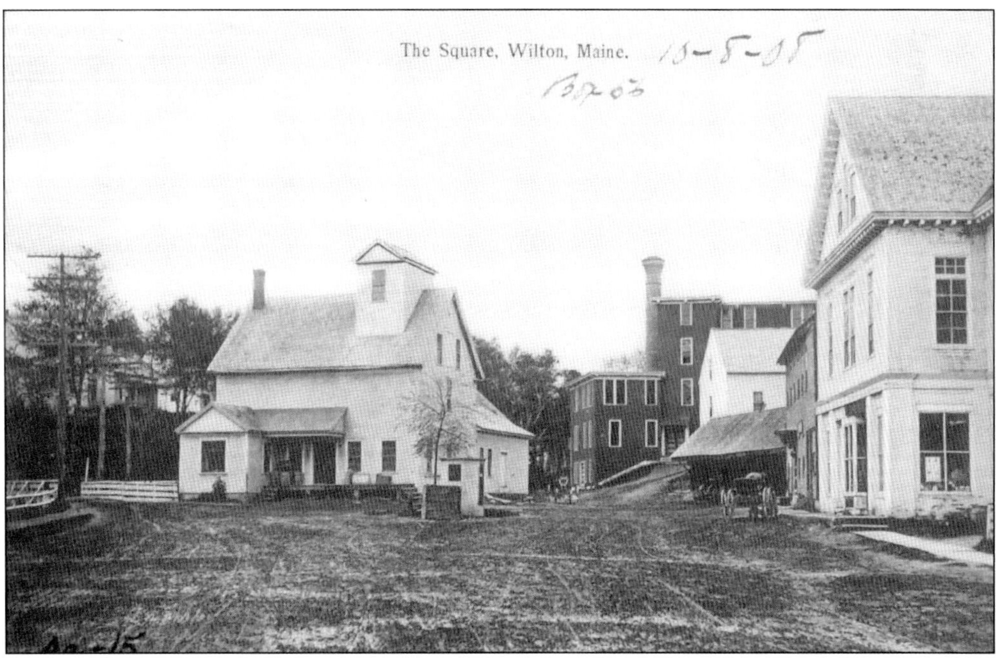

Wilton Square, *c.* 1908. Note the condition of the road.

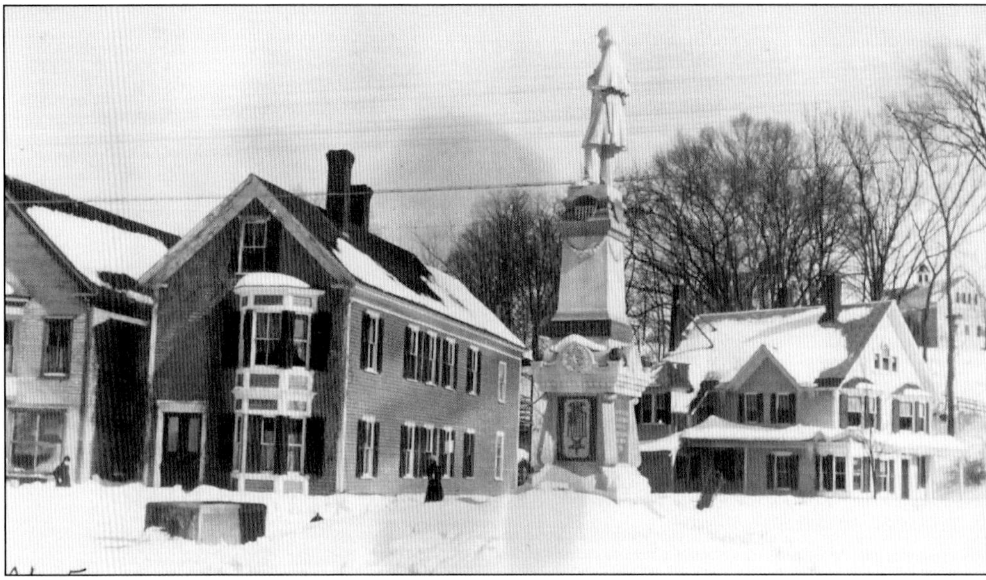

Wilton Square with the Soldiers Monument, *c.* 1920s.

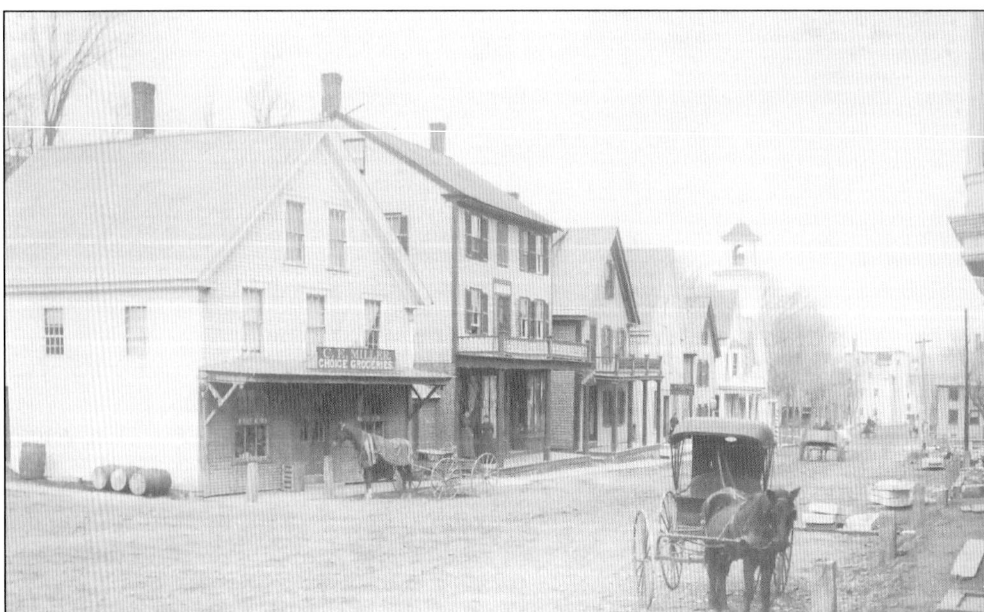

Main Street, Wilton, in 1894. Aunt Ida Miller is standing in front of her store. Further along is a watch shop; still further up the street is L.E. Hiscock, furniture.

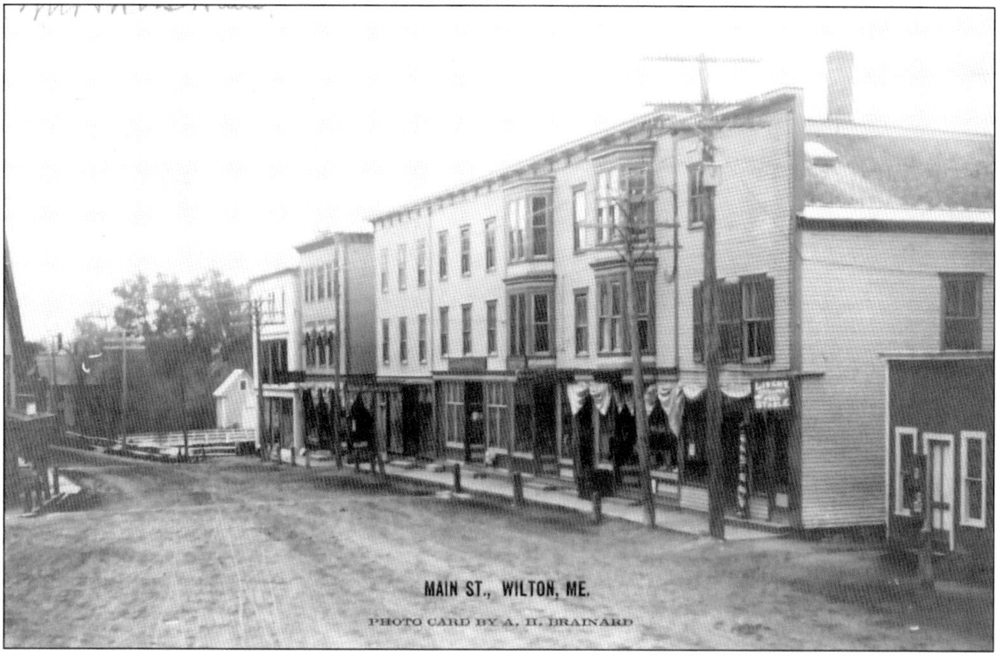

Main Street, Wilton, *c*. 1900. Note the livery stable in the right foreground.

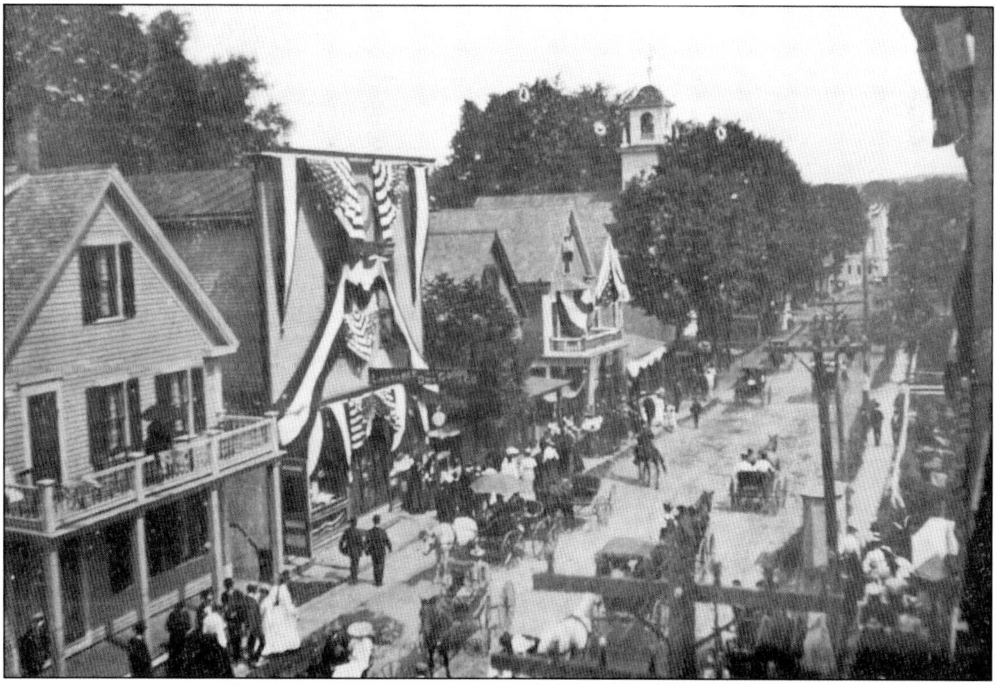

Main Street, Wilton, looking north during the 1903 centennial. We see much bustle including several horses with buggies.

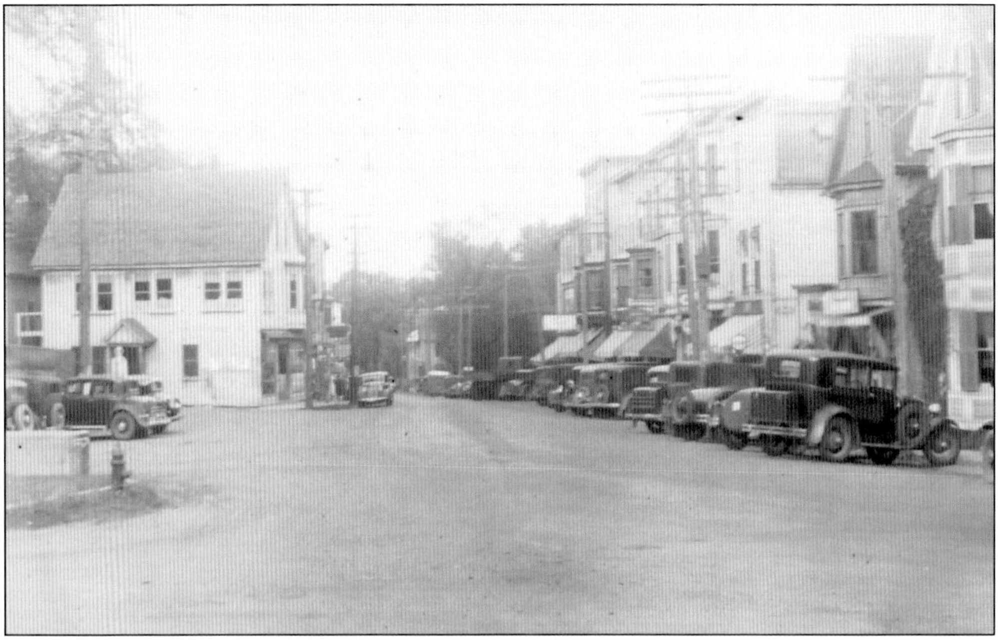

Main Street, Wilton, in the 1930s. Every automobile seen on this postcard is parked.

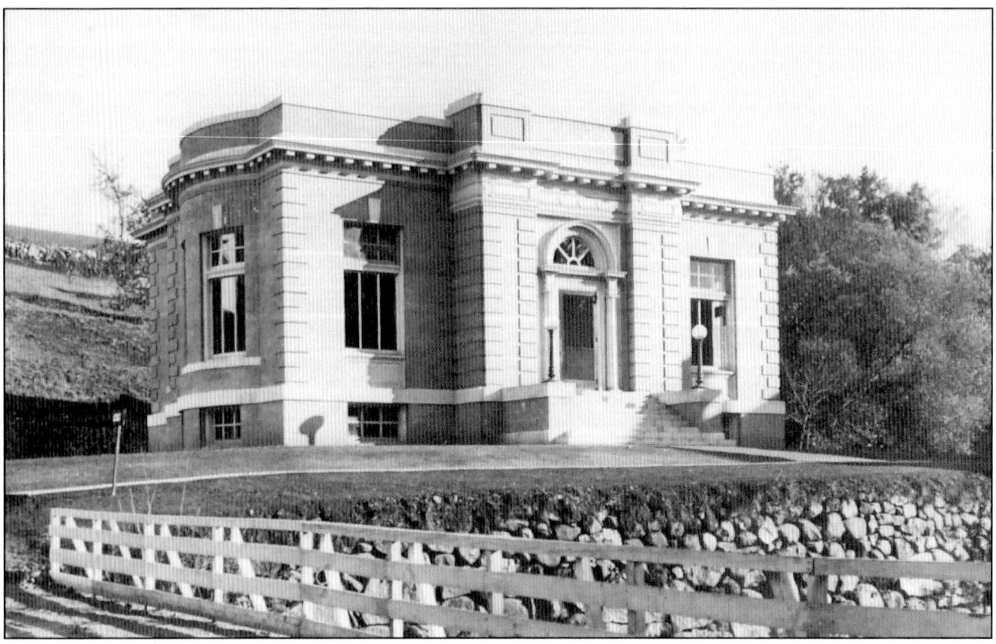

Goodspeed Memorial Library, Wilton, *c.* 1910s. Money for it was given by George and Frank Goodspeed in honor of their parents. The two men were owners of Wilton Woolen Company.

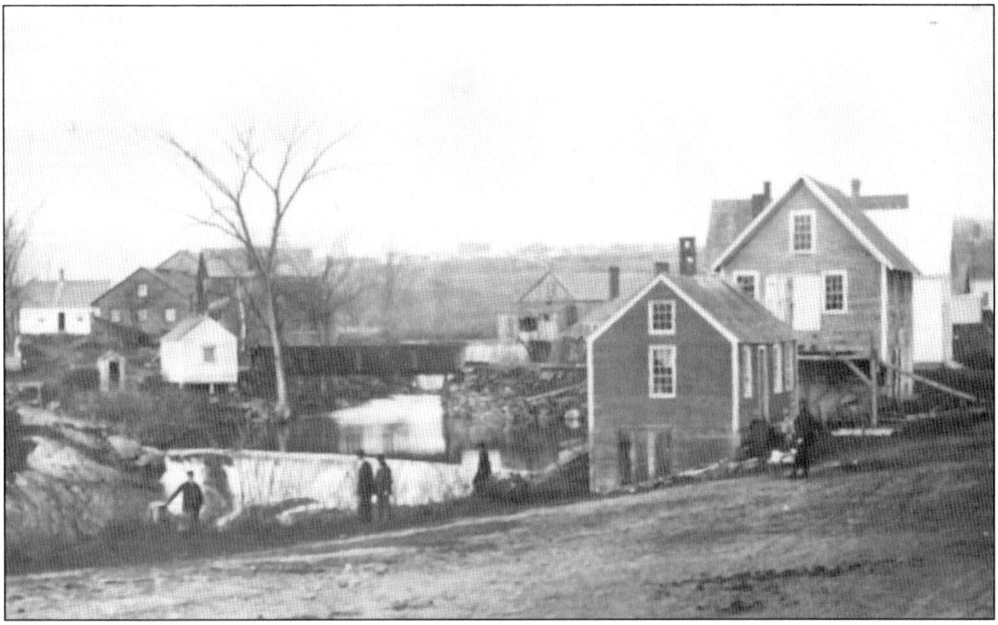

Main Street, East Wilton, *c.* 1880s. The road is, of course, a dirt one.

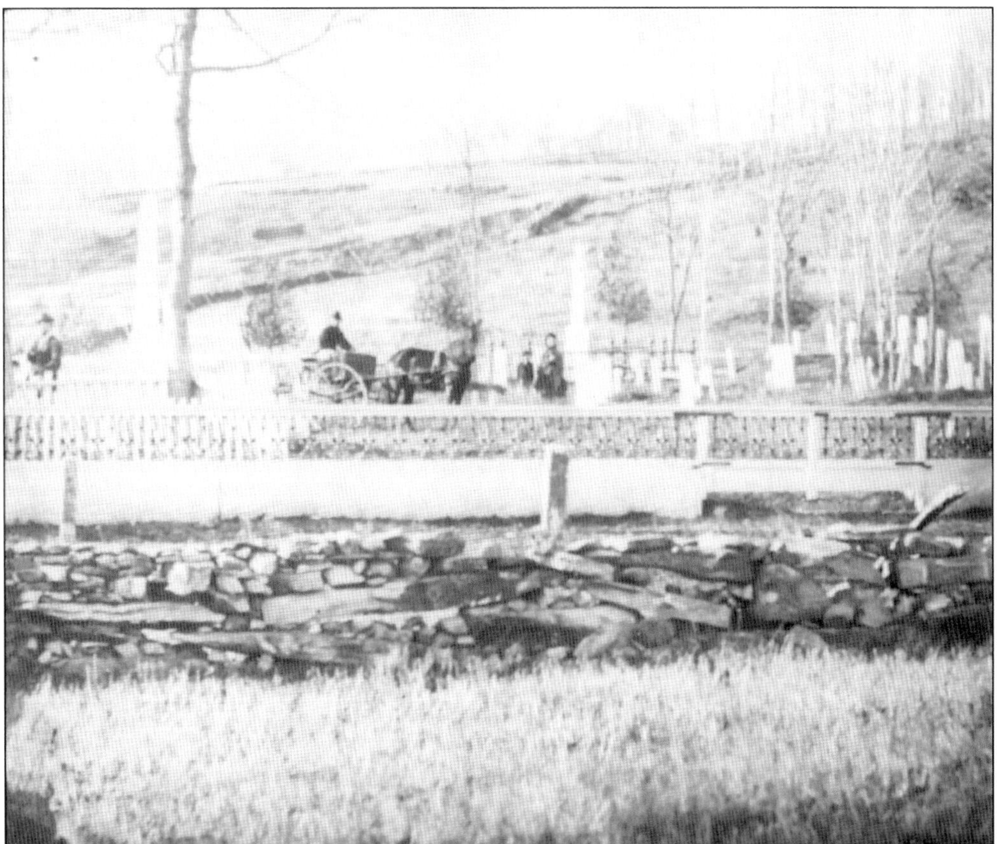

The East Wilton cemetery, *c.* 1880s.

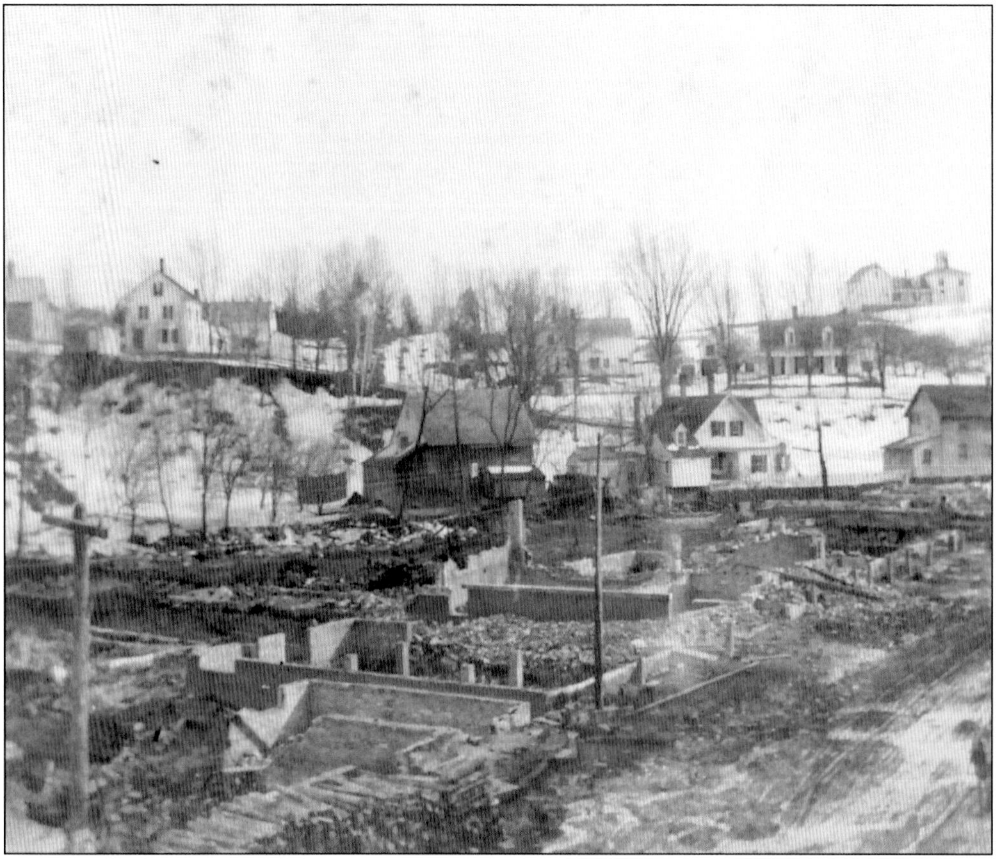

After the fire of 1893 in Wilton. We're looking toward Bass Hill and beyond.

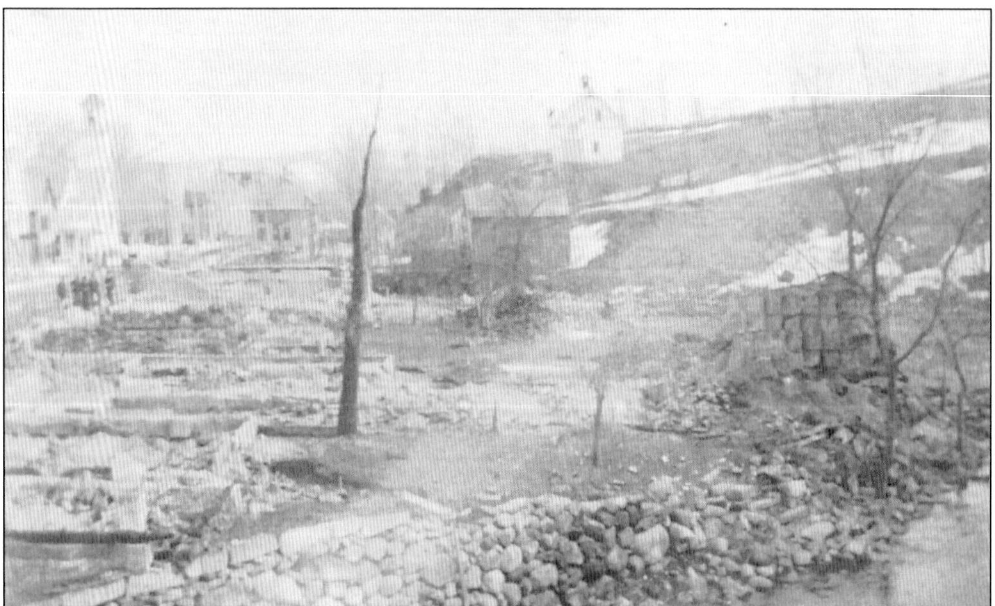

Another view of the ruins from the 1893 fire.

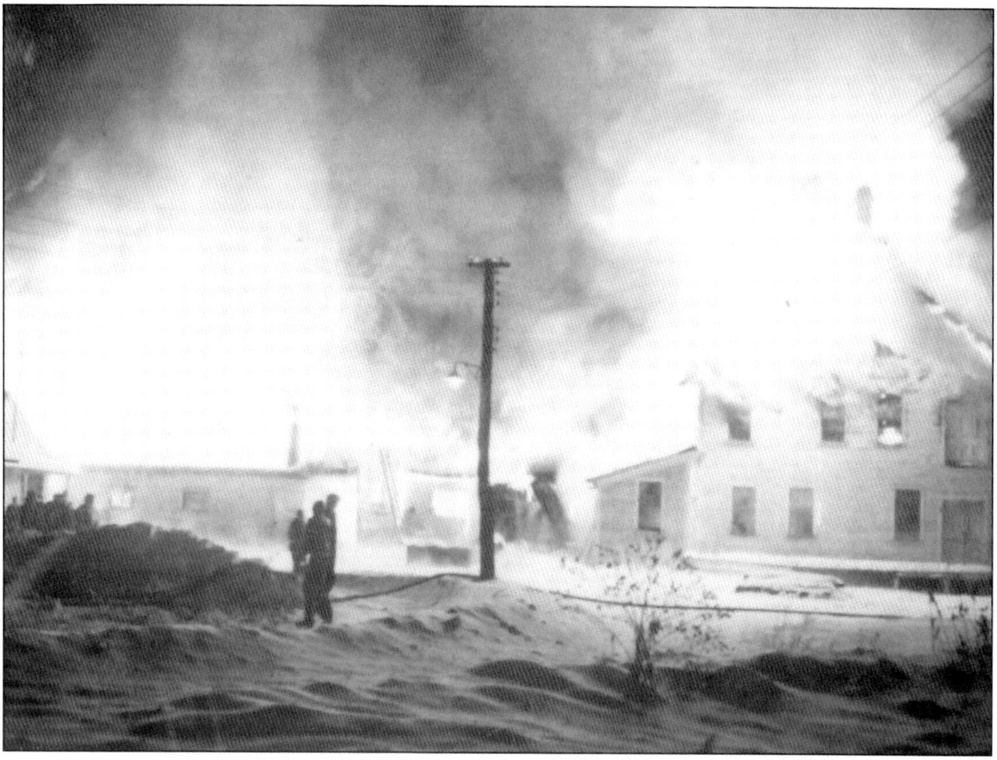

As in every community, there have been disasters that wiped out businesses. In 1960, the Thomas & Marble Cannery in Wilton burned. The business had been in the town many years.

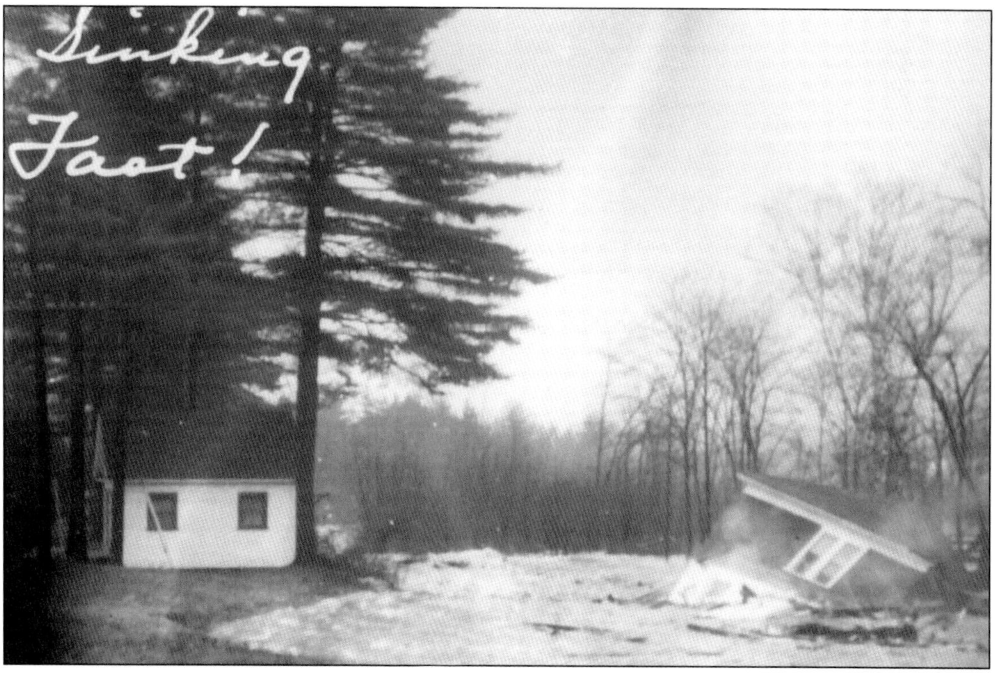

The Harnden house in Dryden was washed away during a 1953 flood.

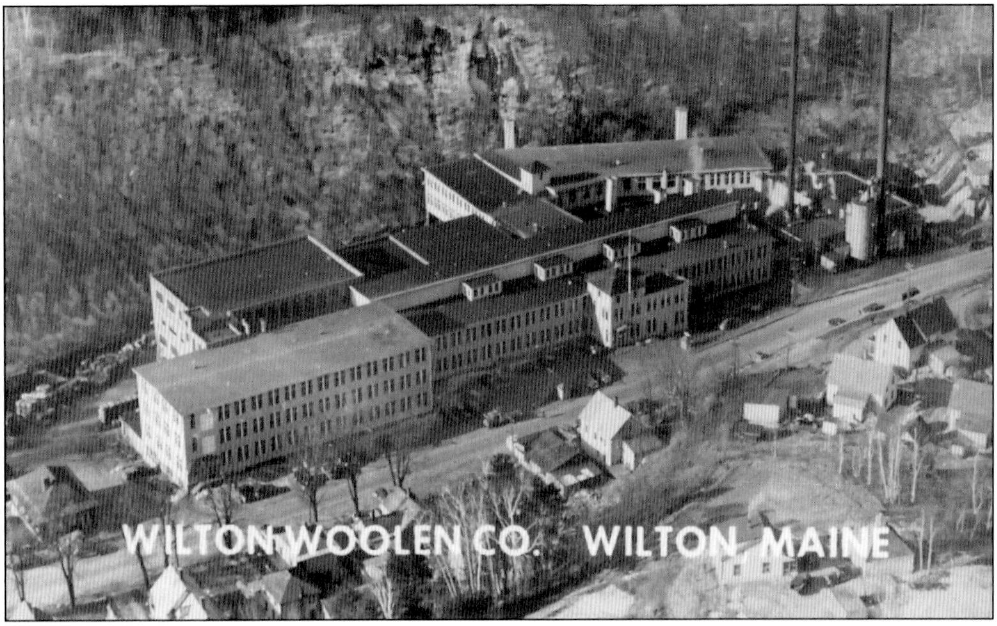

Many industries and businesses flourished in Wilton for years. One of the best known was the Wilton Woolen Company shown here *c.* 1940s. At this time the mill was nearing the end of its existence as a woolen maker. One of its final owners was the Goldfine family, which owned several Maine woolen mills. The family was best known for Bernard, who was involved with presidential aide Sherman Adams in the vicuna coat episode of the 1950s.

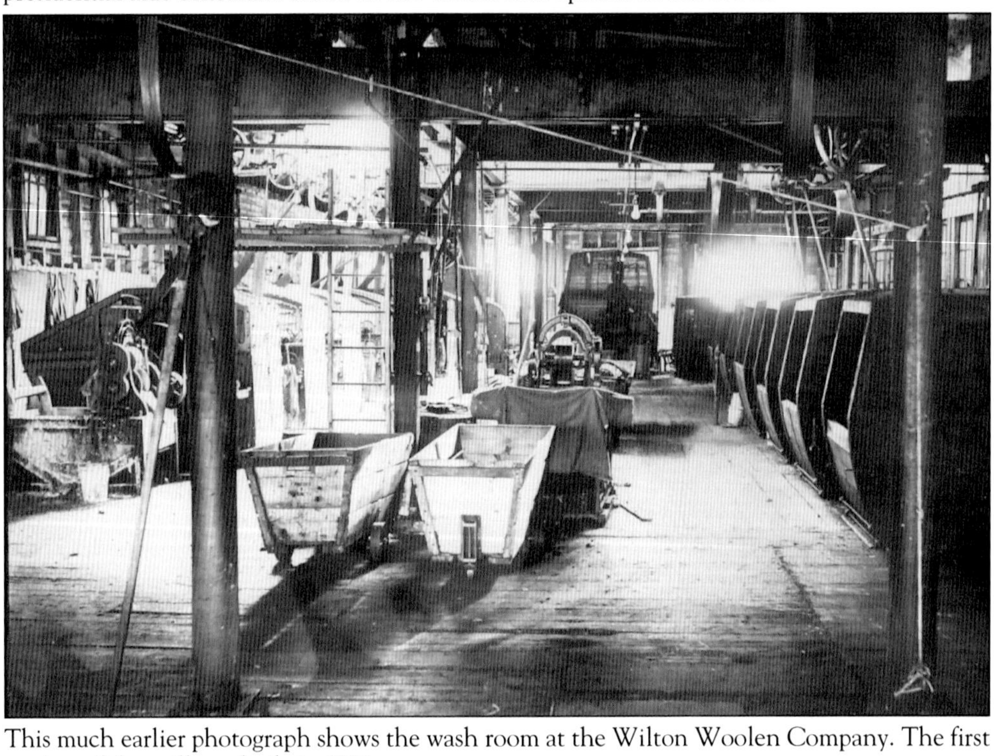

This much earlier photograph shows the wash room at the Wilton Woolen Company. The first section of the mill was built in 1901.

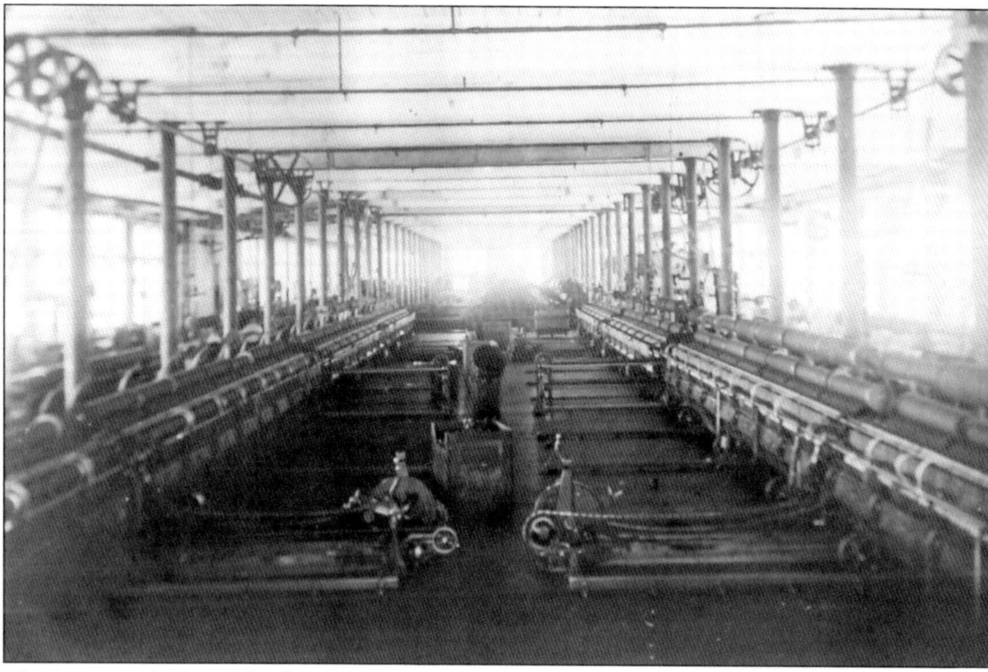

The looms at Wilton Woolen Company, *c.* turn of the century.

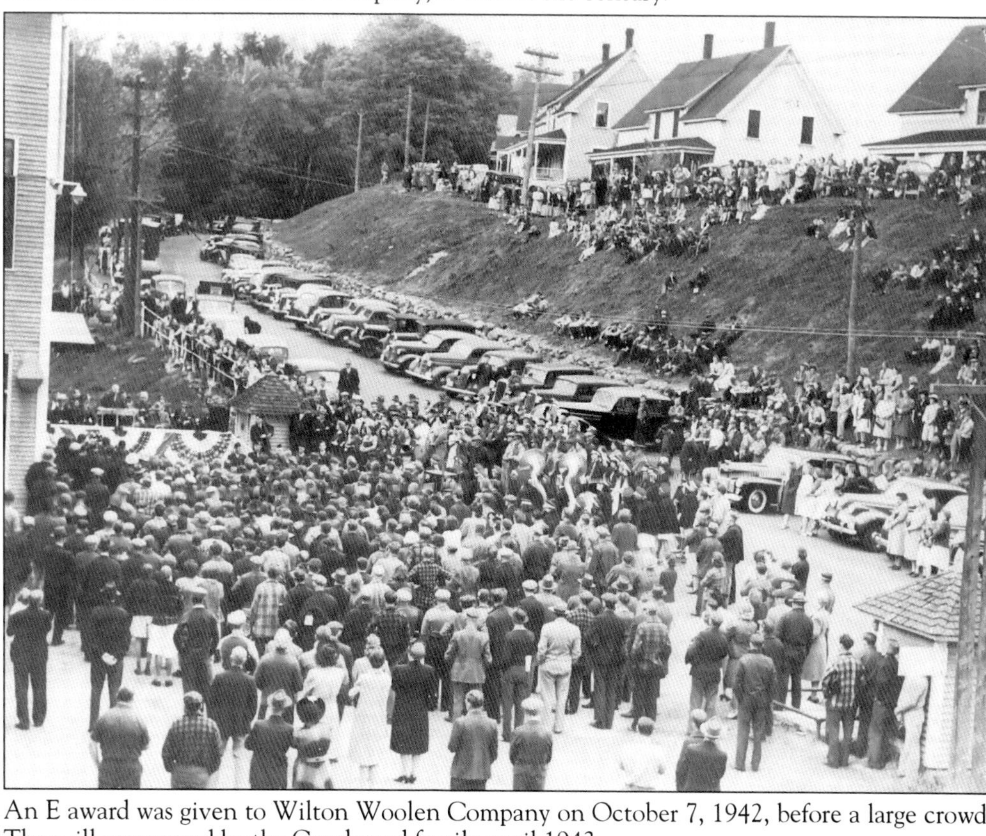

An E award was given to Wilton Woolen Company on October 7, 1942, before a large crowd. The mill was owned by the Goodspeed family until 1943.

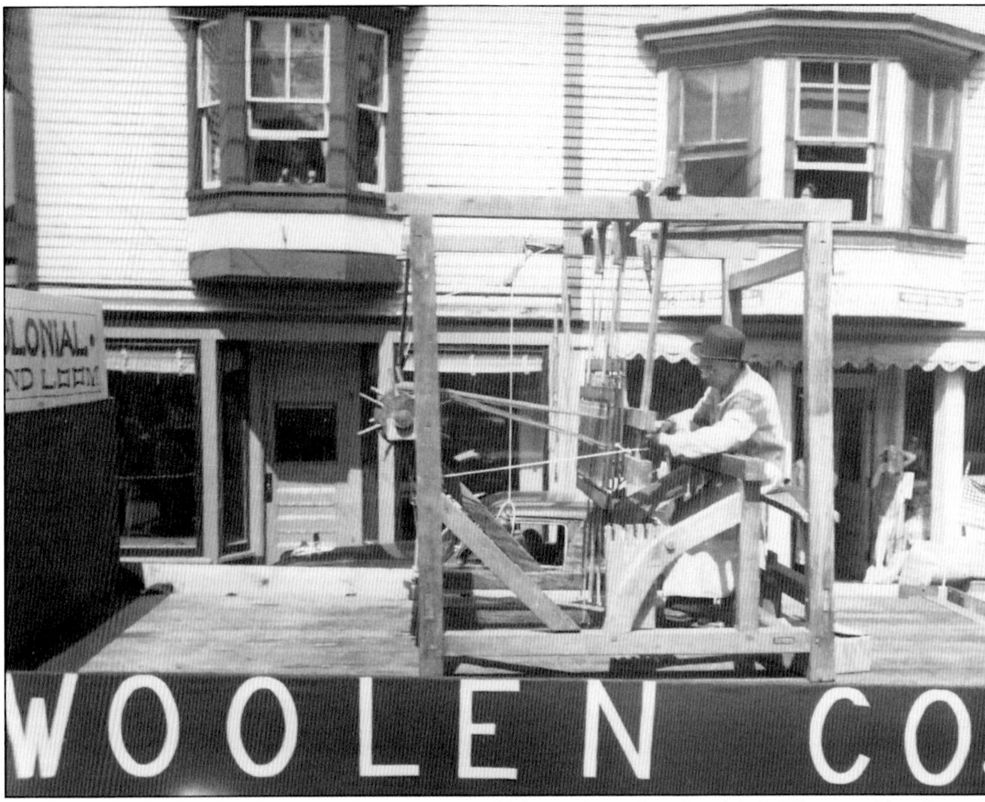

This float in a 1930s Wilton parade carries an old loom from Scotland (1840) owned by George F. Goodspeed, then one of the owners of the Wilton Woolen Company. The man is believed to be Earl Harvey, who worked in the mill's weaving room.

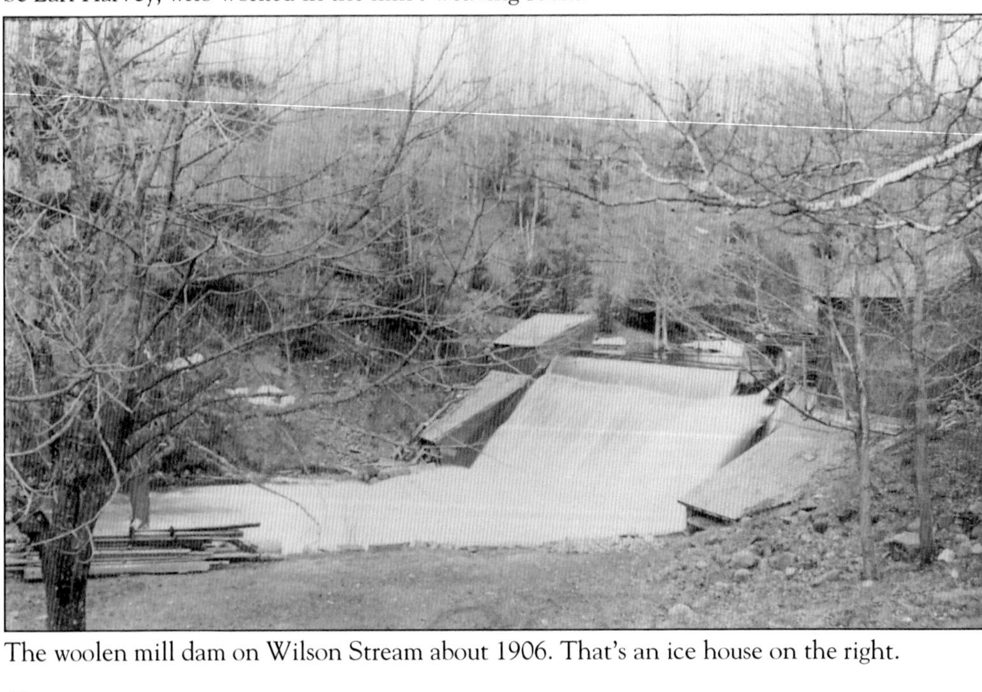

The woolen mill dam on Wilson Stream about 1906. That's an ice house on the right.

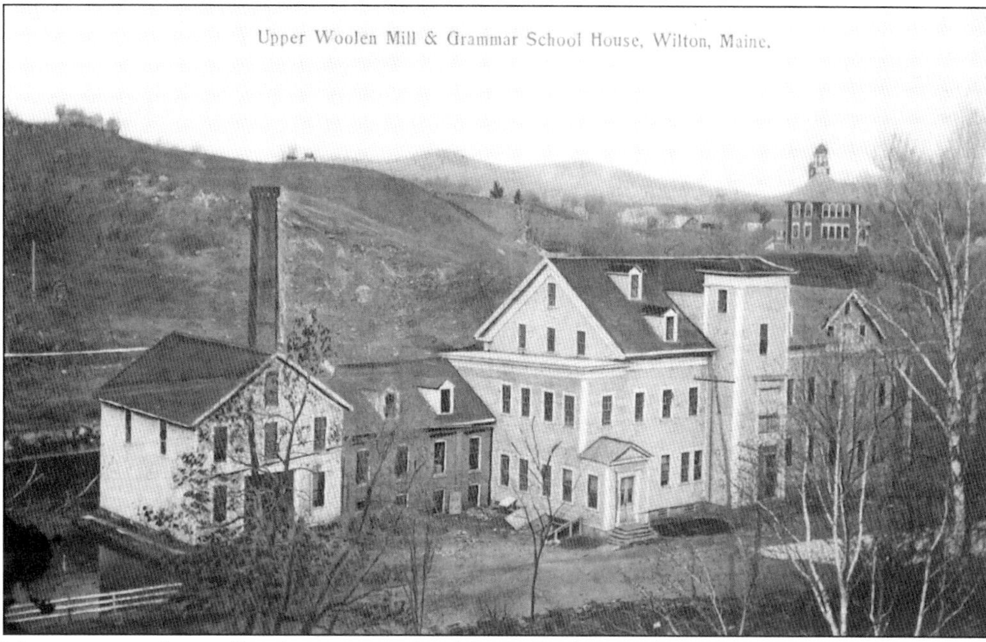

The upper woolen mill and grammar school (right background) in Wilton, *c.* early 1900s.

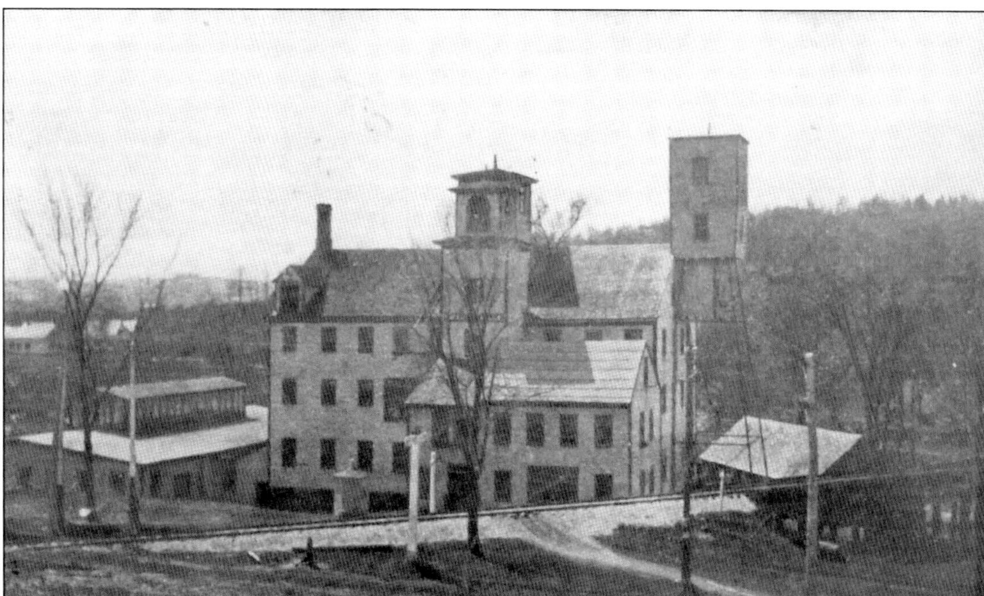
The Walker Mills, East Wilton, *c.* early 1900s. They were built in 1840.

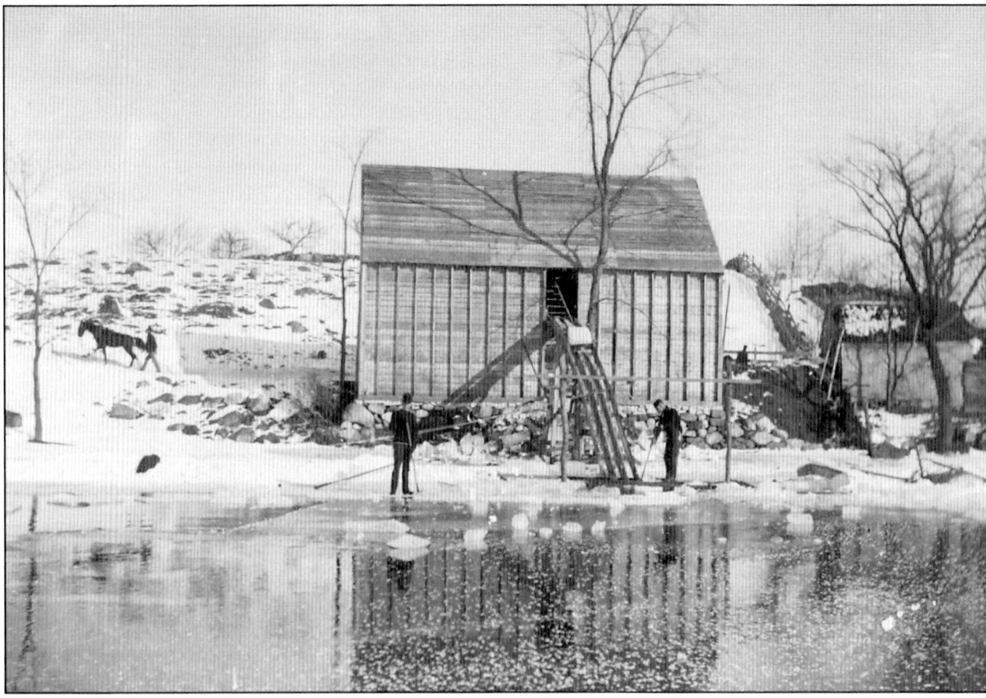

The Sanborn ice house in Wilton, *c.* early 1900s.

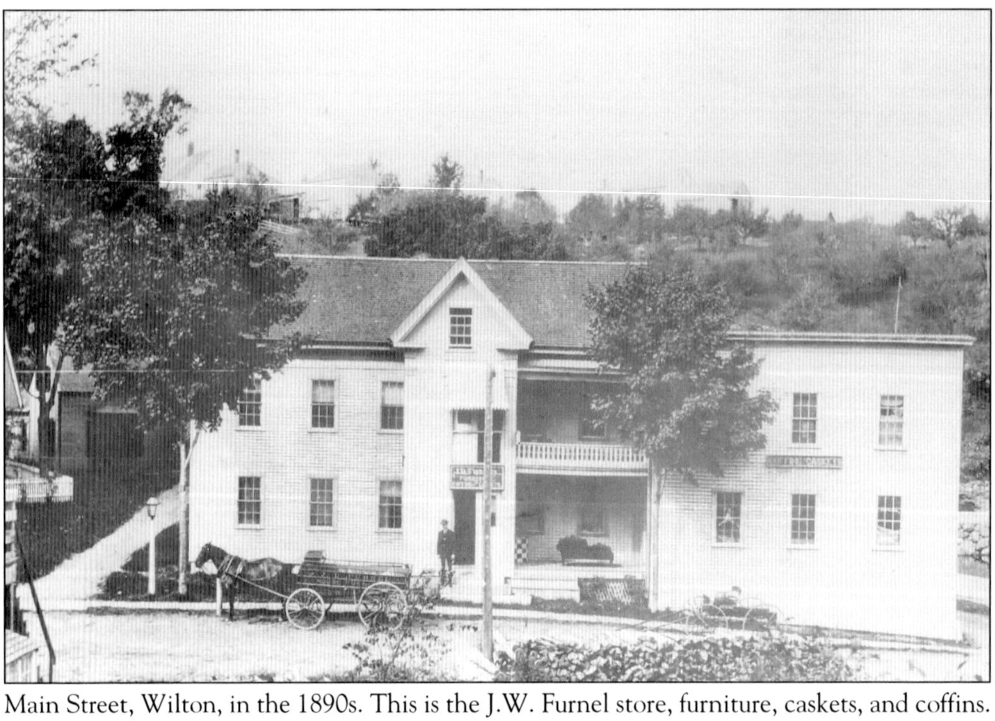

Main Street, Wilton, in the 1890s. This is the J.W. Furnel store, furniture, caskets, and coffins. The post office is located here.

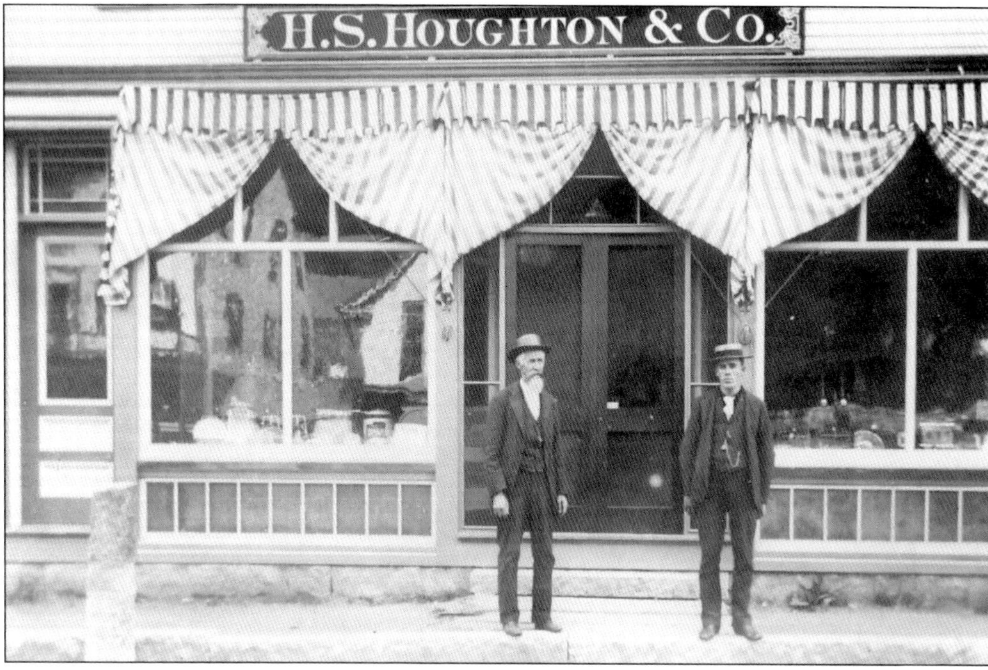

The H.S. Houghton & Company, *c.* 1900s. Herbert Houghton is on the left and his son is on the right. The company was a hardware store.

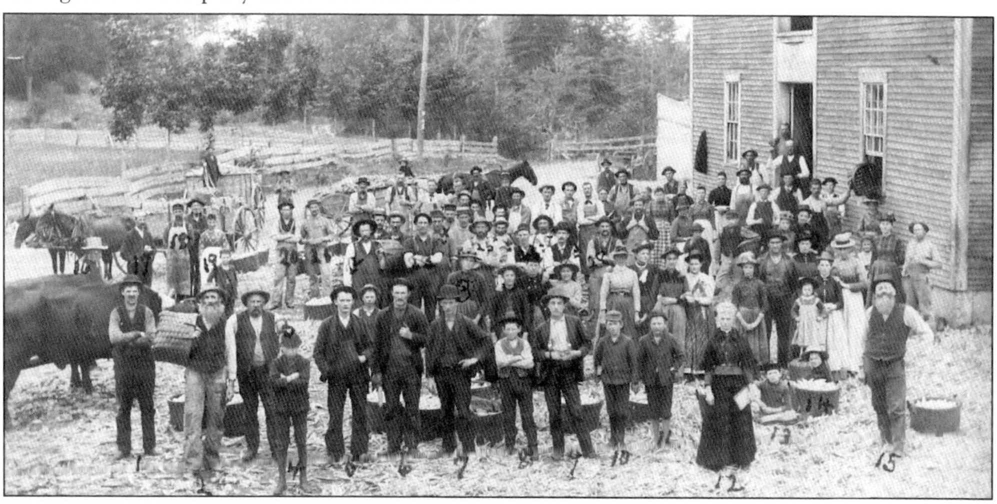

The corn shop, Dryden, in 1890. From left to right are as follows: (front row) unknown, David Thompson, Farrington York, Leon Gilbert, unknown, unknown, unknown, Elmer Merchant, Arthur Wentworth, Fred Townes, Ernest Mayo, Laura Duley, unknown, unknown, and Merrill North; (second row) ? Russell, Dwight Hall, Eugene Davis, Pamelia Davis, John Miller, Will Phillips, Orman Calden, Charles Robbins, Newman Hall, unknown, Milt Davis, Fred Duley, Peter Dascombe, Walter Wells, and Frank Paine. Others include Lucy Mayo, Lill Searles, Lottie Mayo, Amy Howe, Grace Tracy, Lena Green, Annie Howe, Arthur Hodgkins, Ella Corey, Ann Townes, Eva York (in gingham apron), Martha Allen, Alice Thompson, Mrs. Staples, Frank Ireland, John Duley, Thomas Dudley (boss of the shop), Horace Staples, Roscoe Dudley, Vance Calden, Ezra Melendy, Abbie Welch, Nettie Ranger, Jimmie Hibbard, Connie Davis, Blanche Hodgkins, and Angie Hodgkins.

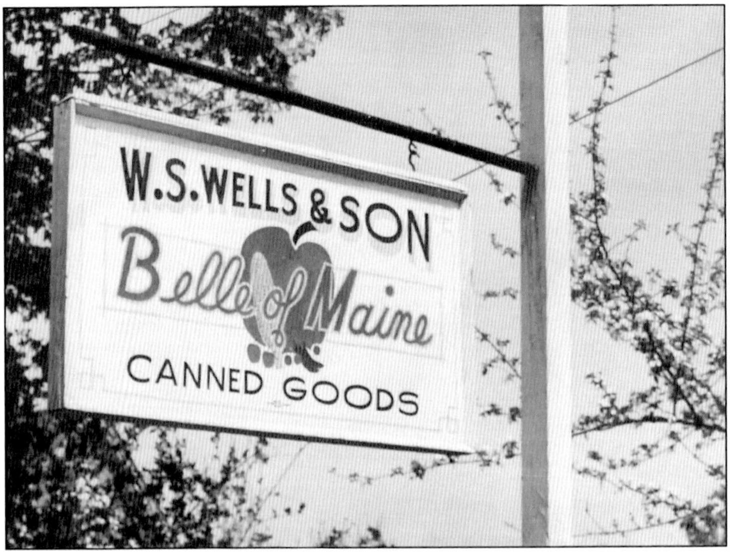

A W.S. Wells & Son sign, c. 1953. The company's canned goods include fiddleheads and it continues to operate. Dandelion greens are another specialty.

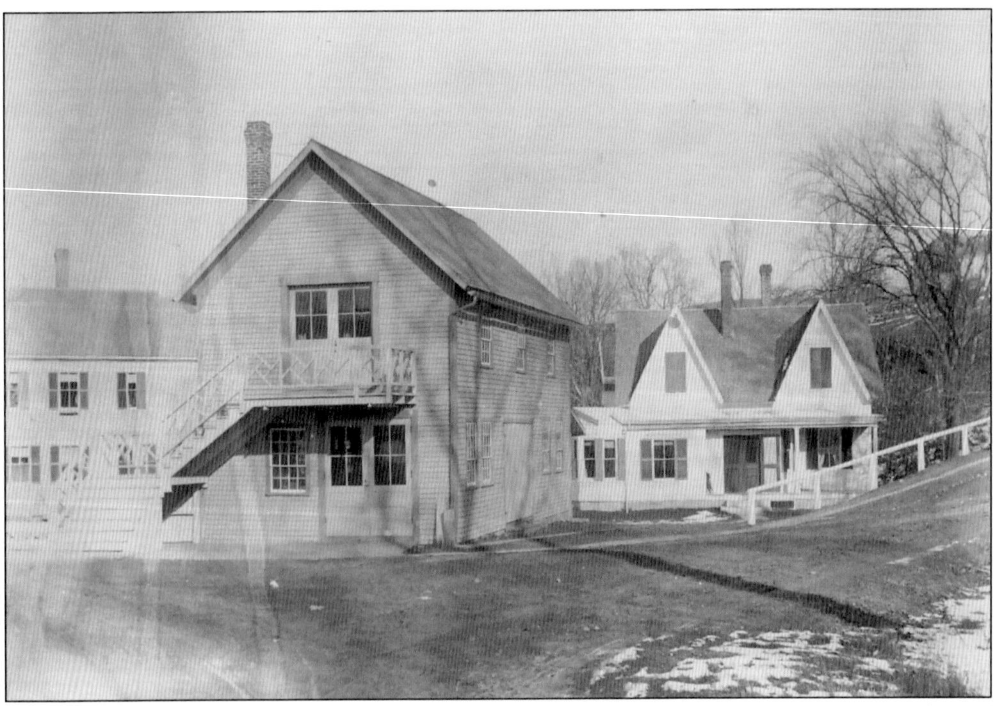

The J.E. Hiscock Shop and residence, c. 1920s. Hiscock served many years as superintendent of the Wilton Water Company and as town clerk. The residence is still occupied by his family.

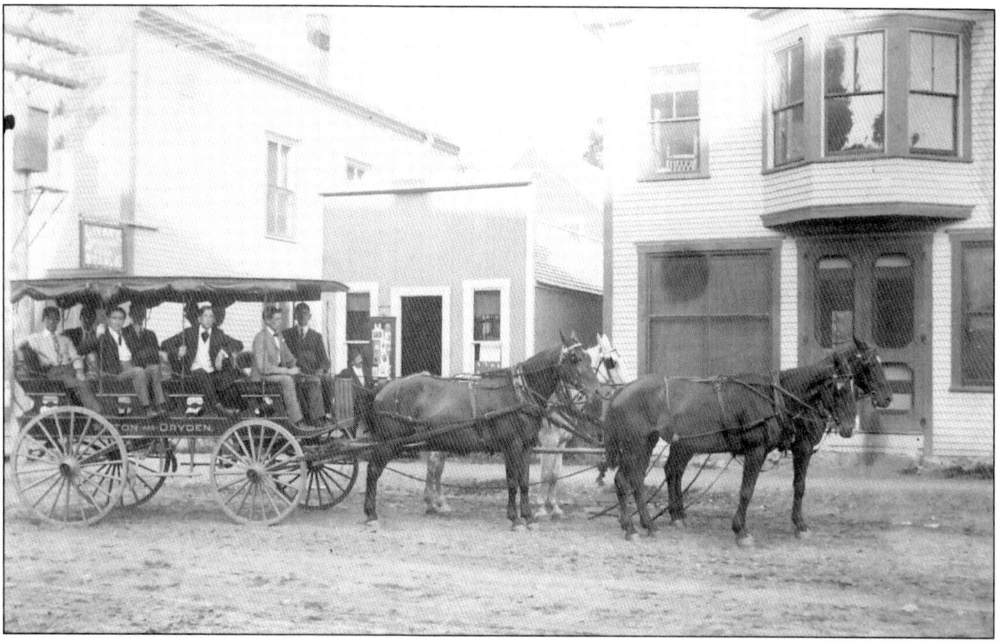

Bert Sanborn's Shoe Repair was located in the small shop. A sign on the left says "Livery Exchange and Feed Stable." In front is the Wilton-Dryden stage which met trains, *c.* early 1900s.

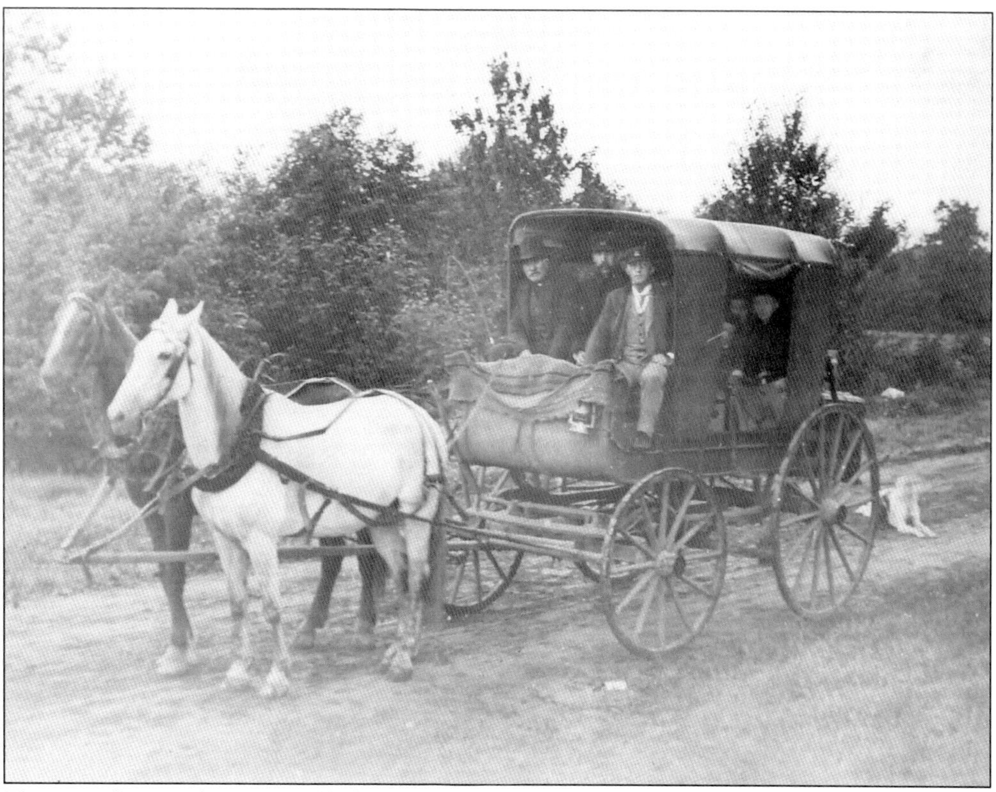

The stage from Wilton to Weld, driven by Uncle John Pickens, *c.* 1890s.

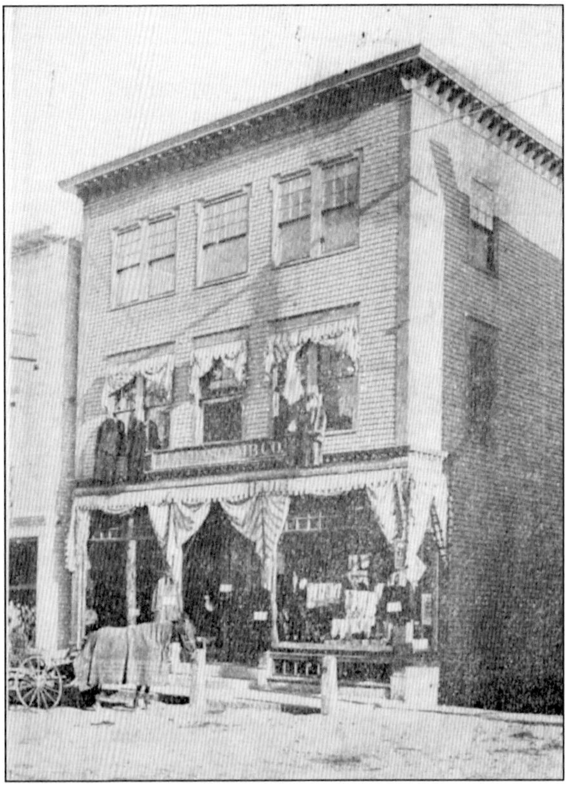

The H.R. Dascomb Company, Wilton. "This card is good for 5 percent discount on or before December 20, 1905," it reads.

Earl Carr cuts the cake November 14, 1960, celebrating his 50th year in business in Wilton. He was a clerk in the Larabee Dry Goods Store and later purchased it. From left to right are Robert N. Bass and Leon Ogilvie. Patricia Scott is the waitress.

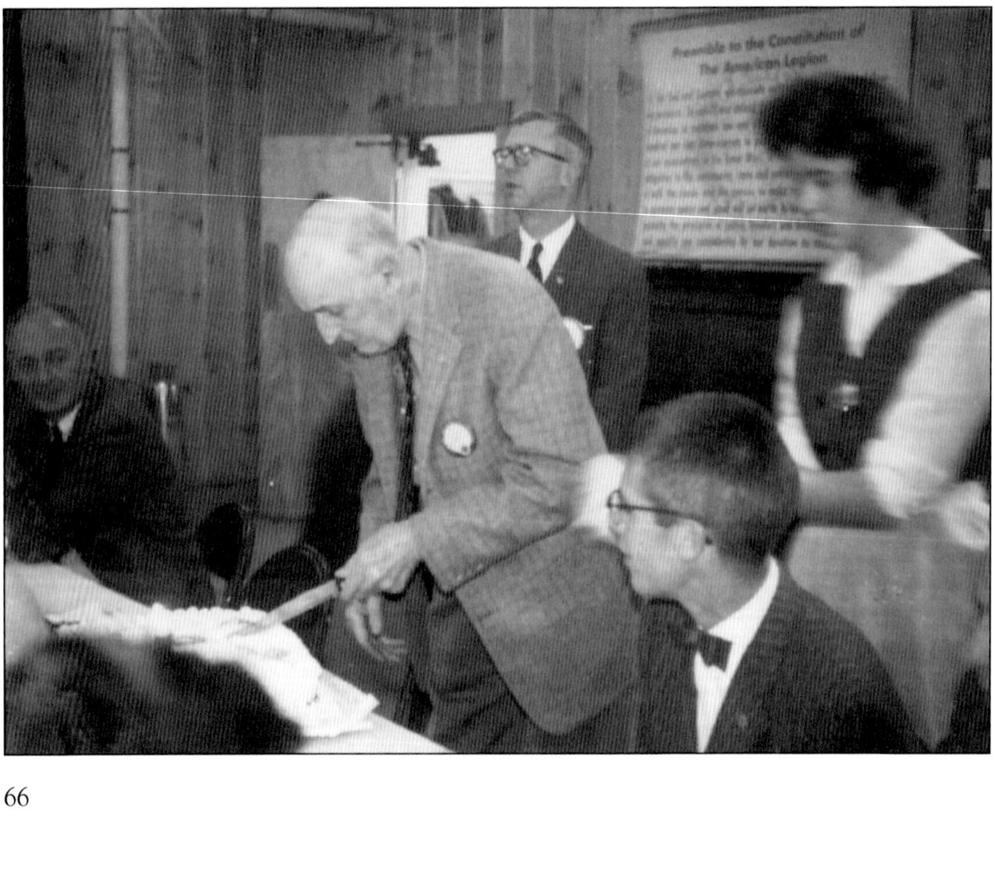

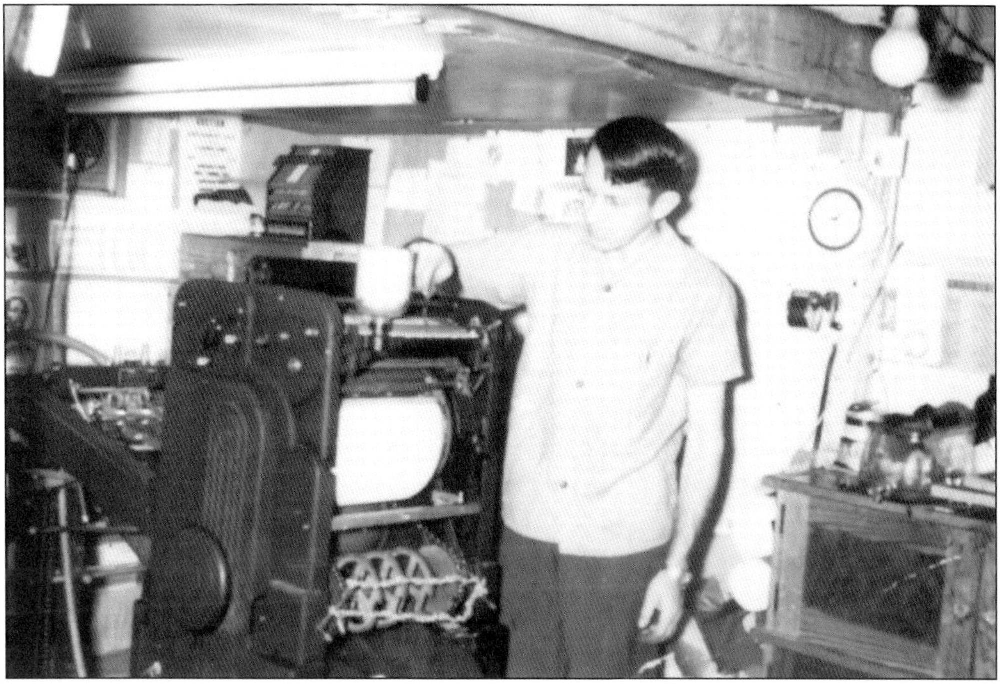

Harold Karkos stands in the basement shop at 37 Allen Street, Wilton, where he started Wilton Printing Service on September 1, 1949. The name was changed to Wilton Printed Products Inc. in 1954.

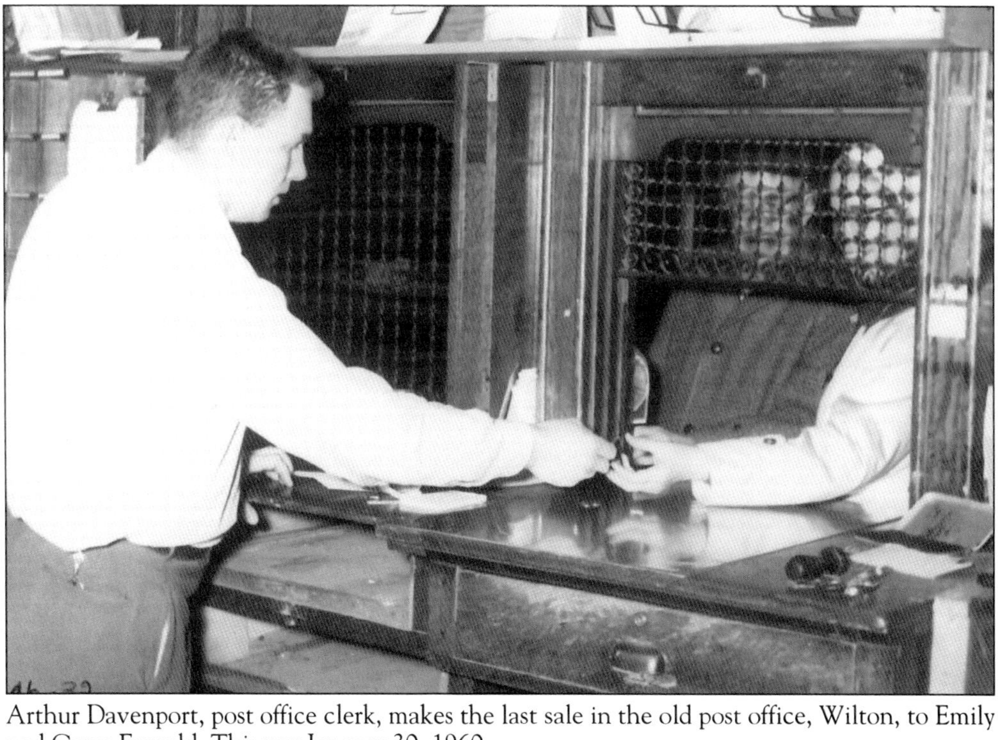

Arthur Davenport, post office clerk, makes the last sale in the old post office, Wilton, to Emily and Cyrus Fernald. This was January 30, 1960.

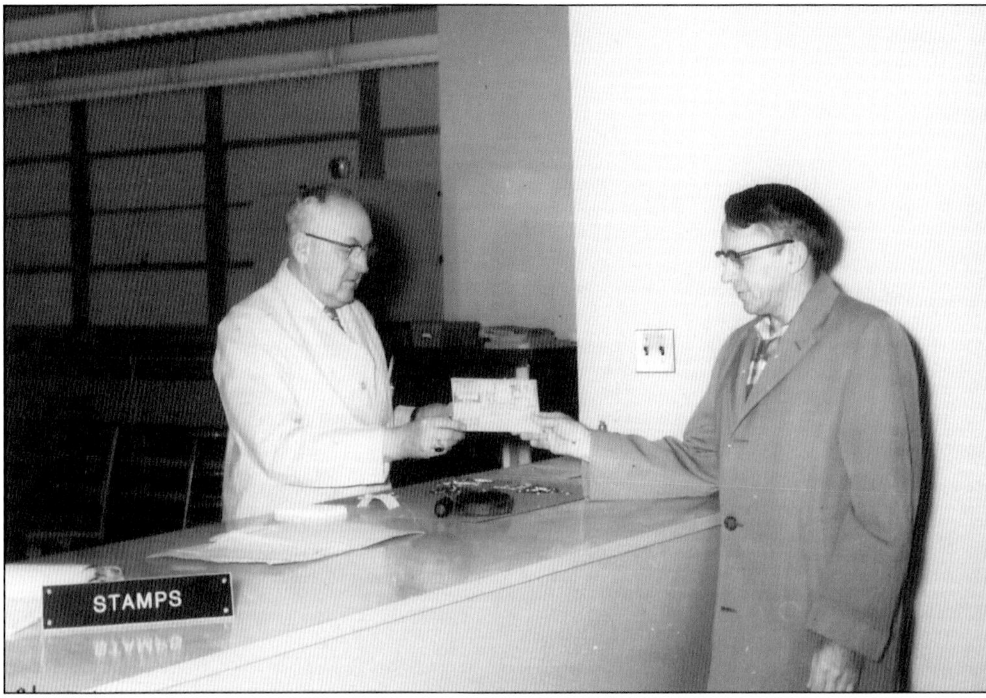

Harry Gould, clerk, delivers the first incoming package at the new post office in Wilton on February 1, 1960, to Harold Karkos.

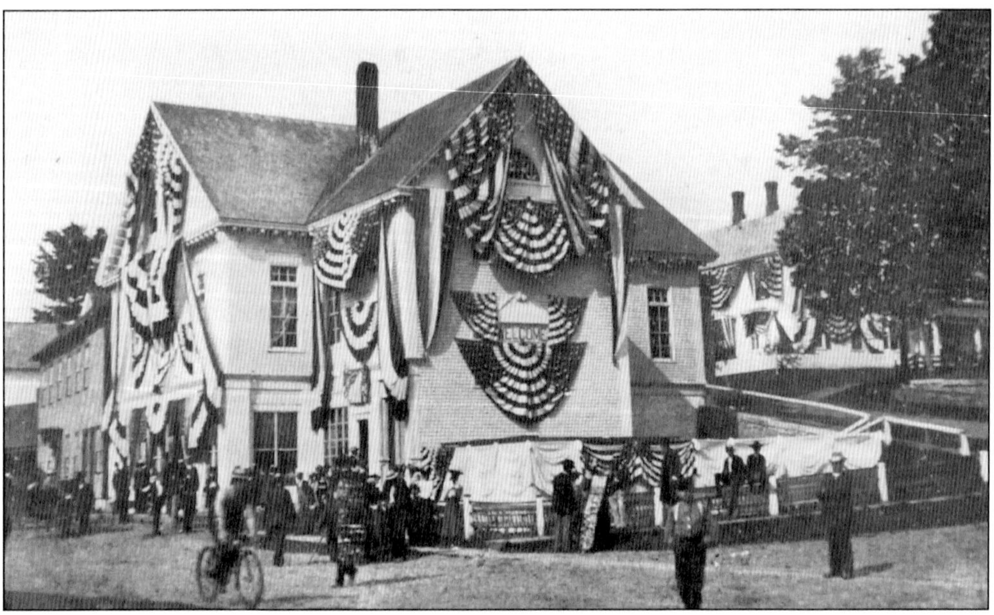
The town hall at Wilton was decorated for the 1903 centennial celebration.

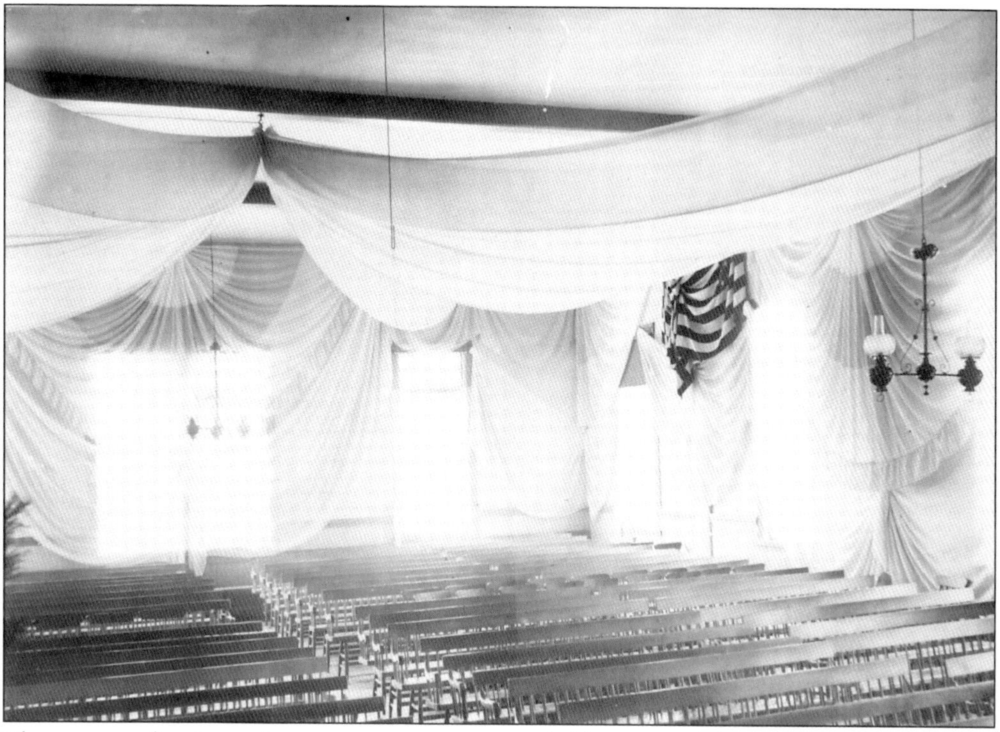

The town auditorium where town meetings were held was on the second floor of the then Wilton Town Hall. The town office was on the first floor in the early 1900s.

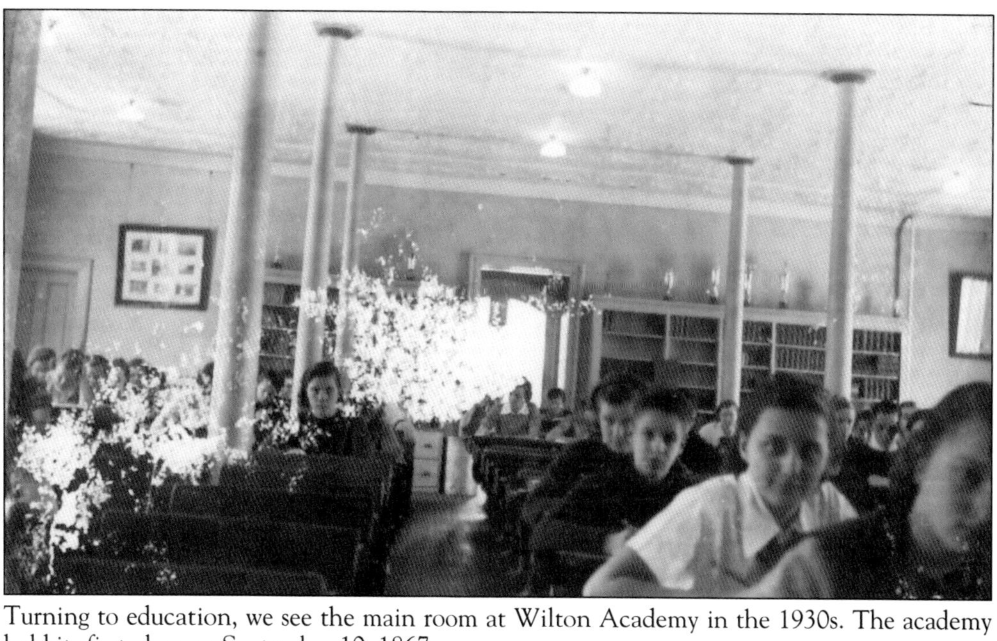

Turning to education, we see the main room at Wilton Academy in the 1930s. The academy held its first class on September 10, 1867.

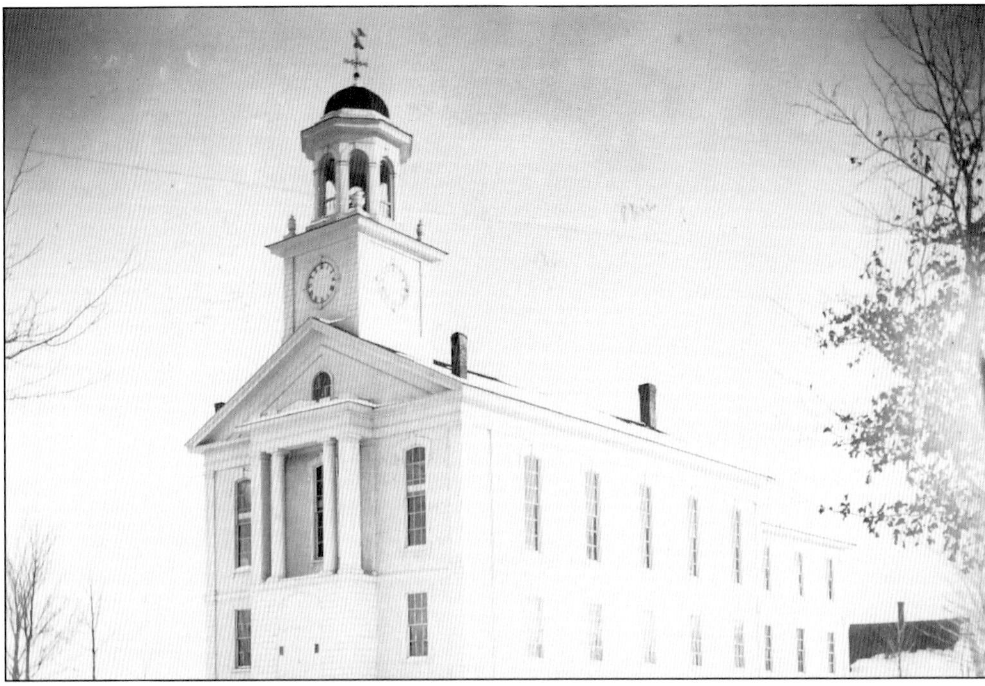

Wilton Academy itself before side entrances were added, no later than 1910.

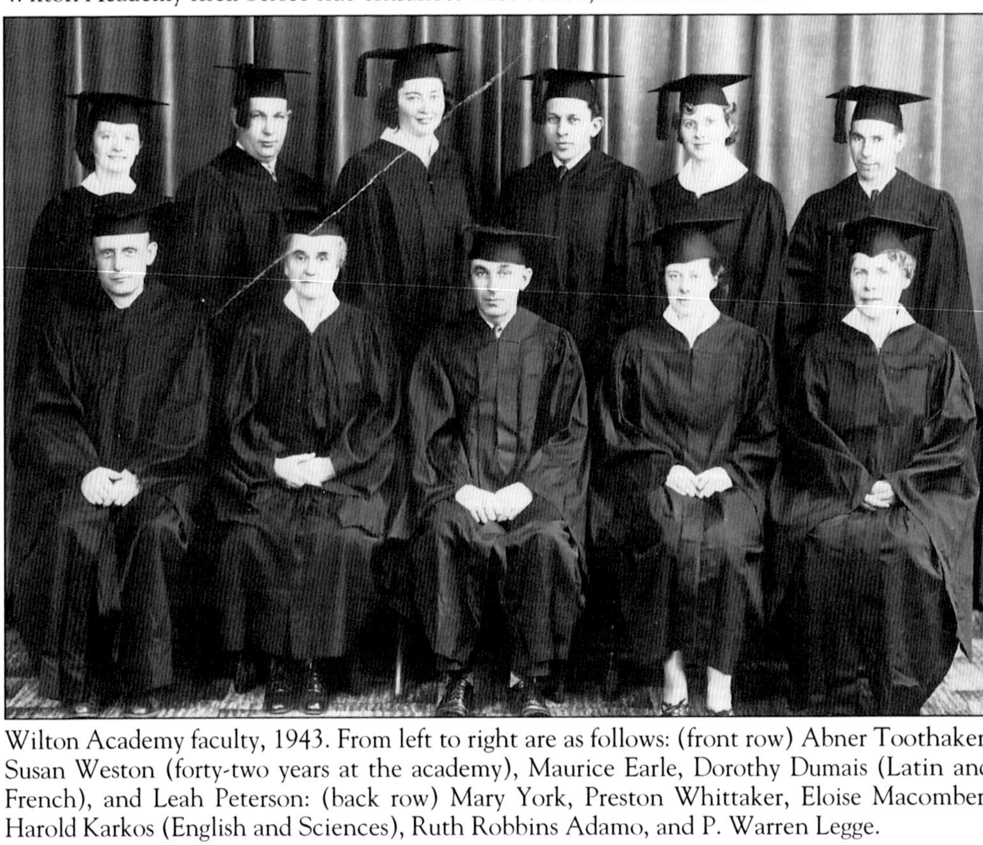

Wilton Academy faculty, 1943. From left to right are as follows: (front row) Abner Toothaker, Susan Weston (forty-two years at the academy), Maurice Earle, Dorothy Dumais (Latin and French), and Leah Peterson: (back row) Mary York, Preston Whittaker, Eloise Macomber, Harold Karkos (English and Sciences), Ruth Robbins Adamo, and P. Warren Legge.

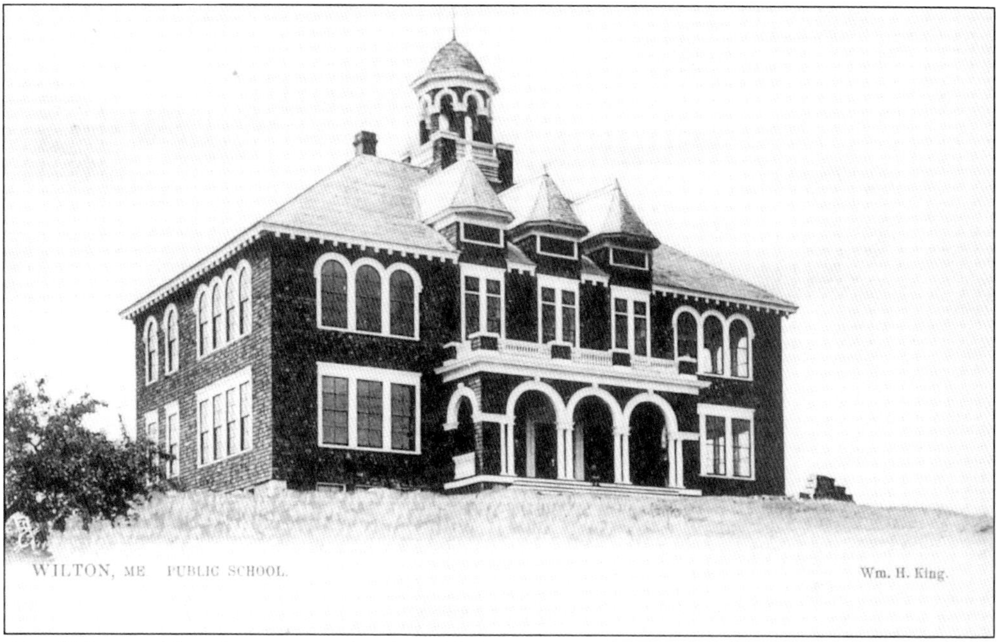

The Wilton public elementary school, *c*. 1890s.

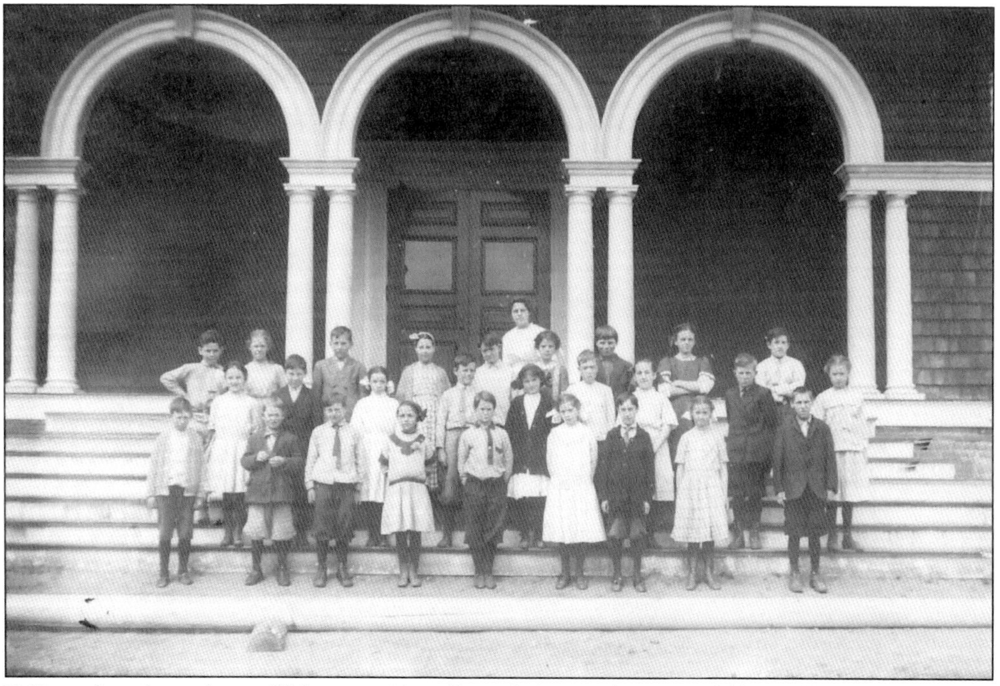

Fifth and sixth grades at Wilton, *c*. 1911. From left to right are as follows: (front row) Walter Miller, Harry Clark, Francis Collins, Harriet Holland, John Swett, Marguerite Hall, Carl Miller, Clara Hathorne, and John Adams: (middle row) Lillian Hamilton, Fulton Johnson, Ruth Bailey, Louie Hall, Marguerite Hiller, Ray Wyman, Florence Holland, Cyrus Fernald, and Bertha Cook; (back row) Weldon Pierce, Agnes Cates, Harry Gould, Vilma Edgar Bump, Maybelle Salisbury, Hiram Crush, Sadie Tibbetts, and Donald Hall.

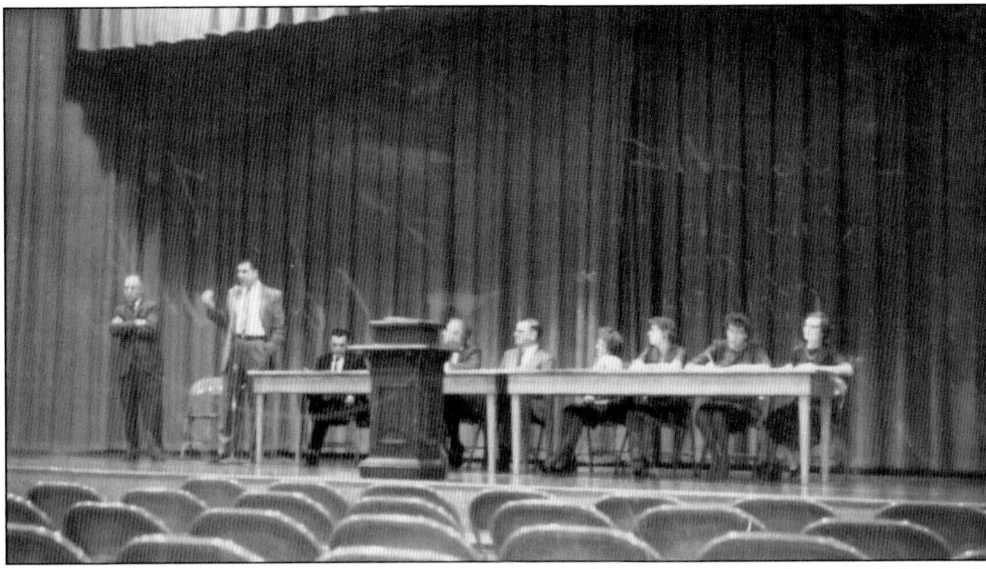

On the stage at Wilton Academy during Education Week in November 1960. From left to right are principal Harland Keay, guidance counselor Harold Kearney, Anthony Jabar, Leon Ogilvie, Norman Hodgkins, Beatrice Mitchell, Maxine Ryan, Maxine Kyes, and Mary Young.

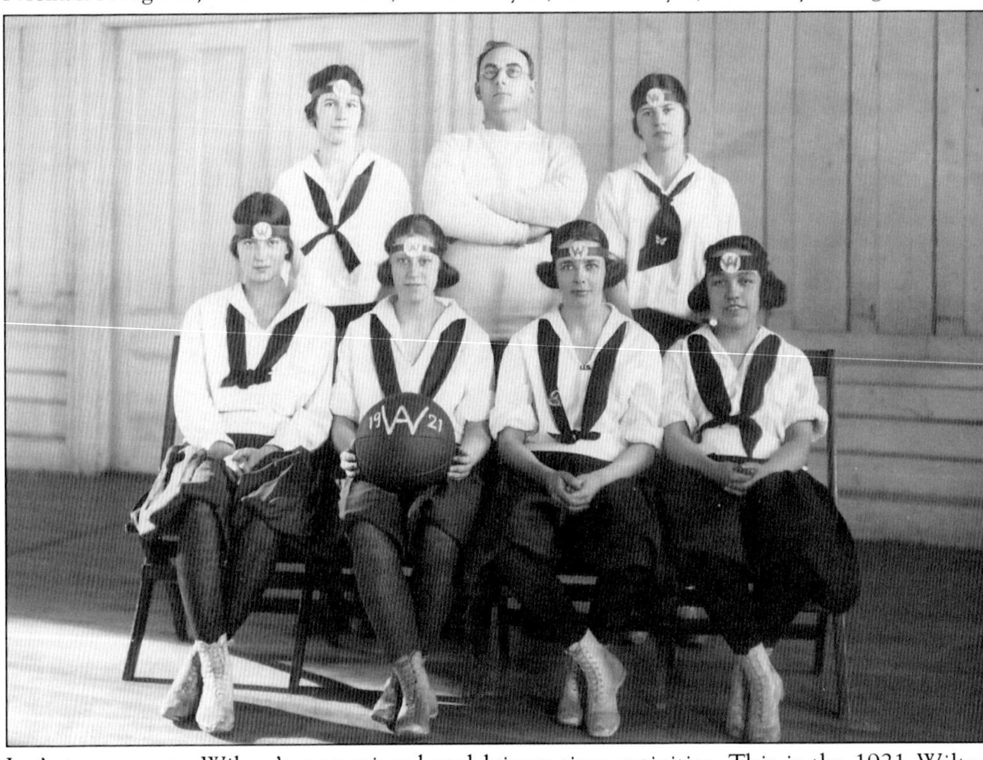

Let's turn now to Wilton's recreational and leisure time activities. This is the 1921 Wilton Academy girls' basketball team which won four of its five games, a school record at the time. From left to right are as follows: (front row) Bertha Cook, Marguerite Hall, captain Sara Robbins, and Harriet Holland; (back row) Leonora Hiscock, coach W.G. Colby, and Geneva Brown.

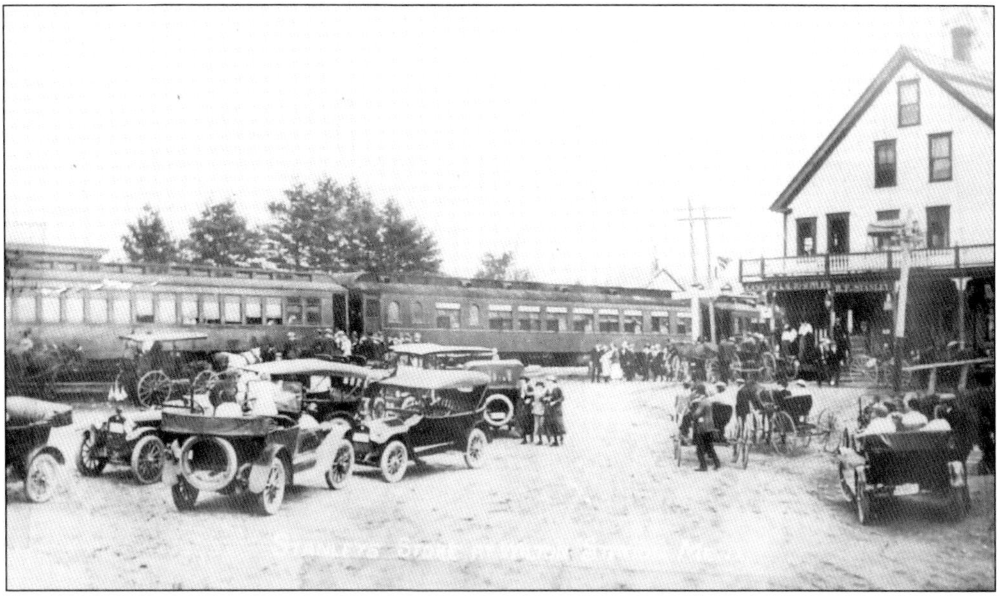

Meeting Joe Knowles after his trip to Boston in 1913 at the station in Dryden. Knowles had entered the Maine woods naked and spent two months there, making his own clothes and pack. There was much publicity when he emerged from the woods and doubt has been cast on the truth of the exploit. Regardless, Knowles eventually became an excellent artist of the West, with his paintings shown in various galleries.

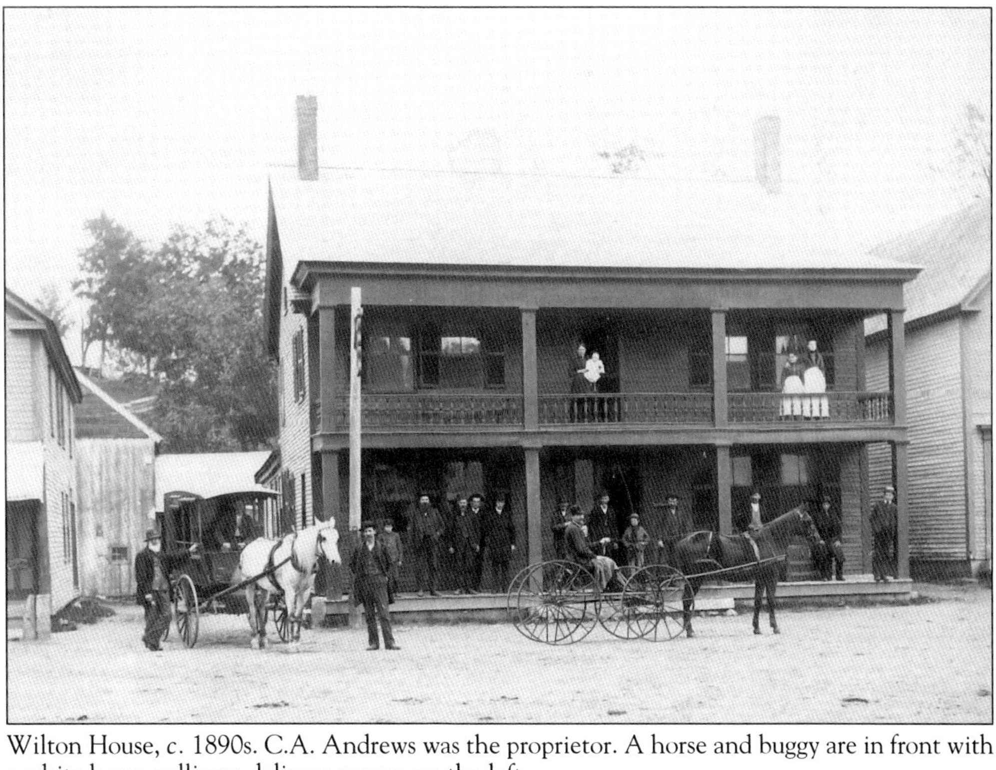

Wilton House, *c.* 1890s. C.A. Andrews was the proprietor. A horse and buggy are in front with a white horse pulling a delivery wagon on the left.

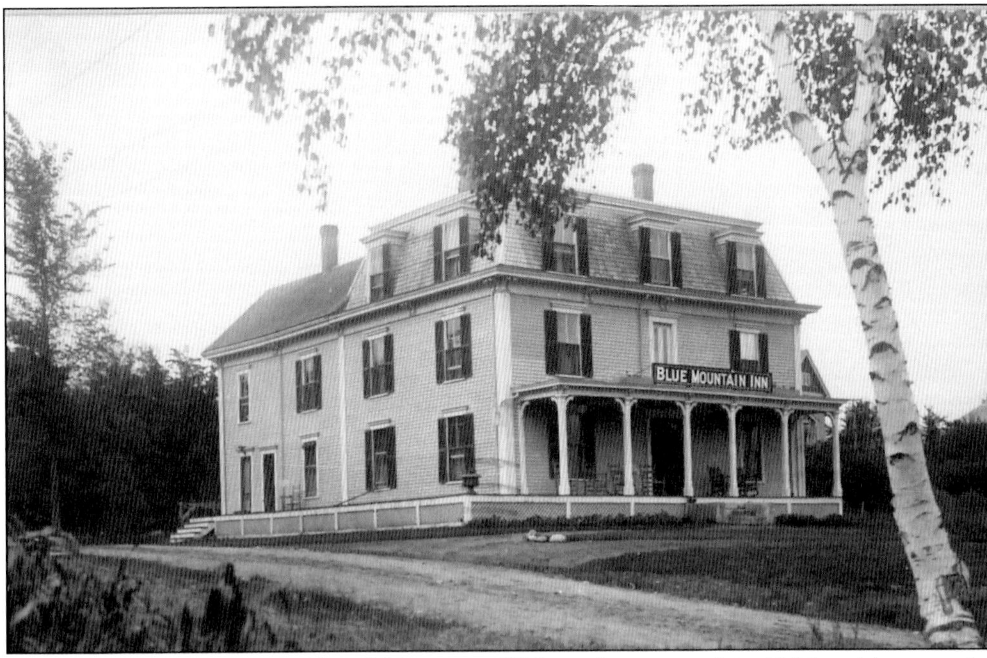

The Blue Mountain Inn on Fernald Street in Wilton. It was razed in 1947 and became the location of the home occupied by Theodore Hodgkins, president of the Forster Manufacturing Company which operated for many years in Wilton and East Wilton.

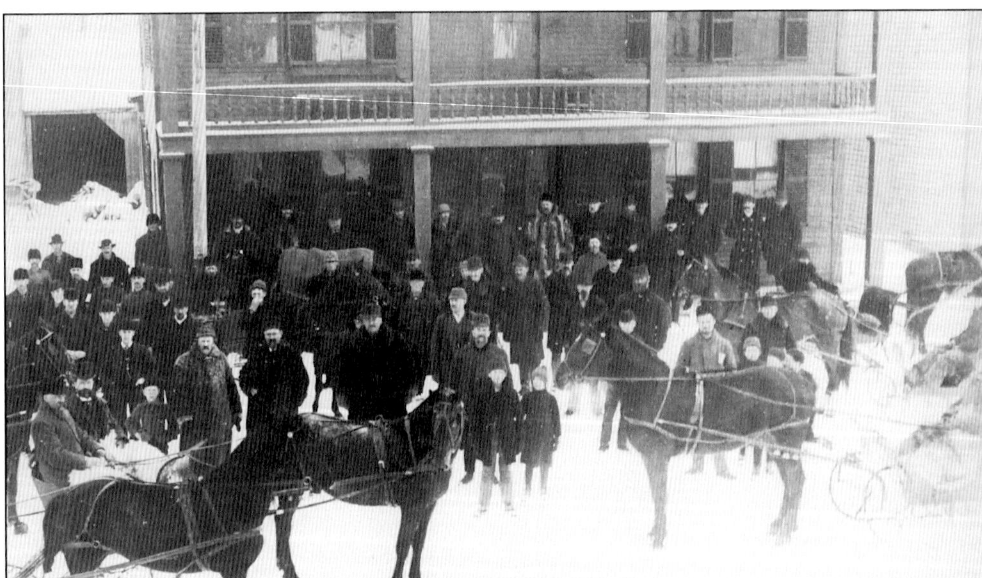

"Horse Day," c. 1889, a showcase for famous Wilton horses. Buyers from Boston were present. The group is in front of the Wilton House.

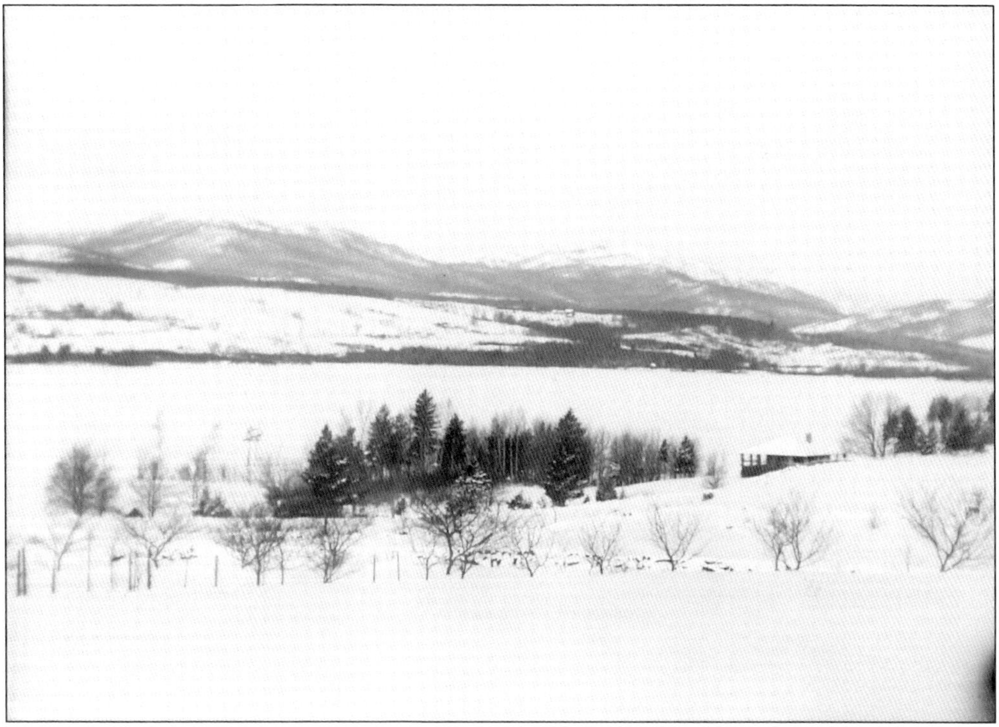

Part of the area's beautiful scenery. This is Wilson Lake, with Saddleback and Bald Mountains in the distance, *c.* early 1900s.

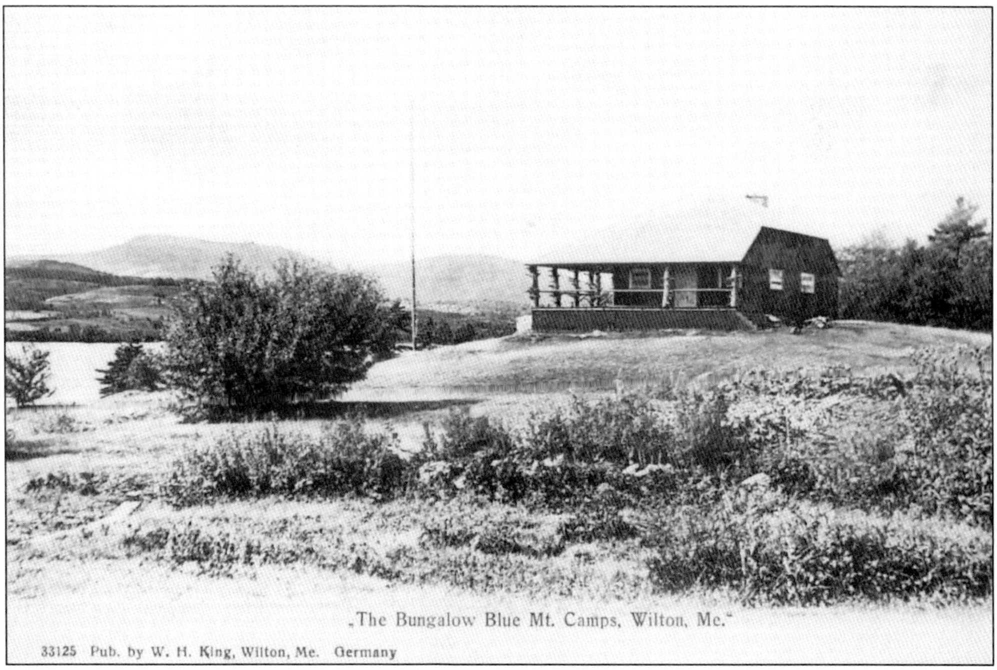

The Bungalow Blue Mountain Camps on Wilson Lake, Wilton, *c.* early 1900s. The Batchelder Music School once was located at these camps. They later became Kineowatha Camps, owned and operated by Anne and Elisabeth Bass.

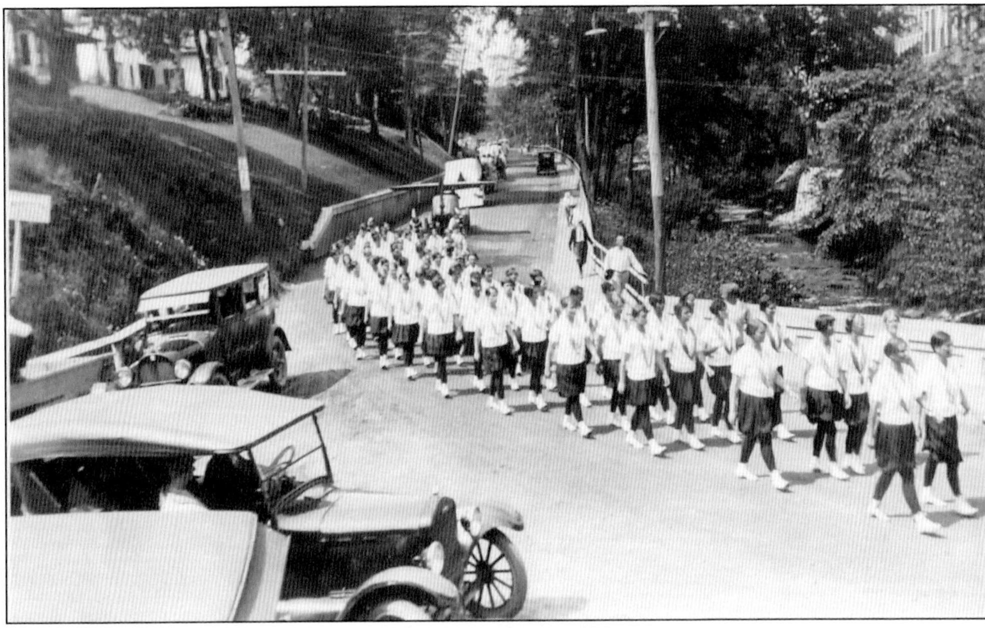

Camp Kineowatha girls march in a Wilton parade, *c.* 1920s.

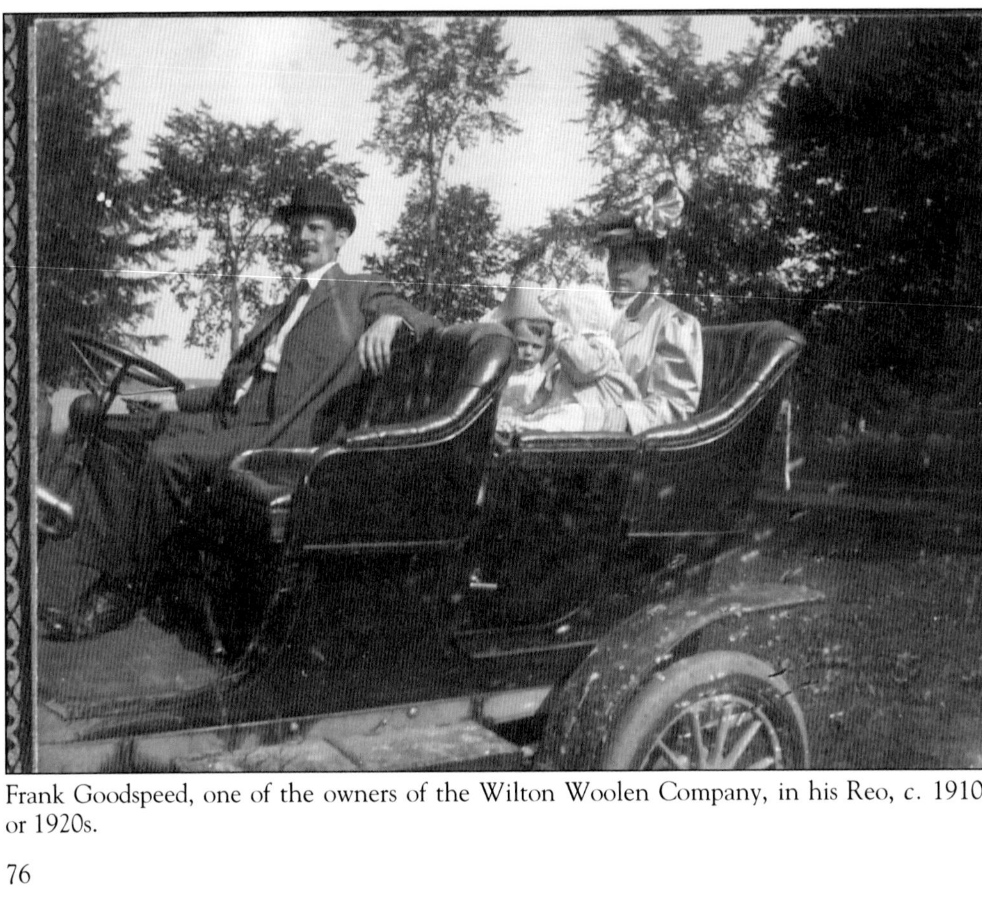

Frank Goodspeed, one of the owners of the Wilton Woolen Company, in his Reo, *c.* 1910s or 1920s.

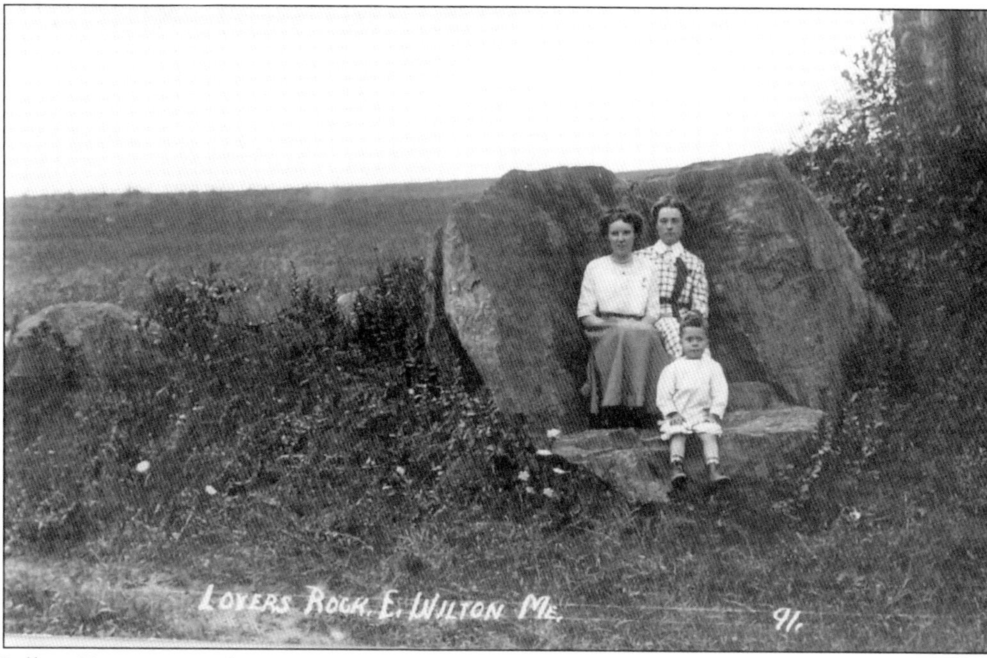

Lillian Farnum Hamilton, Eva Phillips Walker, and Talbot Lockhead are at Lovers Rock, East Wilton, *c.* early 1900s.

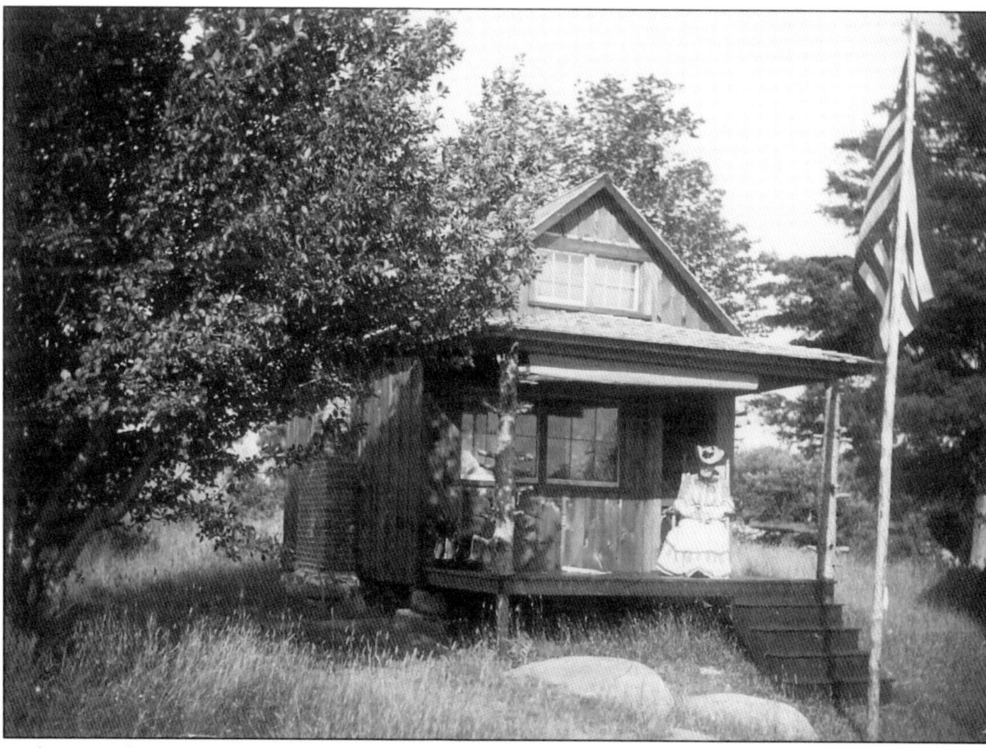

Wiltonites had recreational opportunities right at hand on Wilson Lake. This is one of the Batchelder cottages, *c.* 1900.

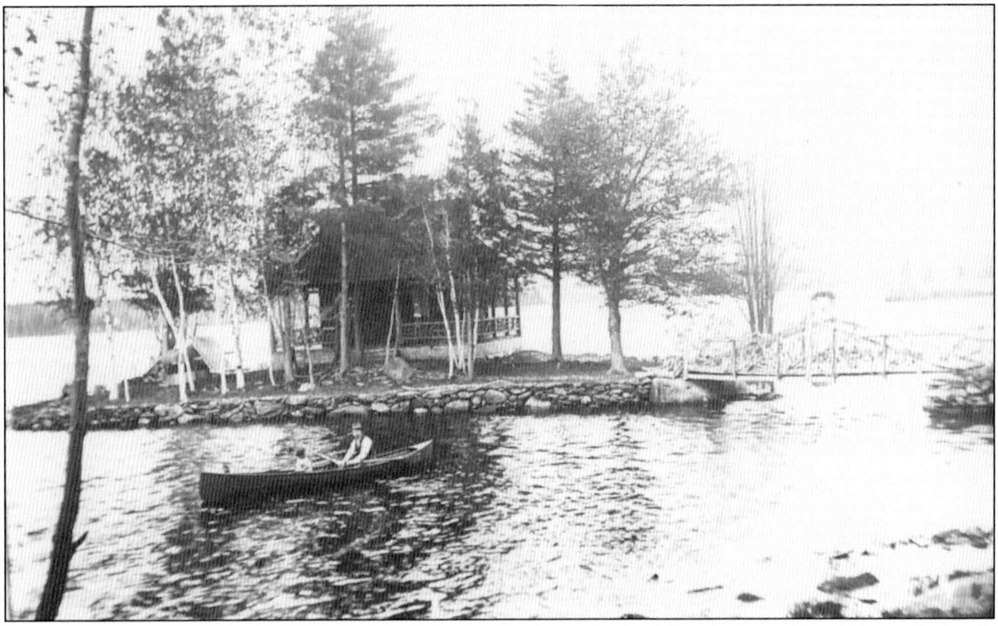

The island cottage on Wilson Lake, *c.* 1910s, was once owned by the Munroe sisters of North Jay. They were related to the people who owned the quarry there. By 1977, it was owned by the Rev. Lawrence Washburn.

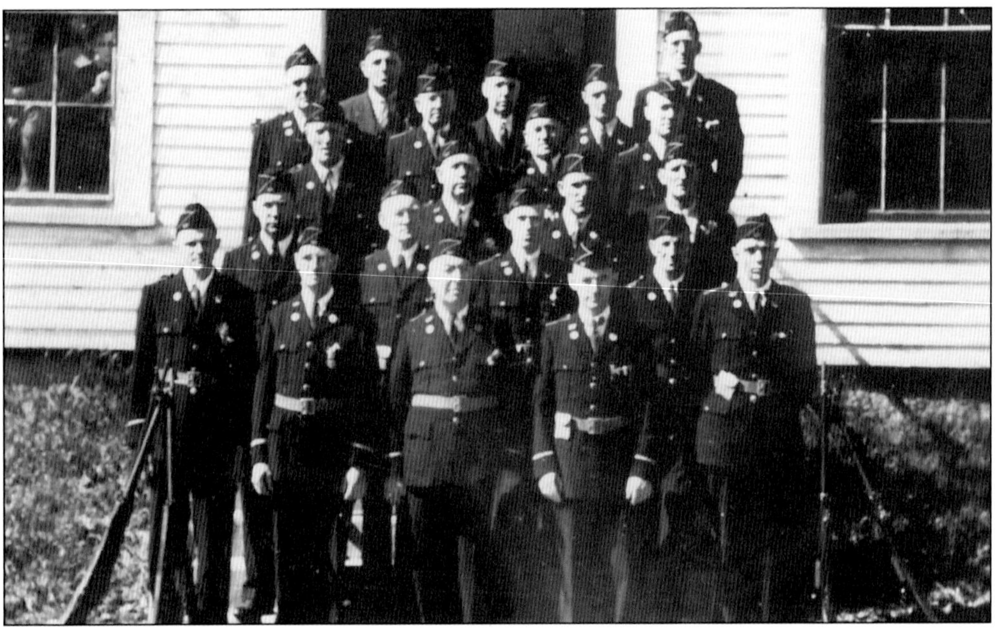

Finally, we have the organizations and groups people belonged to in Wilton. This was a group at the May 30, 1939 Memorial Day meeting of the Wilton American Legion post. From left to right are as follows: (front row) Maurice Fletcher, Wilmer Bryant, Leon Farnum (commander), Alton Farnham, and Harold Melendy: (second row) Howard Kyes, Charles Edwards, Thomas Lake, and Honore Fournier; (third row) Pete Swett, Carroll (Carl) Tobin, Dean Perry, and Joe Mooar; (fourth row) Newton Cochran, Joseph Fite, Ralph Gould, and Earle Harnden; (back row) Everett Smith, Harry Foster, Wesley Spear, and Maurice Wilkins.

Four

The Basses: Economic Savvy

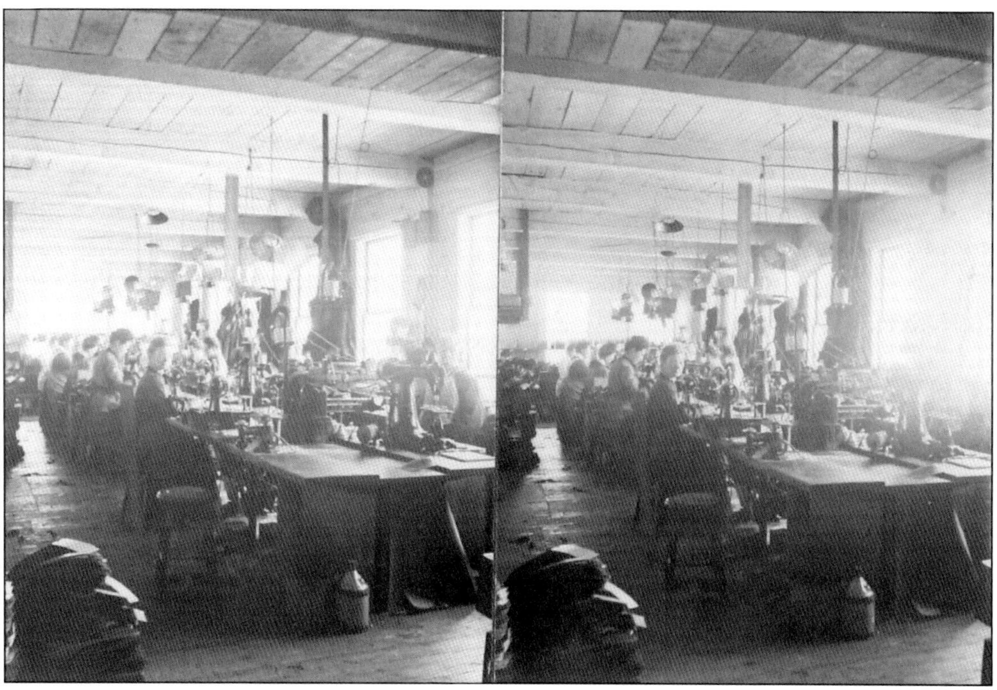

The stitching room at the G.H. Bass and Company shoe factory in 1905 at Wilton.

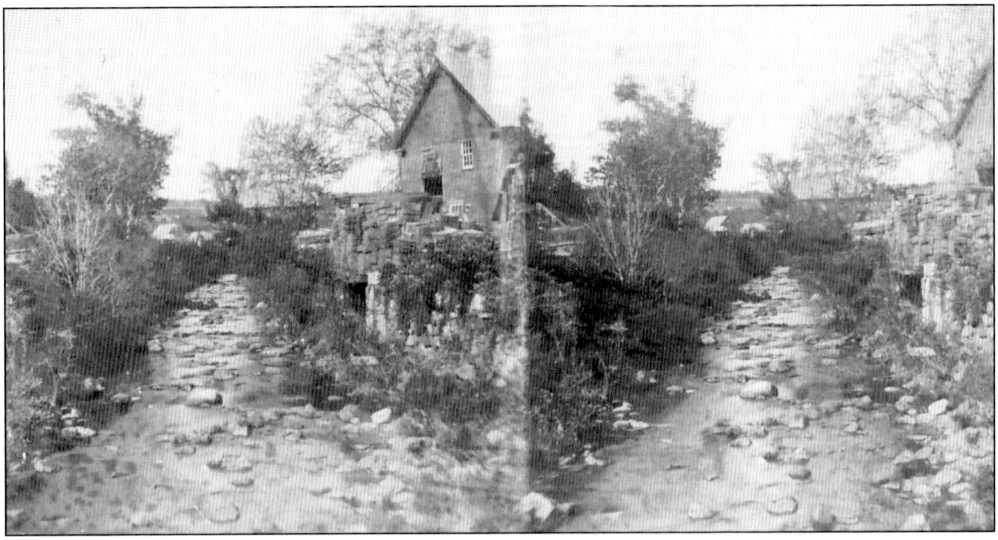

An old sawmill at Wilton where one of the Bass factories later stood.

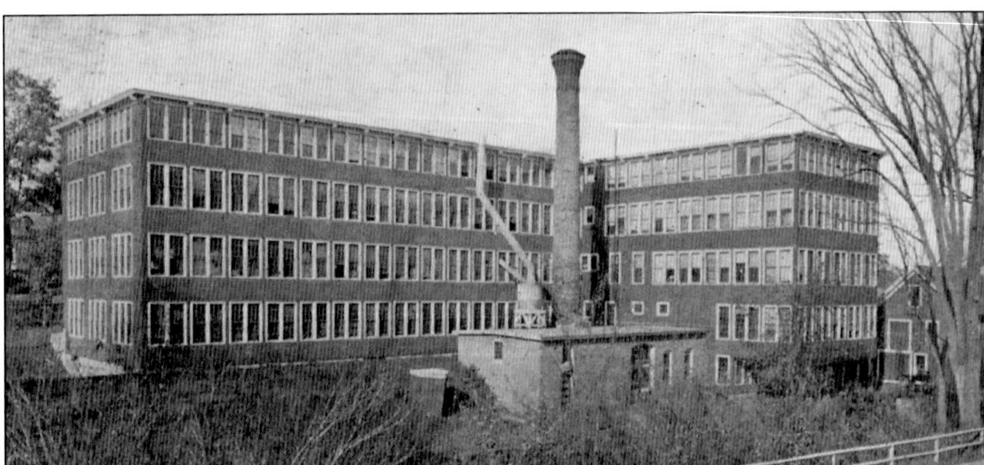

The G.H. Bass and Company shoe factory built in 1904–1905, c. 1915. It was commonly known as Number One and was eventually replaced by an even larger plant.

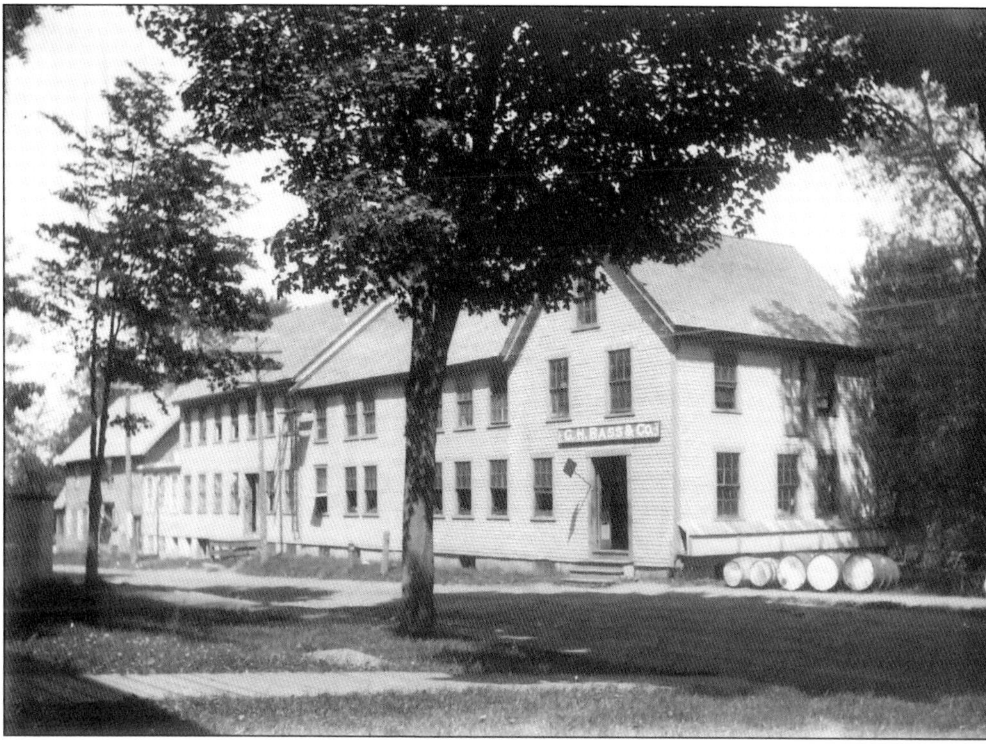

The second location of G.H. Bass and Company in Wilton, *c.* 1892. When started in 1876, the company had eight employees.

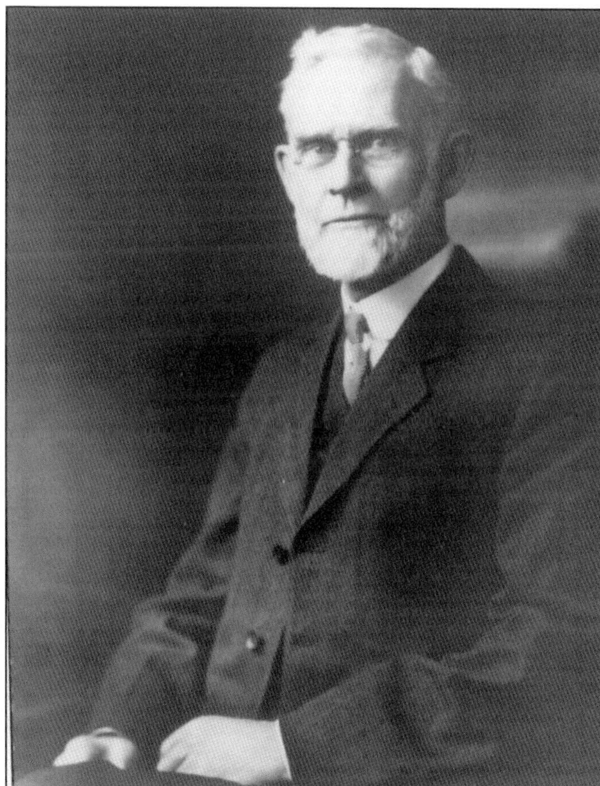

George Henry Bass, founder of G.H. Bass and Company in 1876, is shown here *c.* early 1910s.

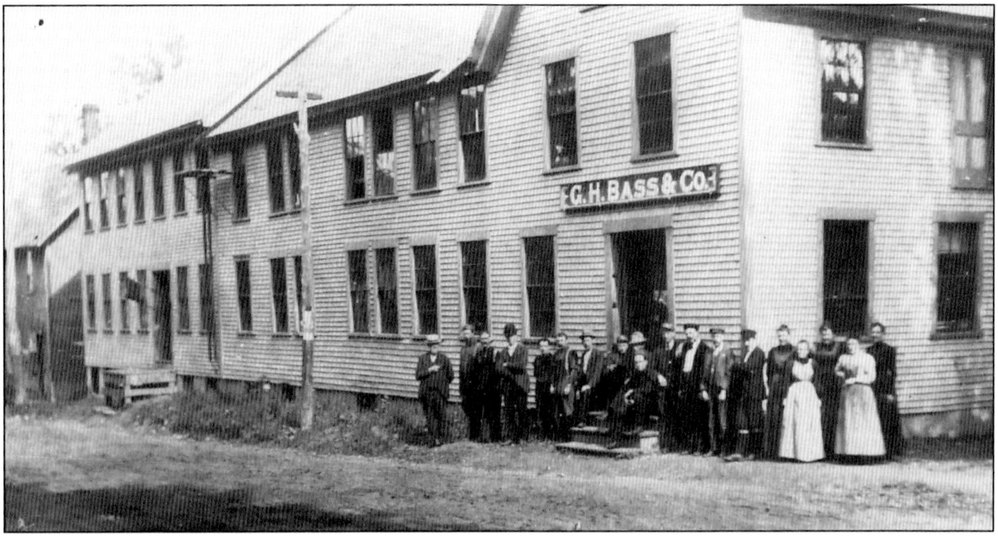

A group poses in front of G.H. Bass and Company, Wilton, *c.* 1892. The firm's ownership for years paid higher wages than the average shoe industry wages in New England.

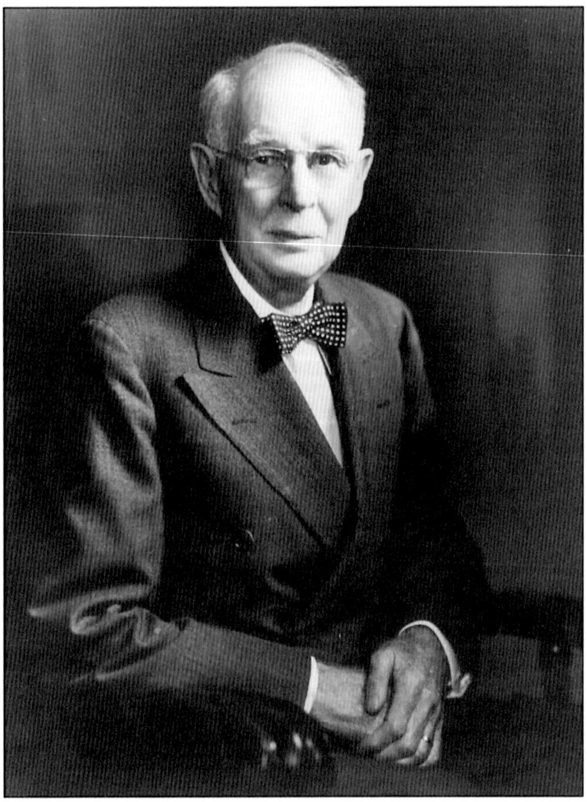

Willard Streeter Bass, president of G.H. Bass and Company from 1925 to 1956, is shown here *c.* 1950s.

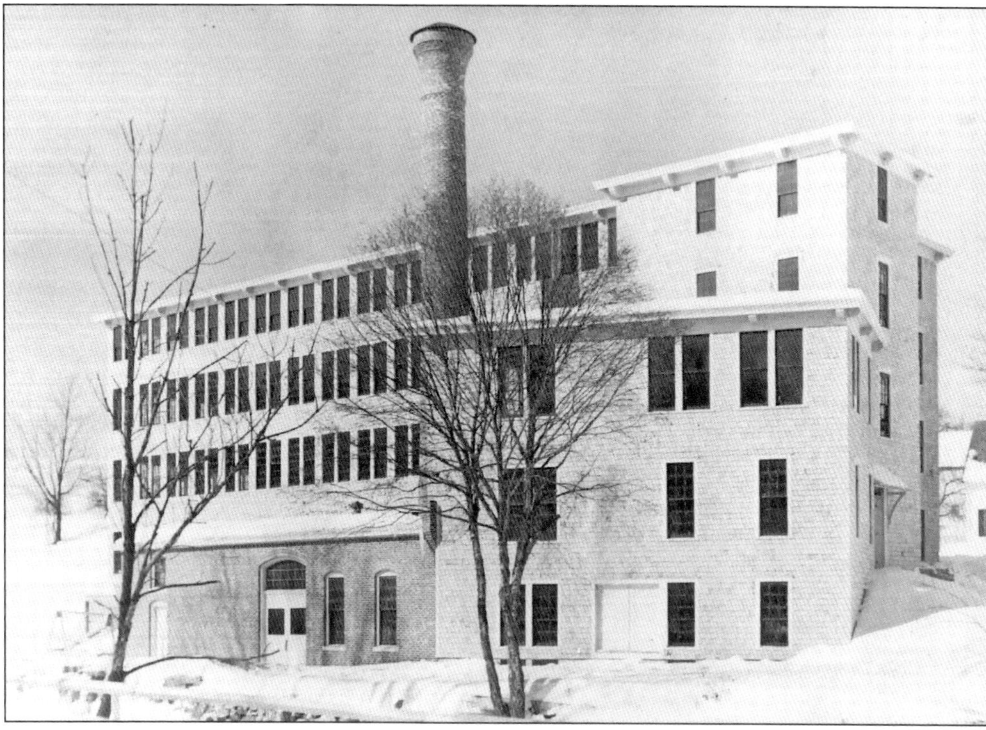

The Number One factory just after it was built in 1904–1905. Several additions were later made.

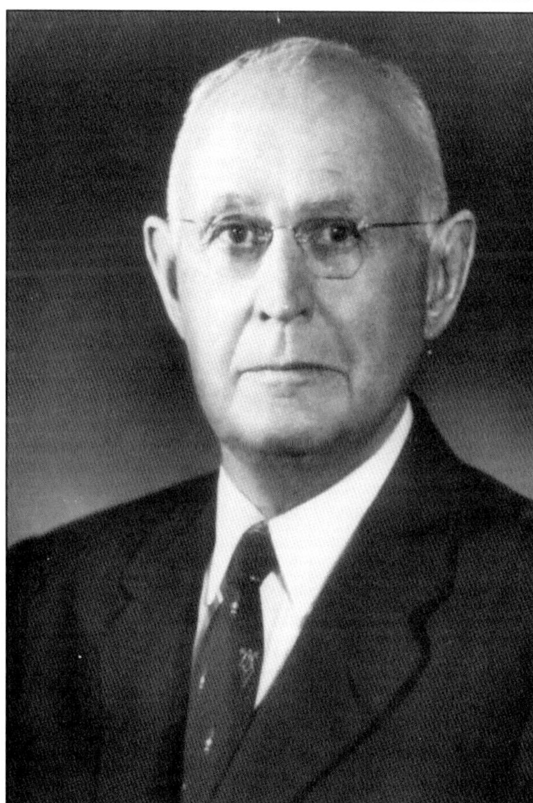

John Bass, treasurer of G.H. Bass and Company from 1900 to 1963, in a *c.* 1950s photograph.

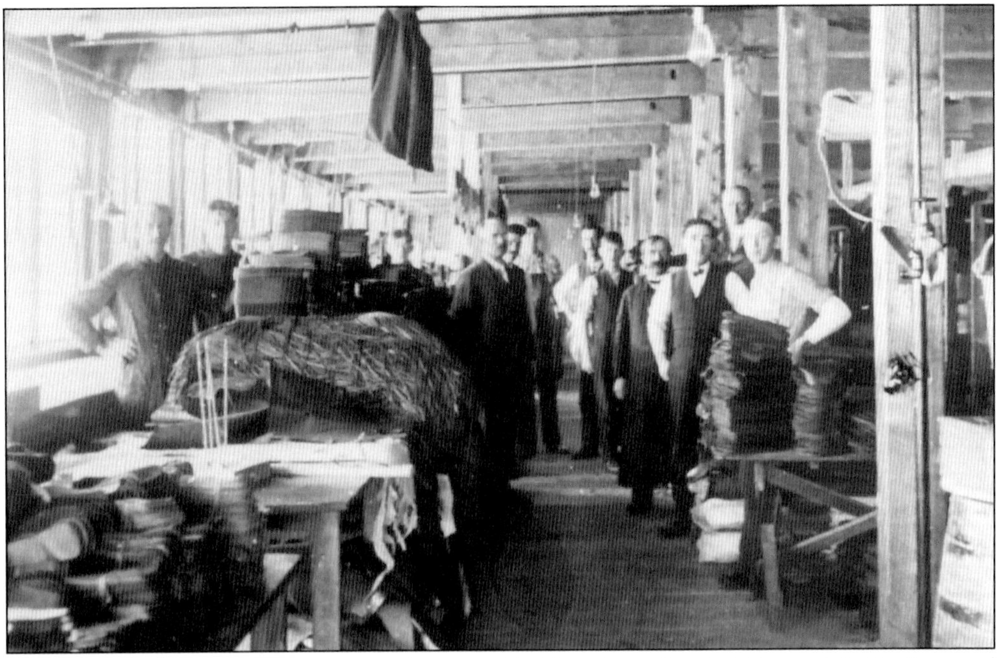

Sole leather in the cutting room at the so-called bowling alley building of G.H. Bass and Company, *c.* late 1890s.

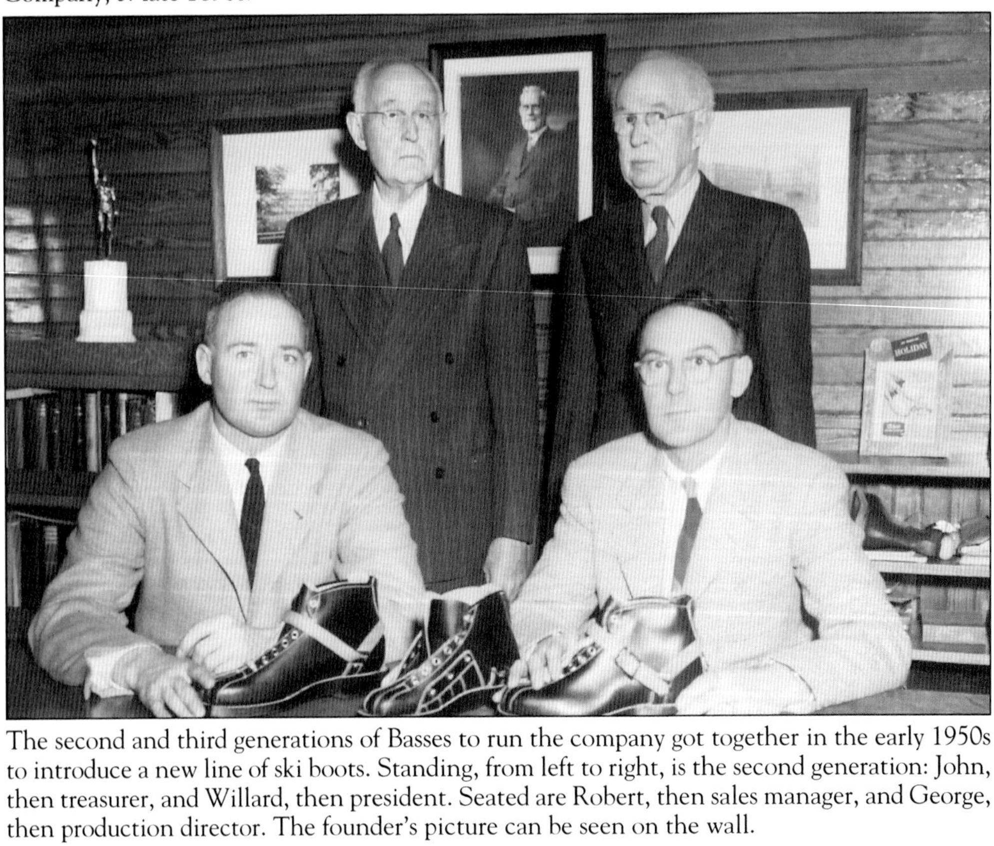

The second and third generations of Basses to run the company got together in the early 1950s to introduce a new line of ski boots. Standing, from left to right, is the second generation: John, then treasurer, and Willard, then president. Seated are Robert, then sales manager, and George, then production director. The founder's picture can be seen on the wall.

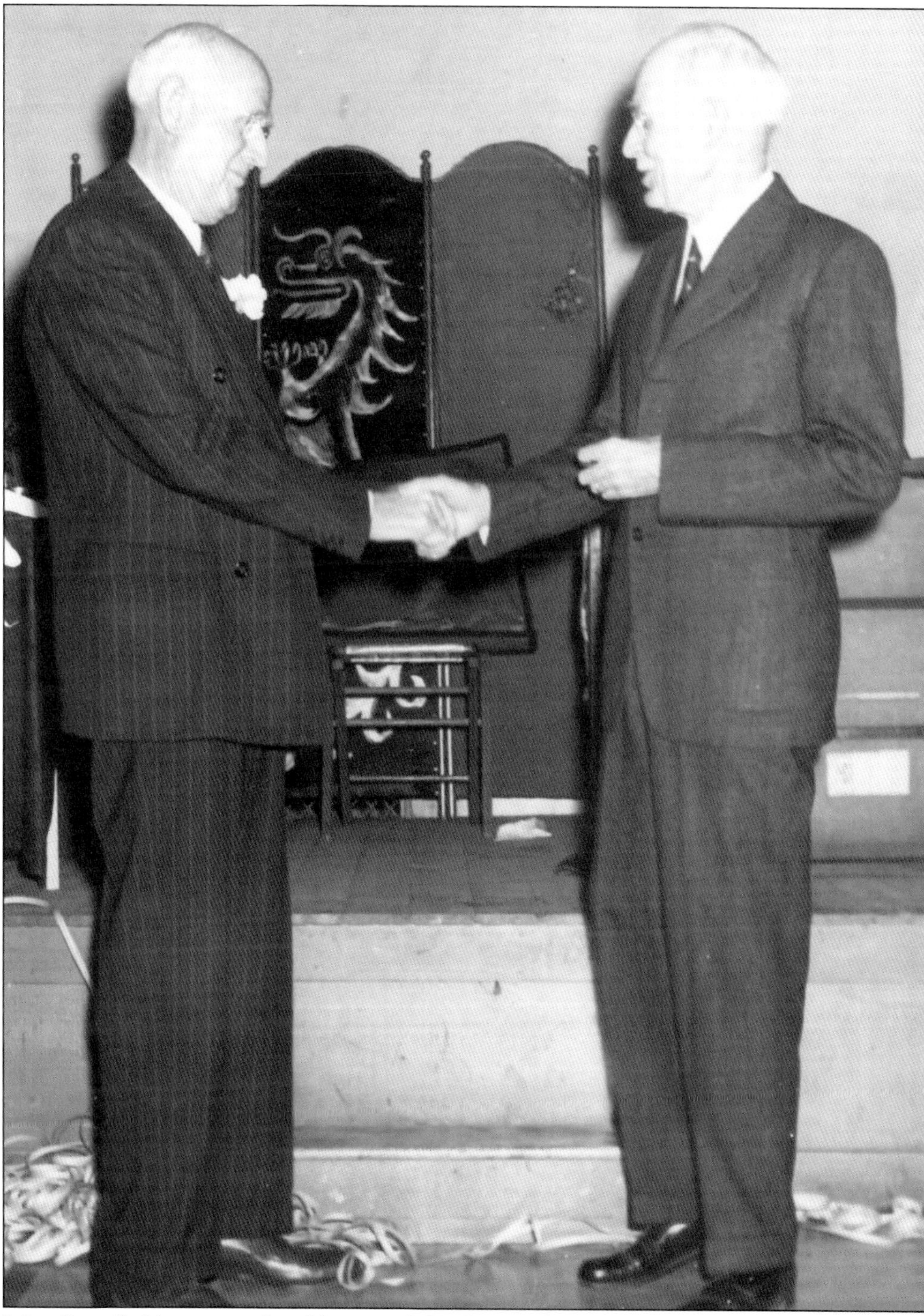

John Bass (left) receives his fifty-year G.H. Bass and Company employment pin from his brother, Willard Bass, in 1951. In those fifty years, John Bass had seen the great success of Bass Weejuns and watched the company make loggers' and hunters' boots, boots that Lindbergh wore on his 1927 solo flight to Paris, boots that Admiral Byrd used on his Antarctic trips, and shoes of many kinds.

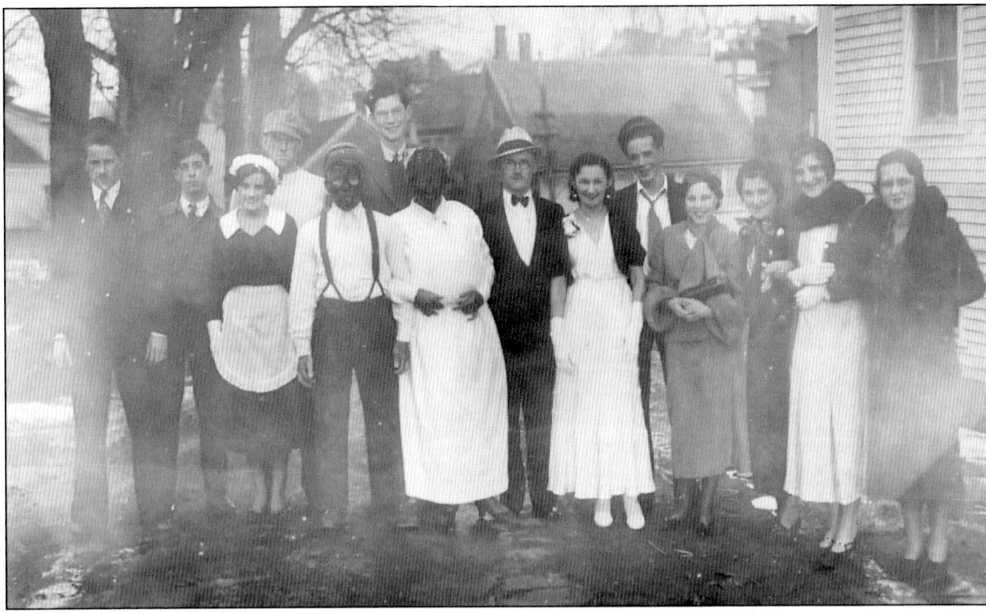

The Basses were part of the Wilton community. In the cast of *Laugh Clown* given by the 1933 senior class of Wilton Academy was Streeter Bass. Others in the cast include Buck Benson, Aaron Parker, Theo Scott, Glenn Mosher, Bob York, Theo Whittemore, Don Kenney, Philia Gondeck, Russ Orr, May Cox, Myra Sawyer, Dorothy Baraby, and Evelyn Lincoln. The play was given on January 6, 1933, at the town hall. Directed by Dorothy Dumais, it made a profit of about $55.

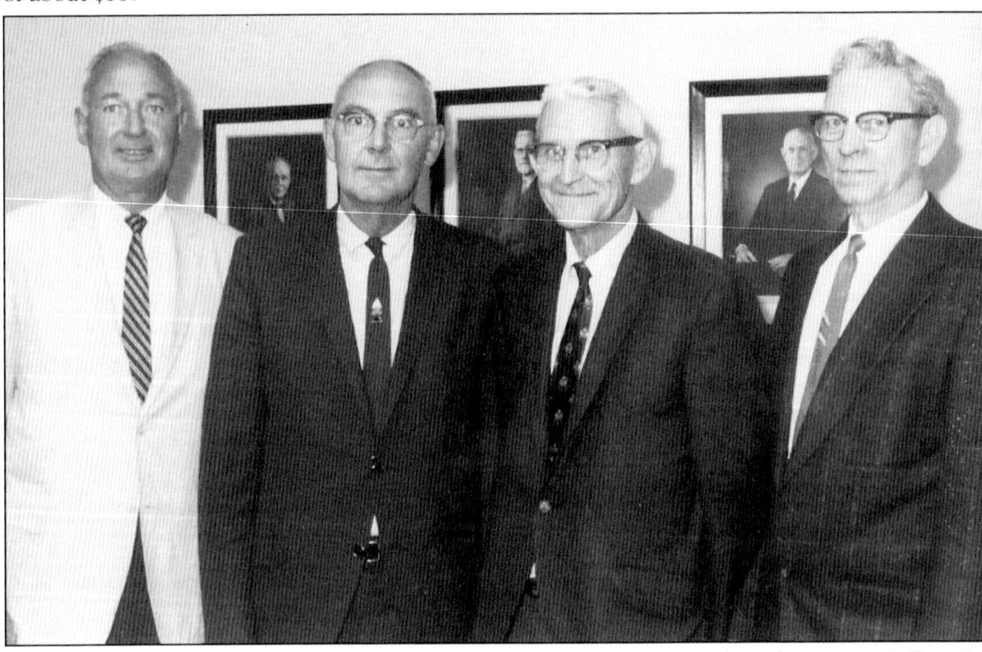

From left to right are Robert N. Bass (sales manager, later treasurer) and George H. Bass III (director of production, later president) of G.H. Bass and Company, with Lyman and Milford Burgess in the late 1950s as the Bass company took over the Burgess Shoe Store in Wilton for money and stock.

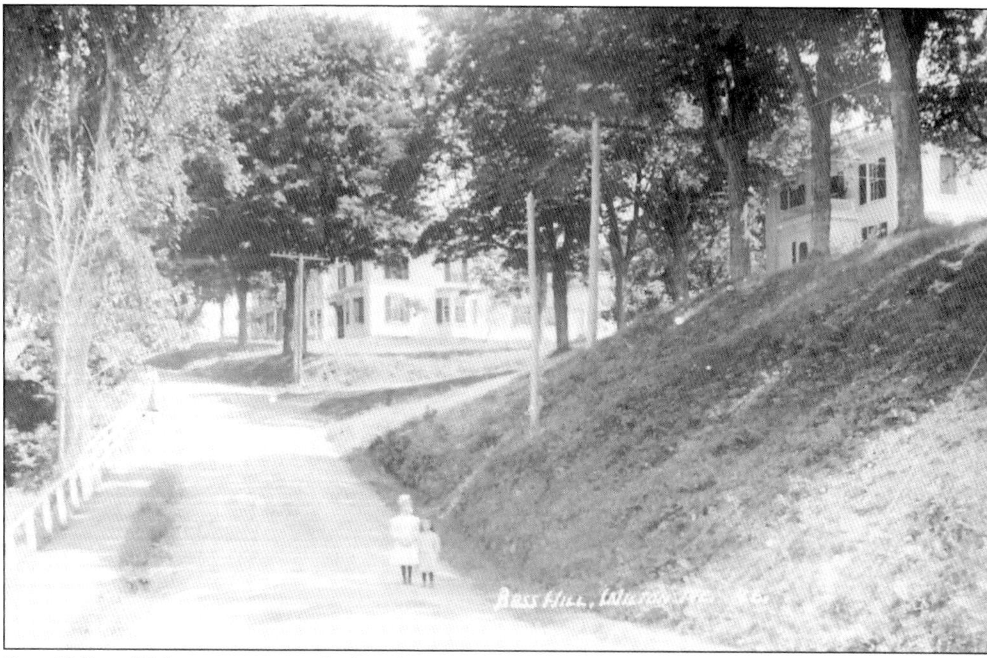

Bass Hill in Wilton was named after the Bass family. At right is part of the house built in 1858 by James Greenwood, bought by S. Savil Bass in 1867, the home for years of Mary and Lizzie Bass. The little girls at the foot of the hill are Leonora and Mabelle Hiscock, *c.* 1910s.

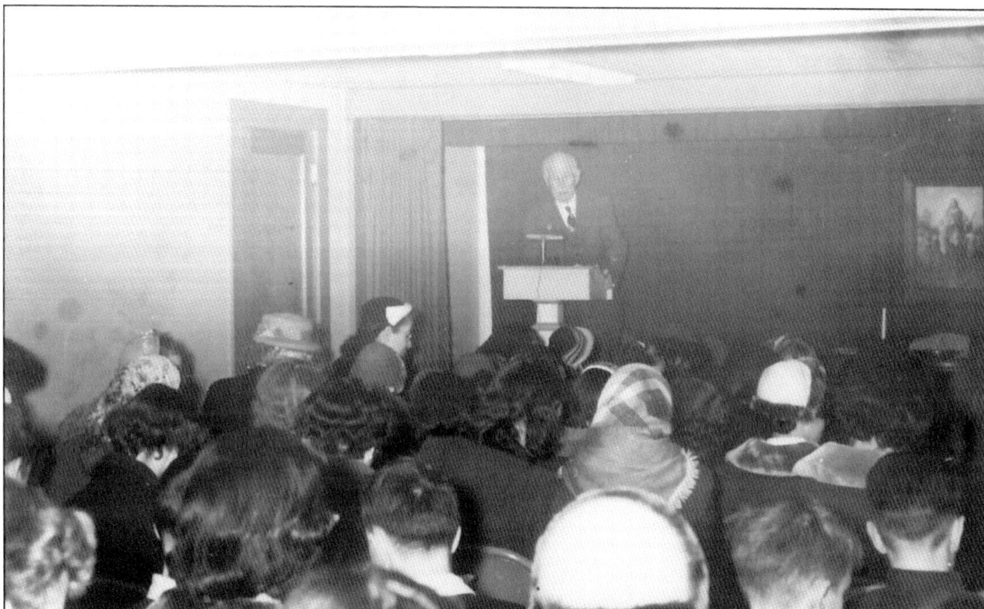

Willard Bass speaks as superintendent of the Congregational Church School in Wilton during the early 1950s. Bass was also very active in the Boy Scouts in Wilton.

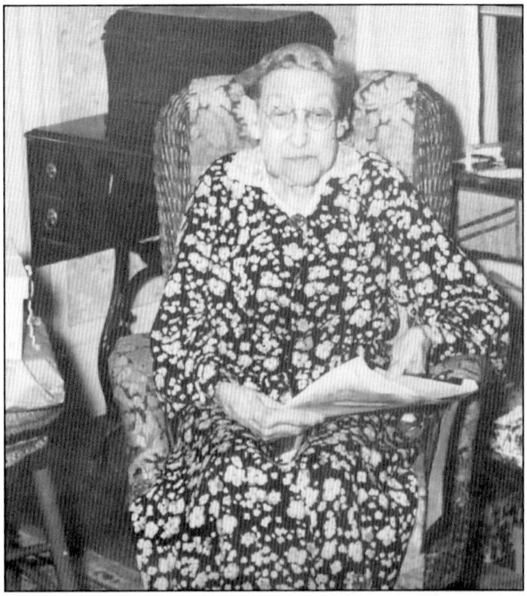

Miss Mary Bass, a cousin of the Basses who ran the company, in the late 1950s. A Wilton Academy graduate, she wrote a history of the First Congregational Church in Wilton and lived to be 105 years old.

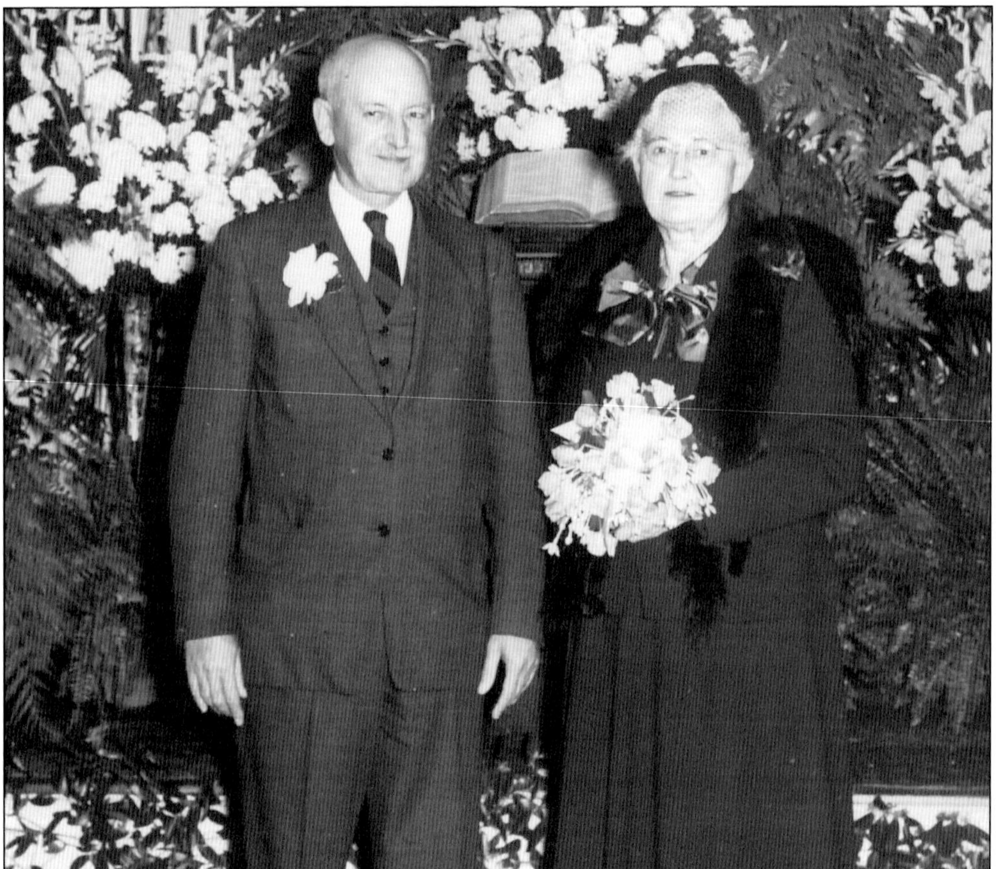

Newlyweds! Anne Bass married J. Willard Bolte in Wilton on November 15, 1952. She was a sister of Willard and John Bass and the daughter of G.H. Bass.

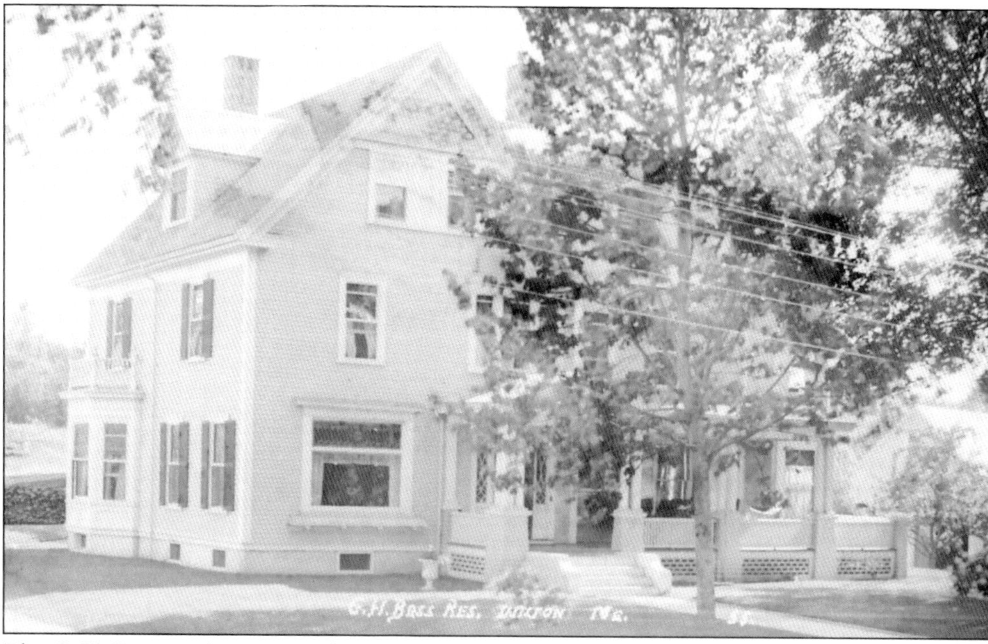

The G.H. Bass residence in Wilton, *c.* 1910s.

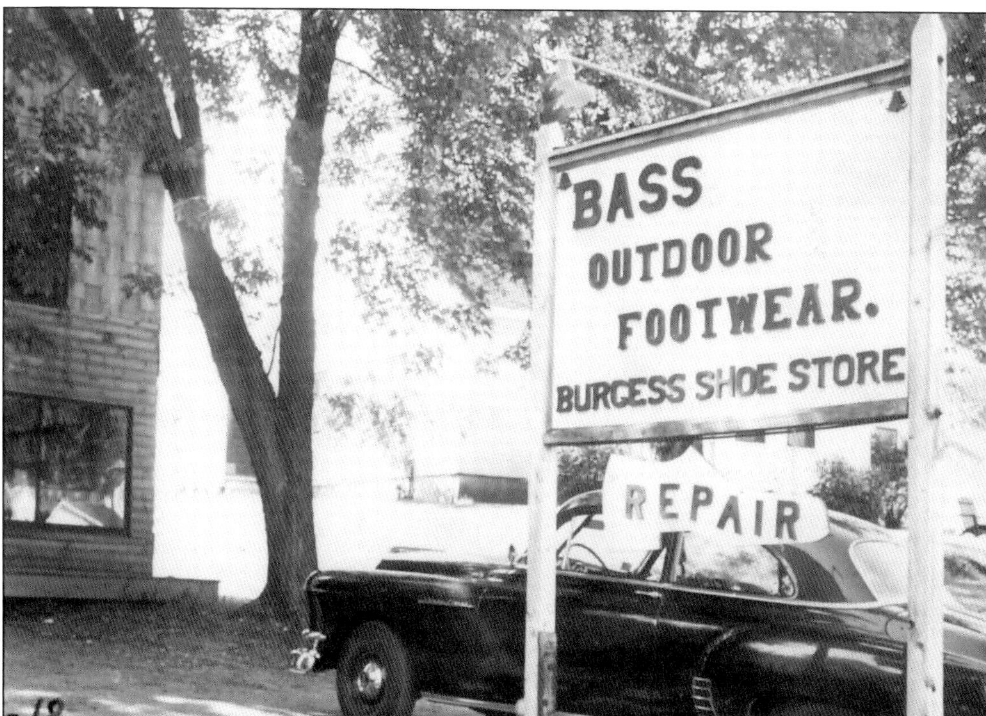

The first Bass outlet store in Wilton, at the Burgess Shoe Store, *c.* 1953. There are now many such outlets. The company was sold in 1978 to Cheseborough-Pond's and, later, to Phillips Van Heusen. There are no longer any Basses living in Wilton. They had lived in the town at least six generations.

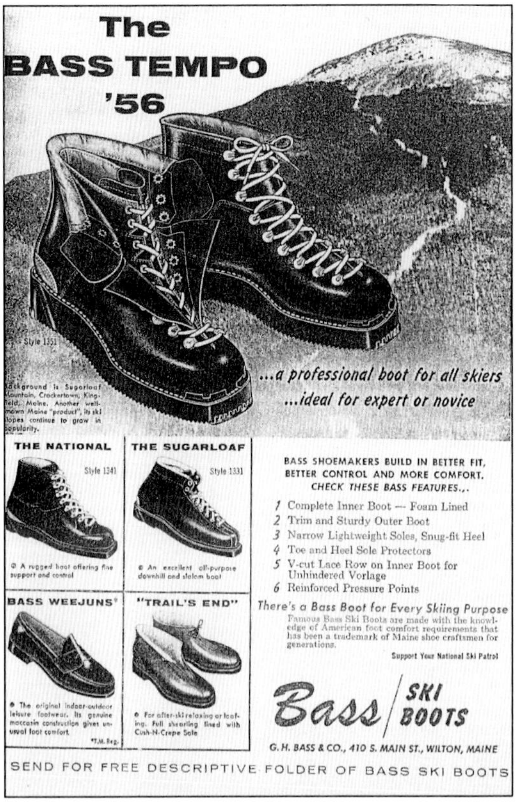

A typical Bass ski boot advertisement, this one from 1956. The company no longer makes ski boots.

This was a sign on Route 4 in the 1950s. It is exactly what the reader is now doing. Note the distances on the sign.

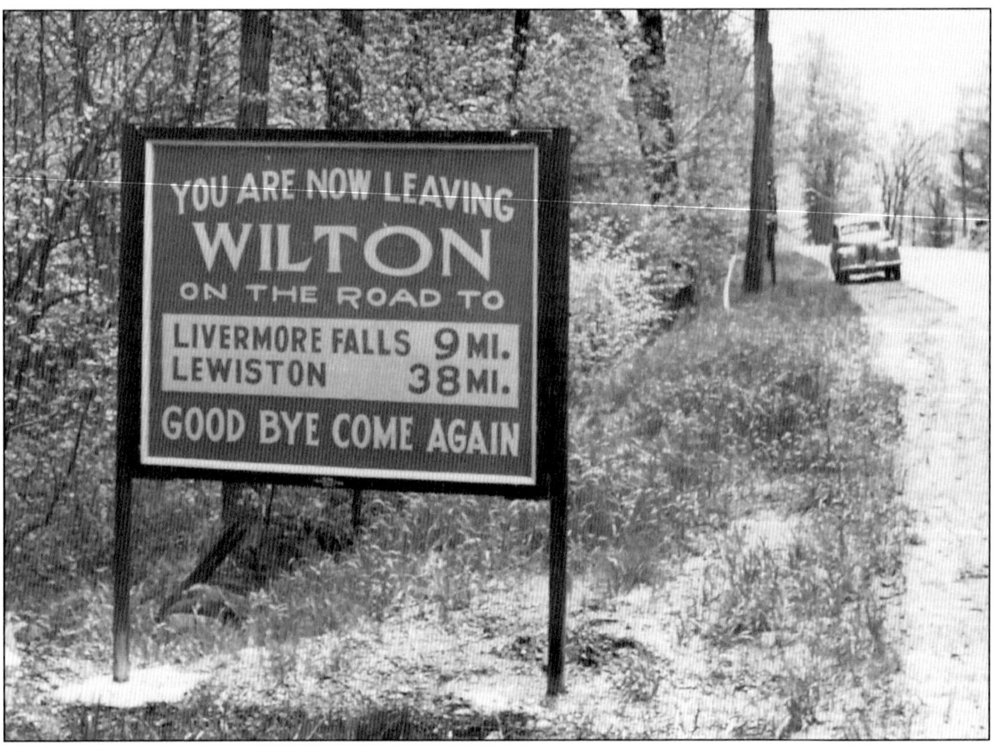

Five

Kingfield and Sugarloaf

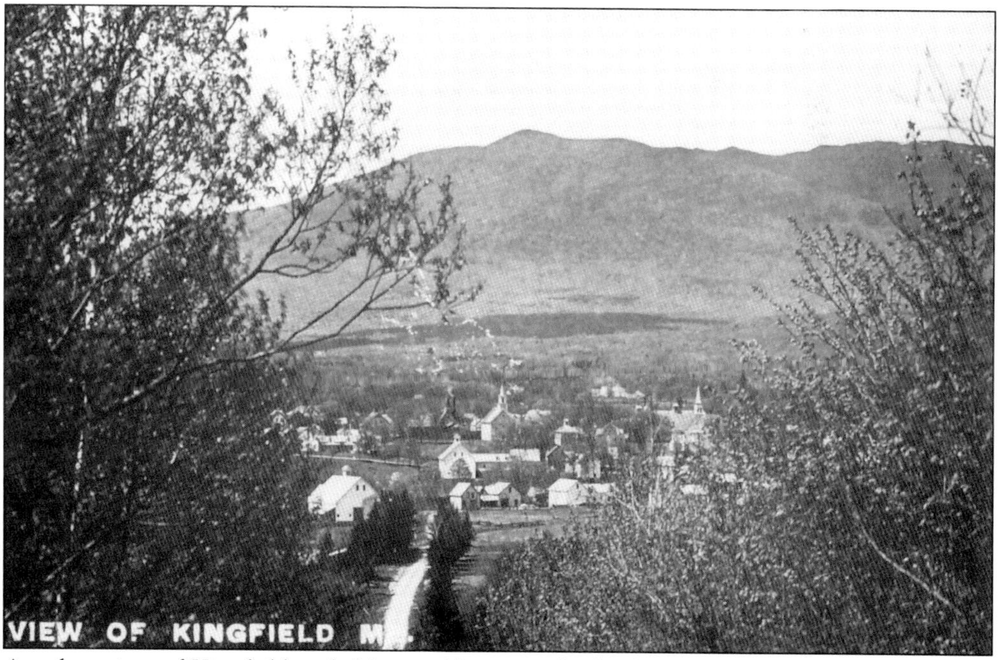

Another view of Kingfield with Mount Abram in the background. This was taken in 1919, about two decades after the picture in the front of the book. The town had grown in those twenty years.

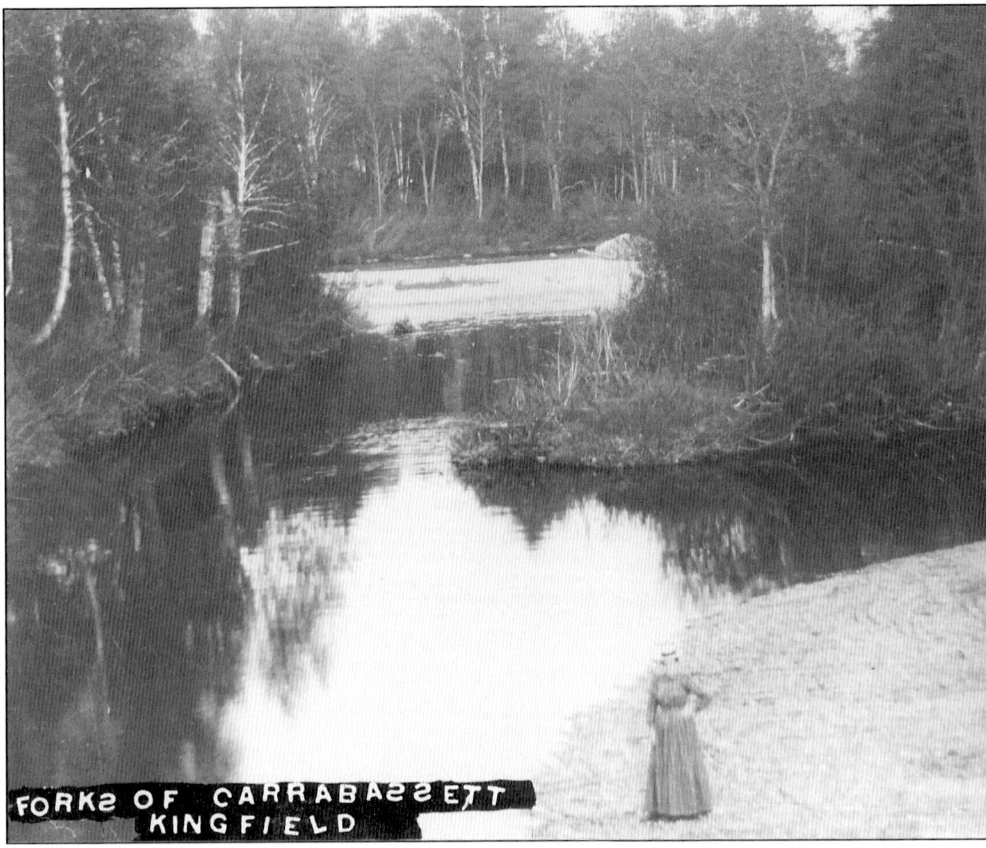

Forks of the Carrabassett River in Kingfield, *c.* early 1890s. The woman is unknown. This is one of a group of stereoptic slides made from the photos of E.P. Locke of Kingfield.

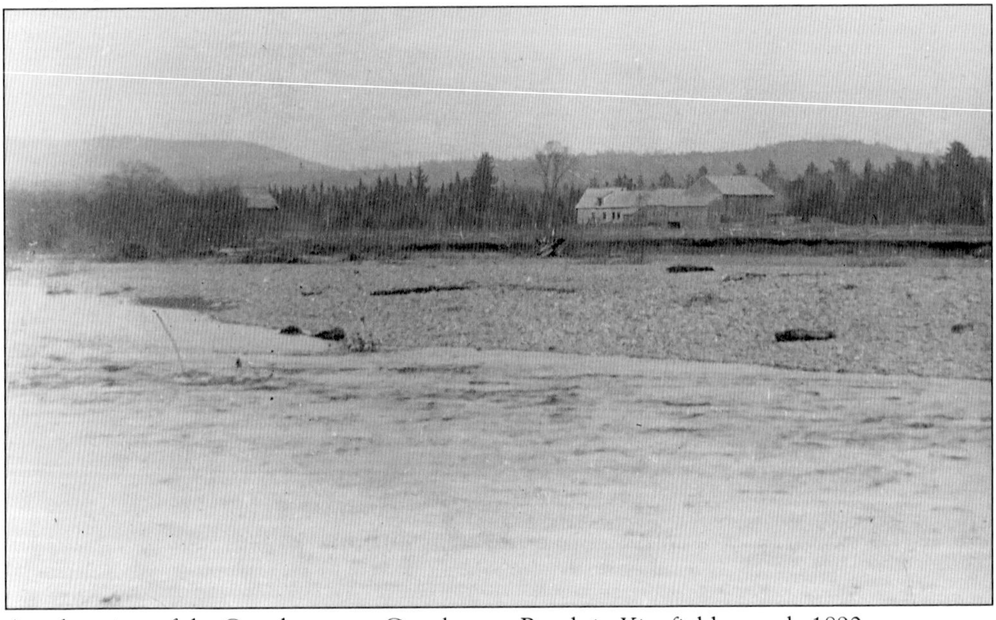

Another view of the Carrabassett at Carrabassett Beach in Kingfield, *c.* early 1890s.

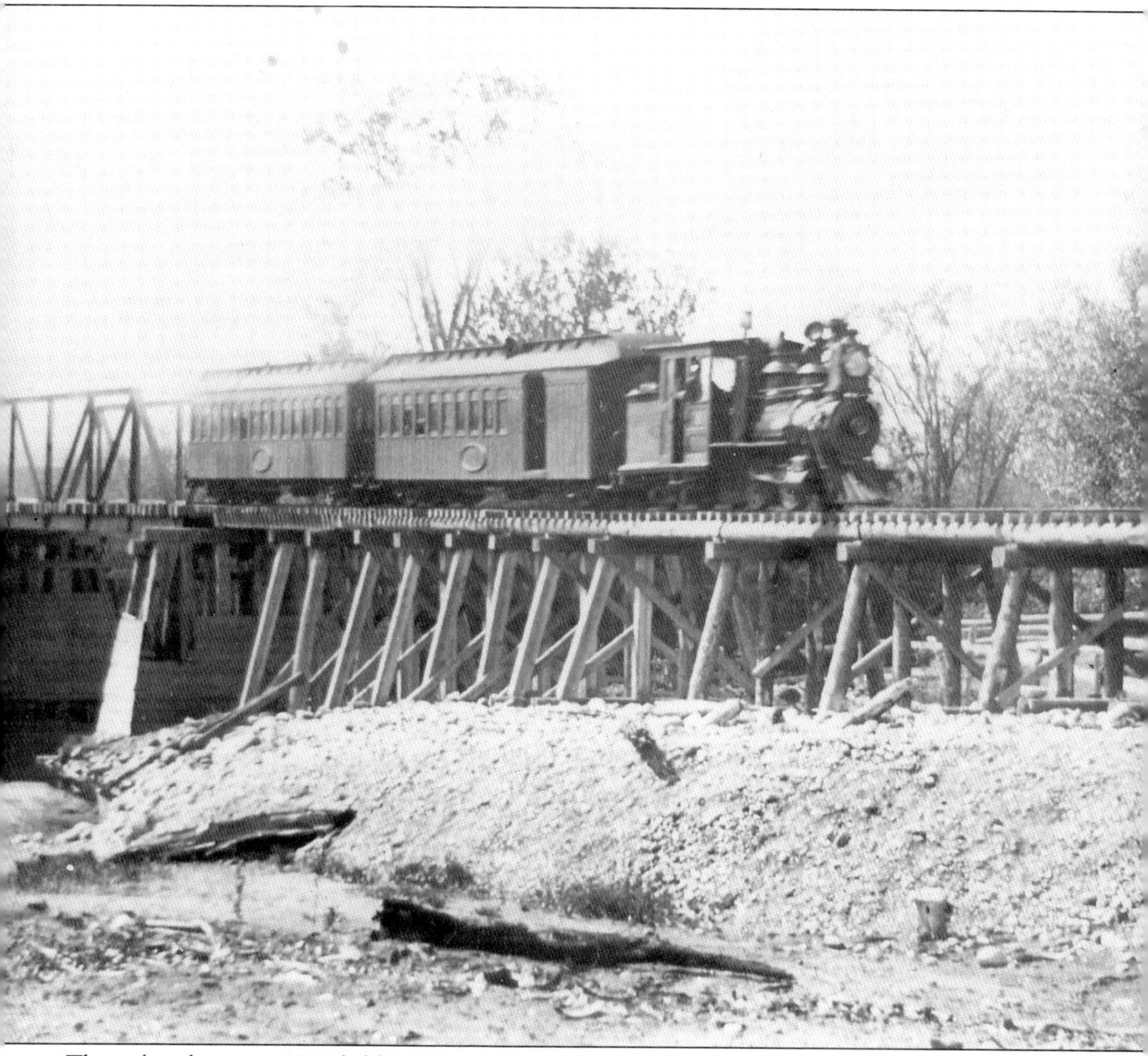

The railroad came to Kingfield in December 1884—but it was a different kind of railroad, narrow gauge. It brought an economic impetus to the town that allowed it to grow when neighboring communities were declining. It was the Franklin & Megantic Railroad when it came in but was later absorbed by the Sandy River and Rangeley Lakes Railroad. Its last run was on July 30, 1936. The trestle was swept away several times, c. early 1890s.

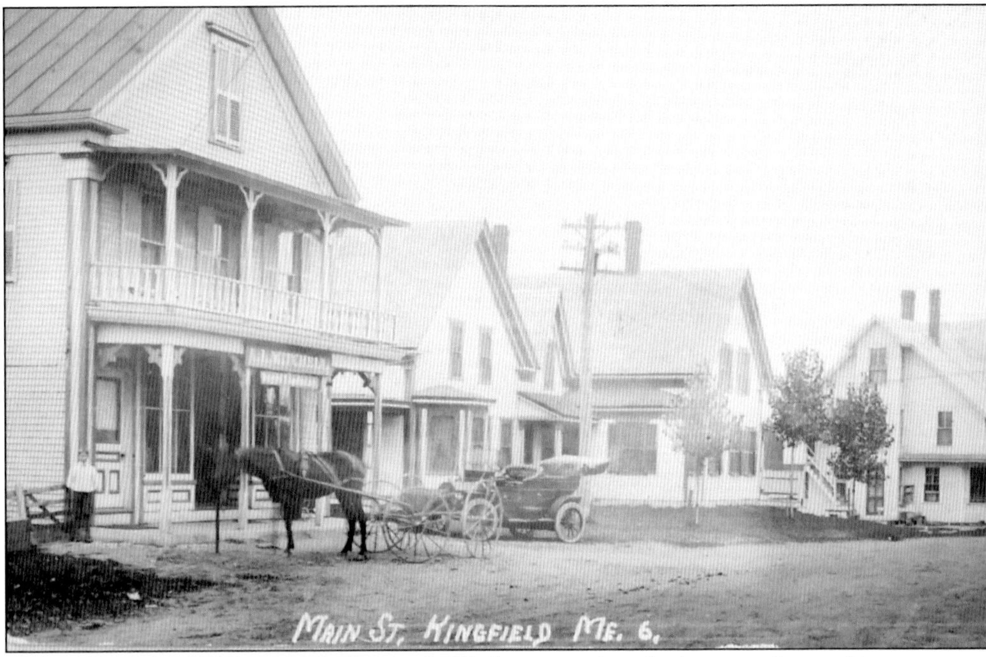

Main Street, Kingfield, *c.* 1910s. L. Mitchell's drug store has the horse in front of it.

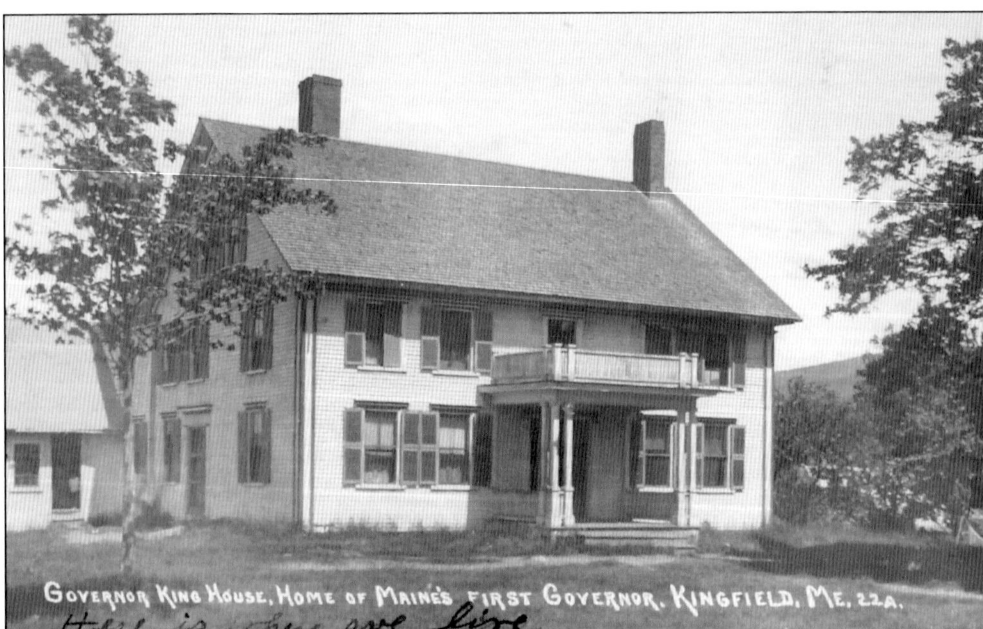

The Kingfield home of Maine's first governor, William King, *c.* 1900s. Kingfield is named after him. Maine's first governor also lived in Scarborough and Bath. As well as governor, he was the first grand master of Maine Masons.

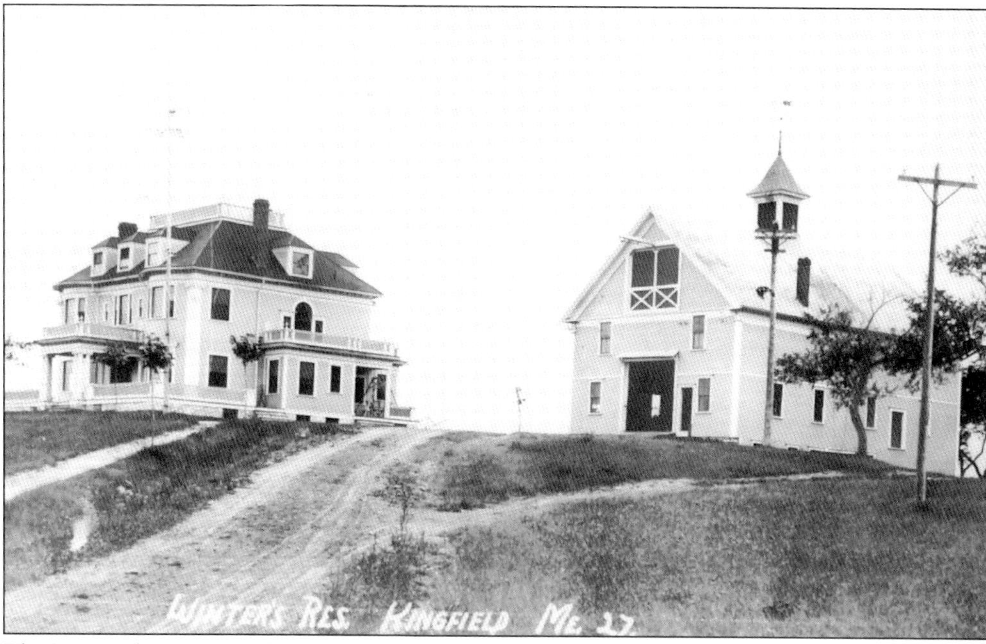

The Winter home, now the Inn At Winter's Hill, c. 1910s.

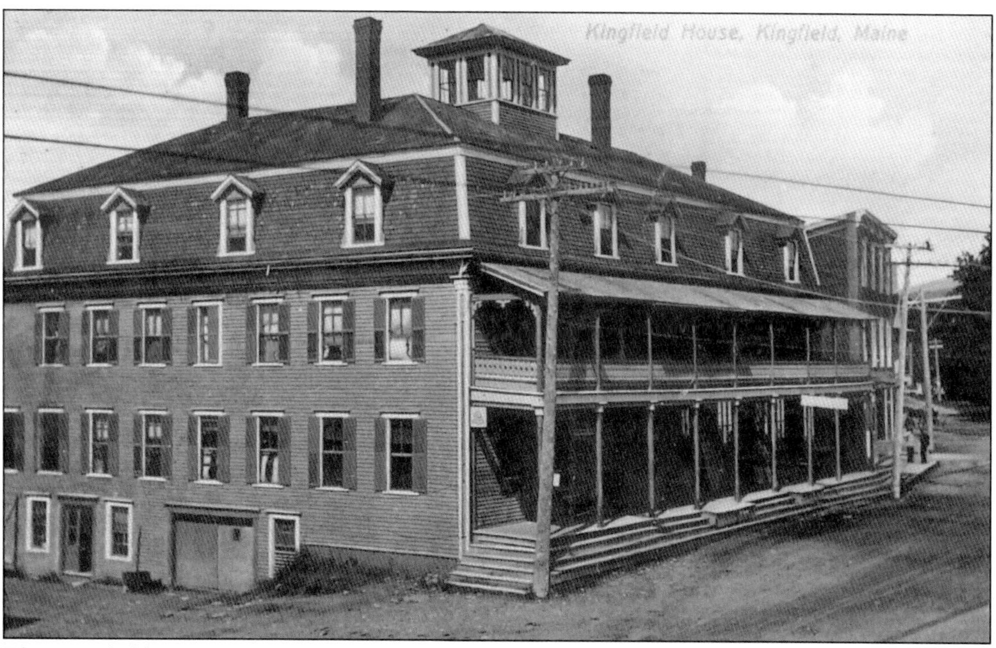

The Kingfield House, c. 1910, was opened in 1886 by John Winter on the site of the present Hotel Herbert. The Franklin House, also on the same site, had burned in 1880.

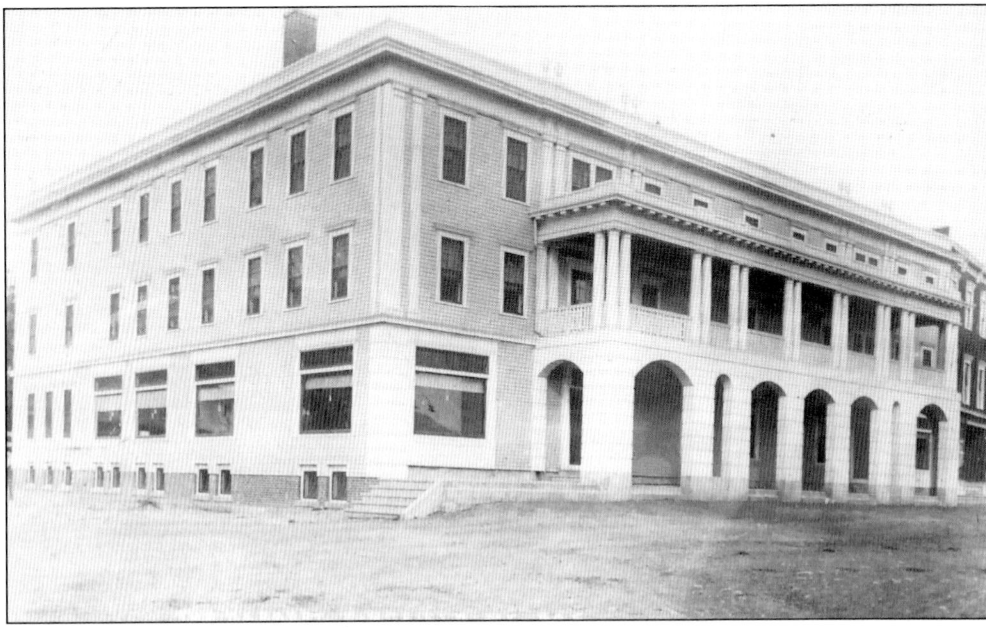

The Hotel Herbert was built for $100,000 in 1918, *c.* 1920.

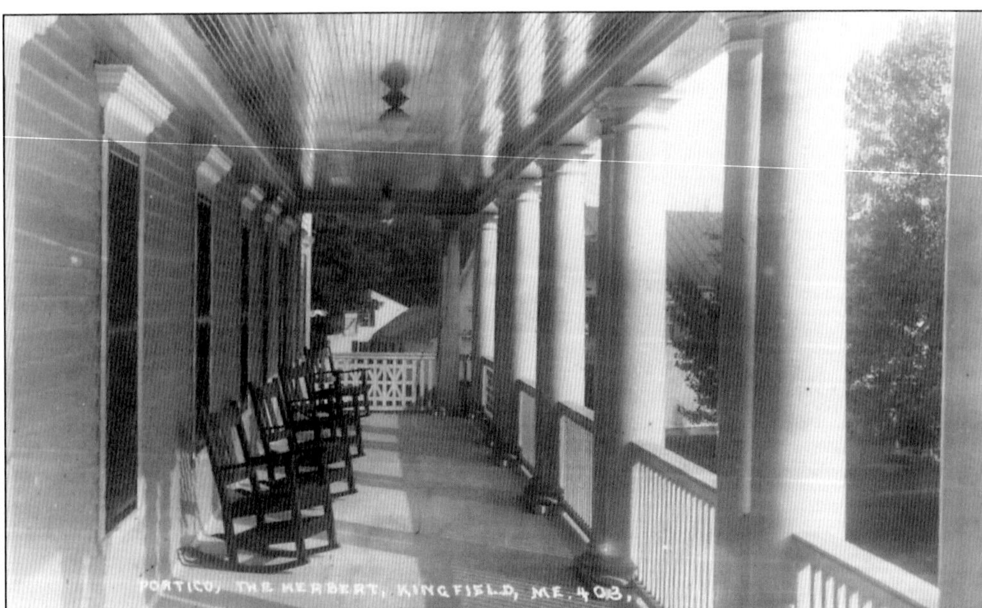

The portico of the Hotel Herbert, *c.* 1920. All the pictures of Kingfield used so far give an idea of the tourist potential that existed here.

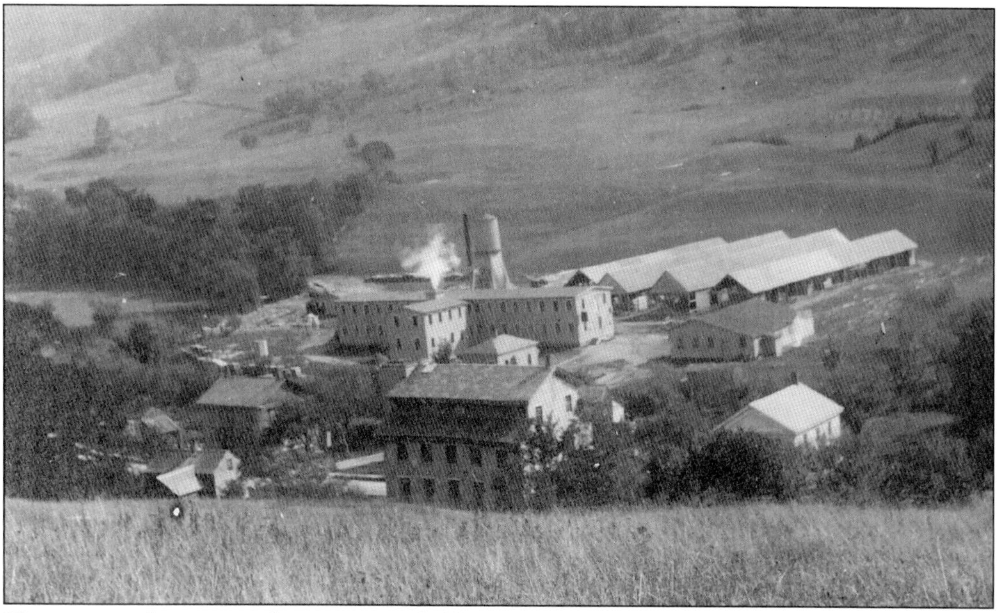

There was and is some industry in Kingfield, most of it wood-related. Here is one of those mills as photographed by E.P. Locke in the 1890s.

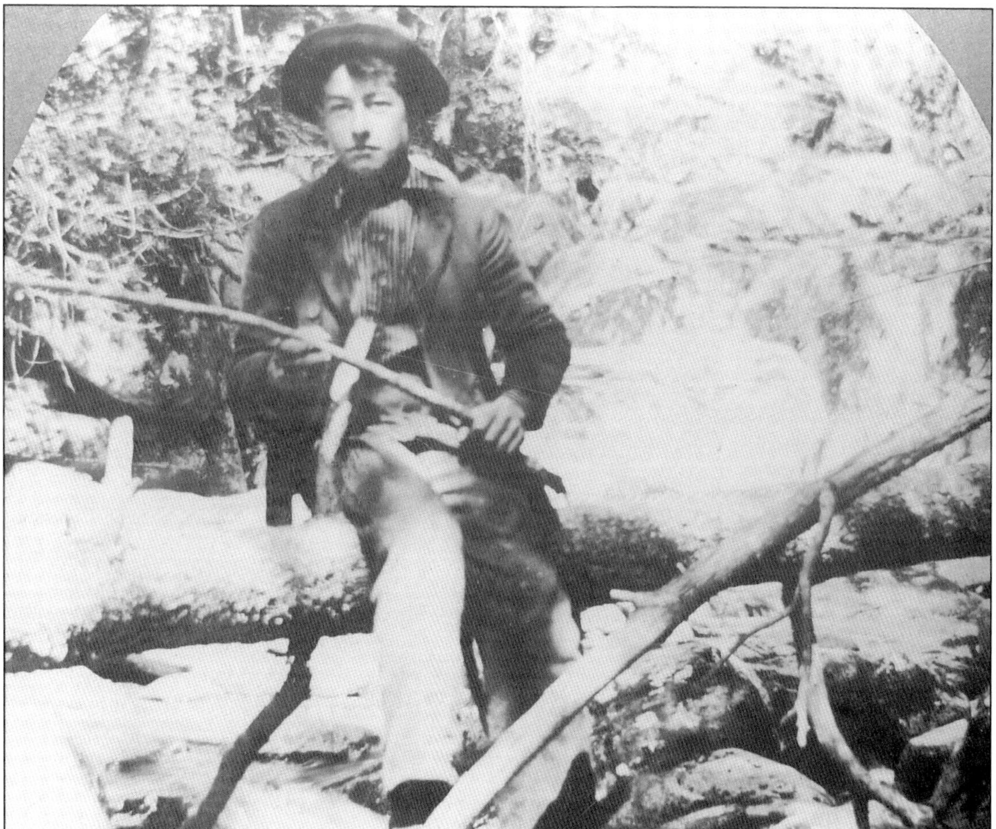

The tourist potential was all around, as this lad fishing on Reed Brook shows in the 1890s.

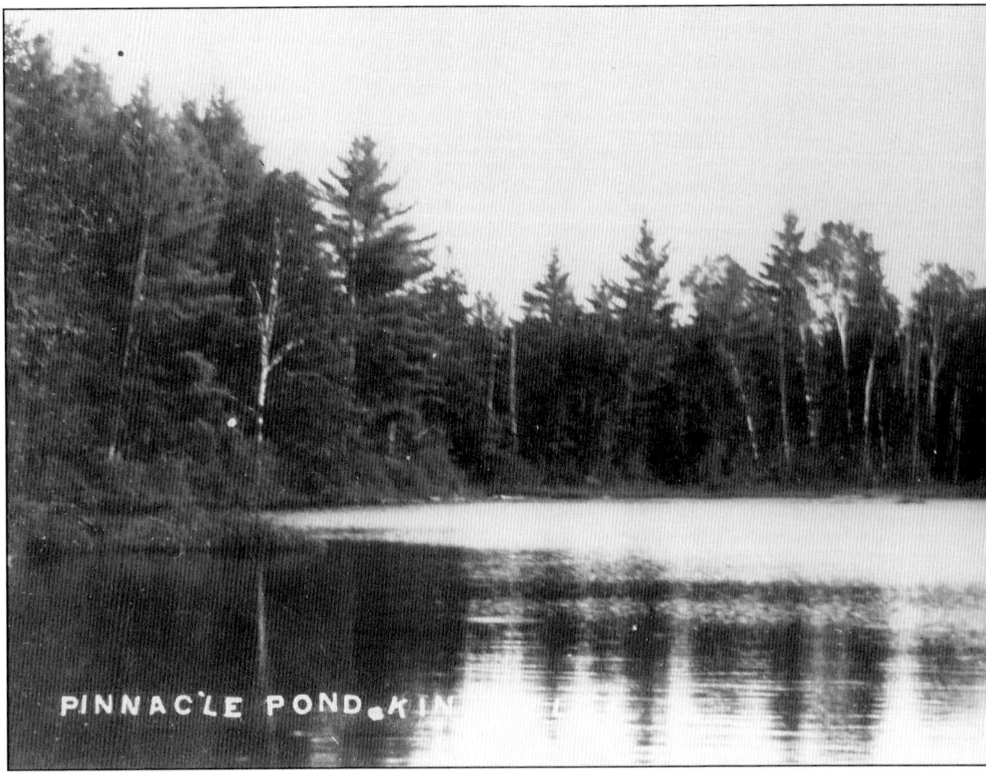

Beautiful Pinnacle Pond in Kingfield in the 1890s.

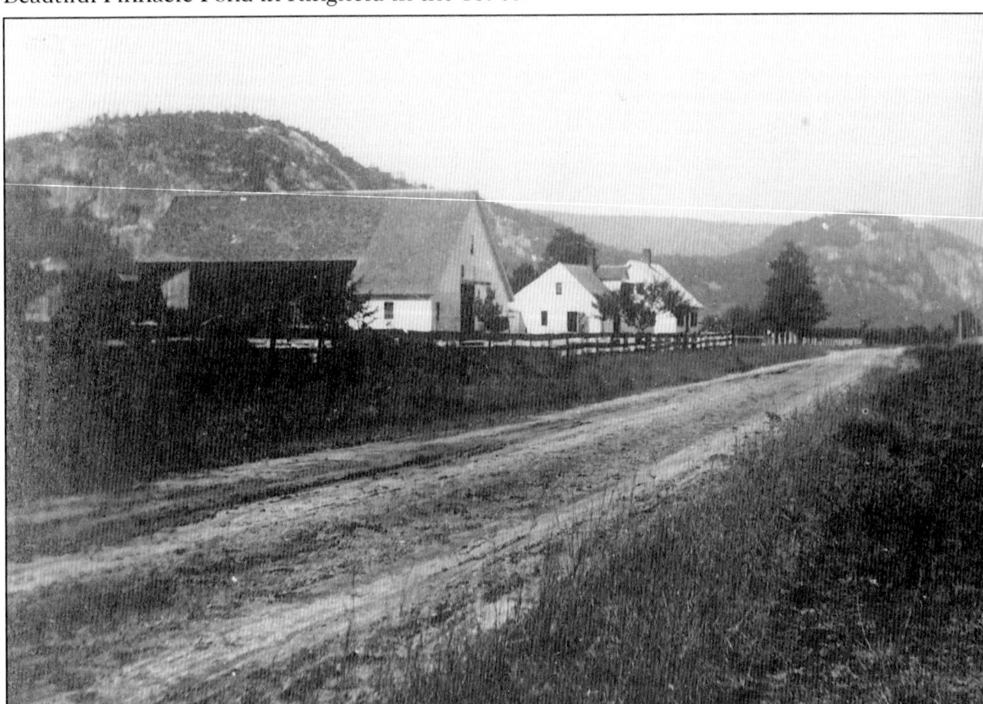
A Kingfield farm scene in the 1890s.

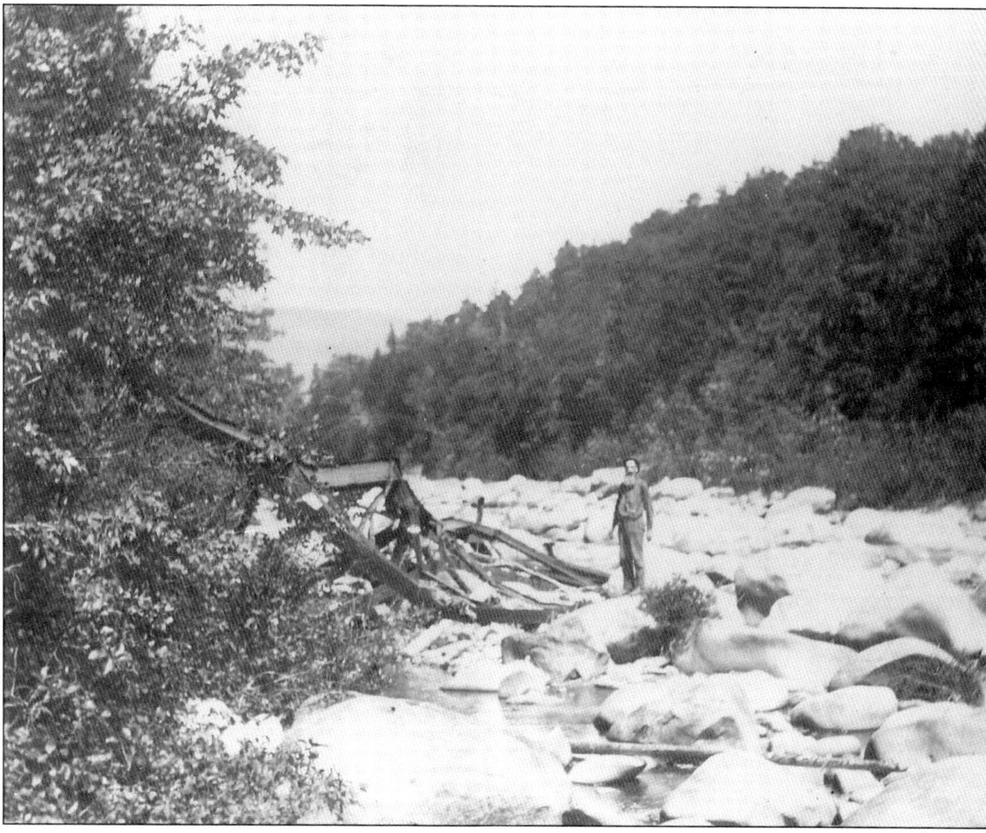

Ruins of the "iron bridge" in Kingfield in the 1890s. Carrabassett River freshets were constantly despoiling bridges in the area about that time. This may have been what was usually called the chain bridge.

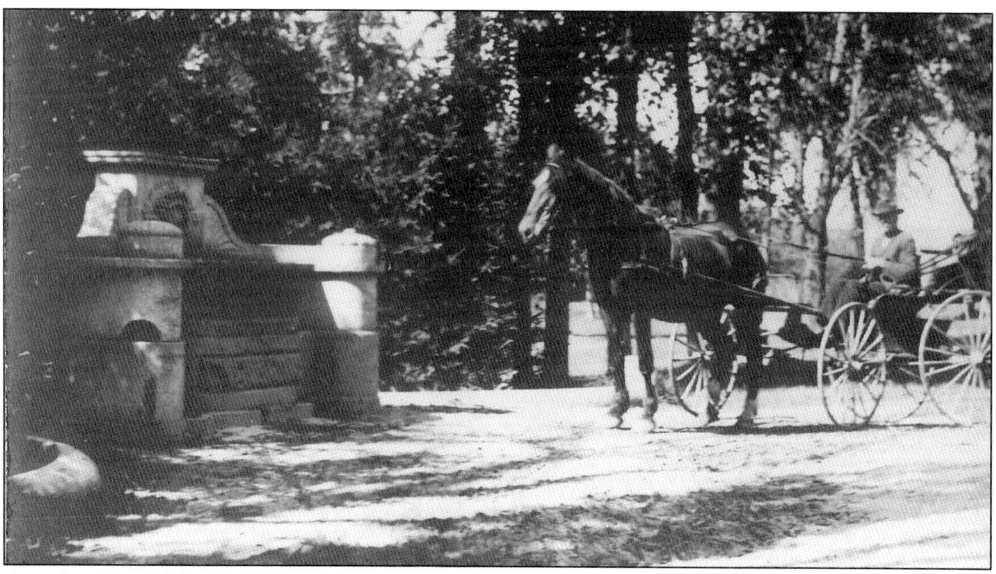

Another peaceful Kingfield scene in the 1890s, with watering trough, horse-drawn buggy, and its driver.

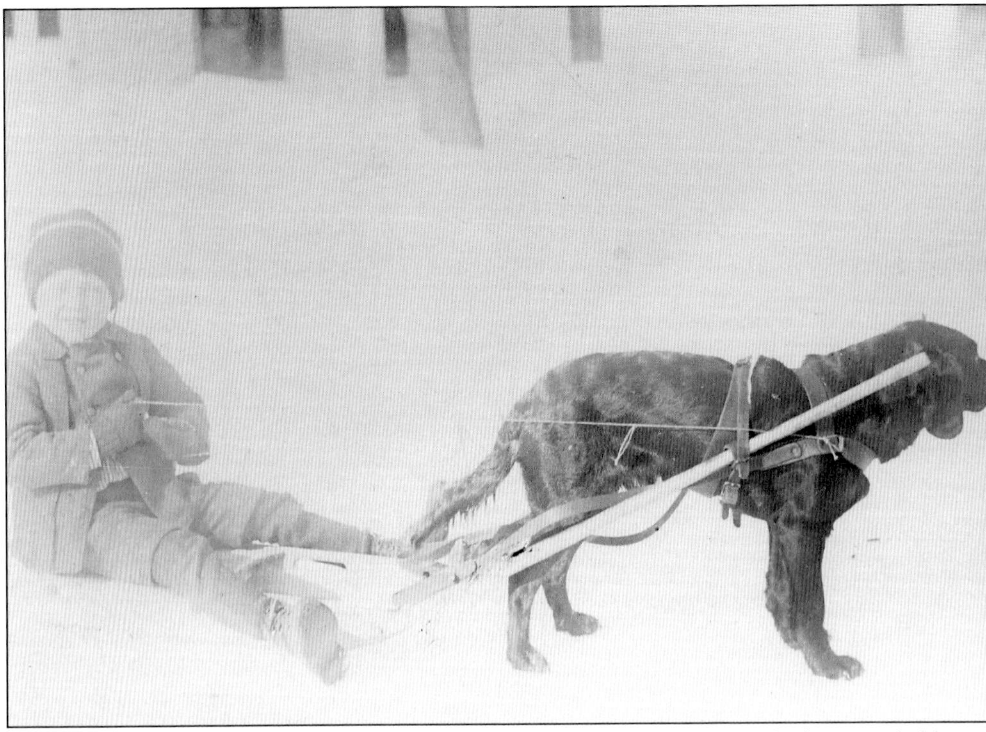

The boy on the sled and his dog illustrate another tourist potential the Kingfield area had—snow.

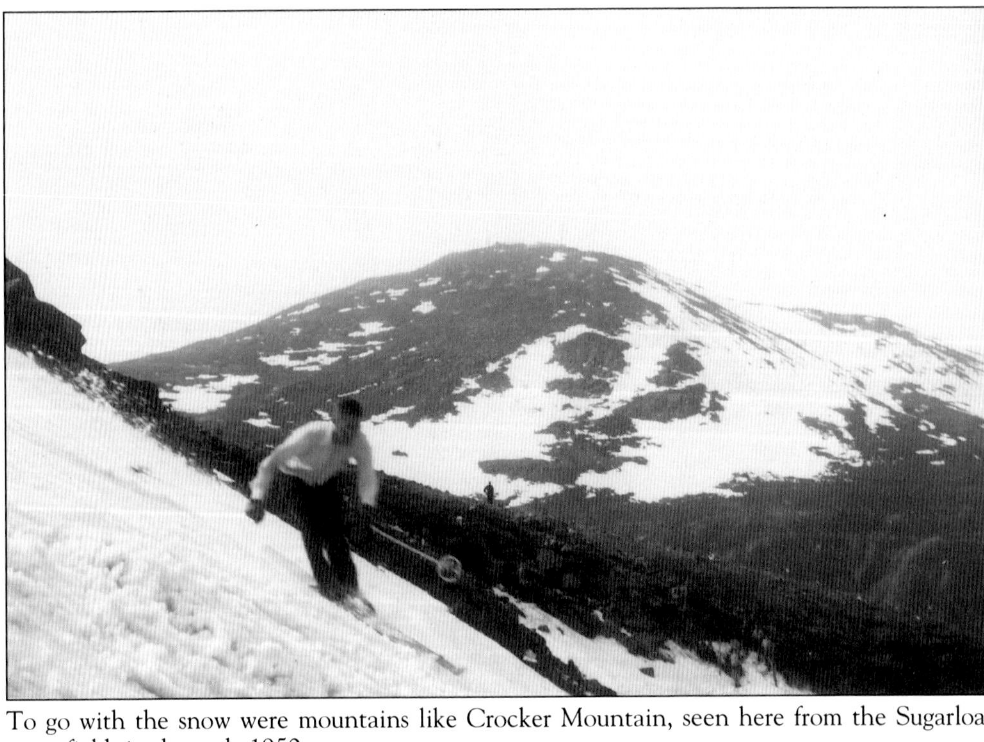

To go with the snow were mountains like Crocker Mountain, seen here from the Sugarloaf snow fields in the early 1950s.

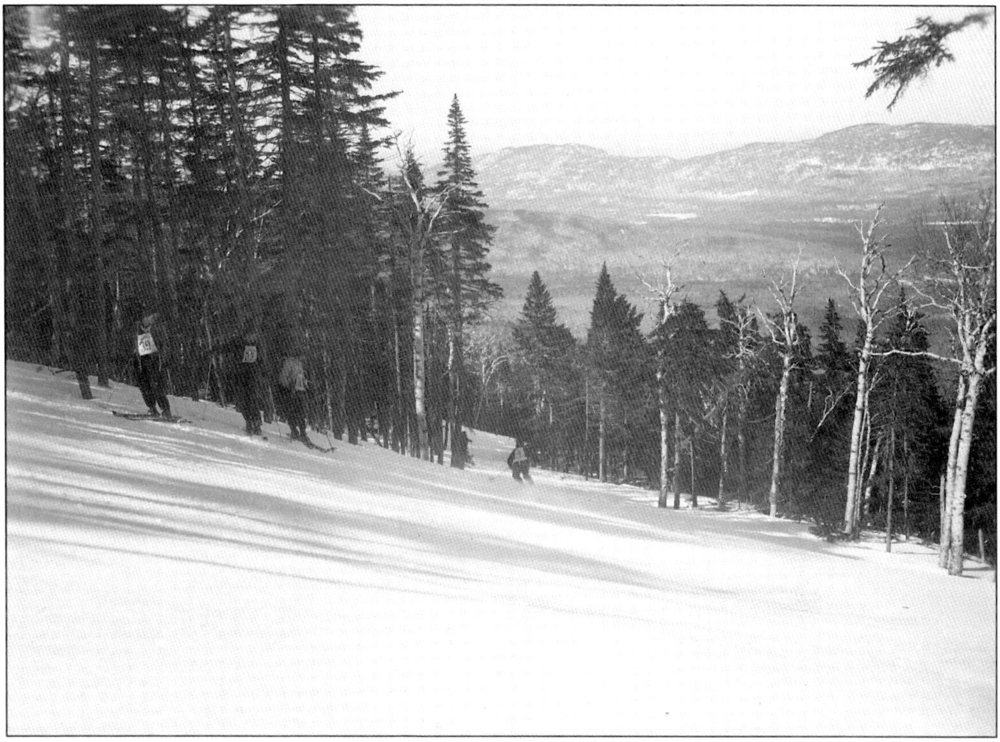

And there was Bigelow Mountain, seen here from one of the Sugarloaf ski trails, probably Winter's Way. As told in Glenn Parkinson's *First Tracks*, Kingfielders preferred to ski Bigelow, where the CCC in the 1930s had cut a trail and built a lodge.

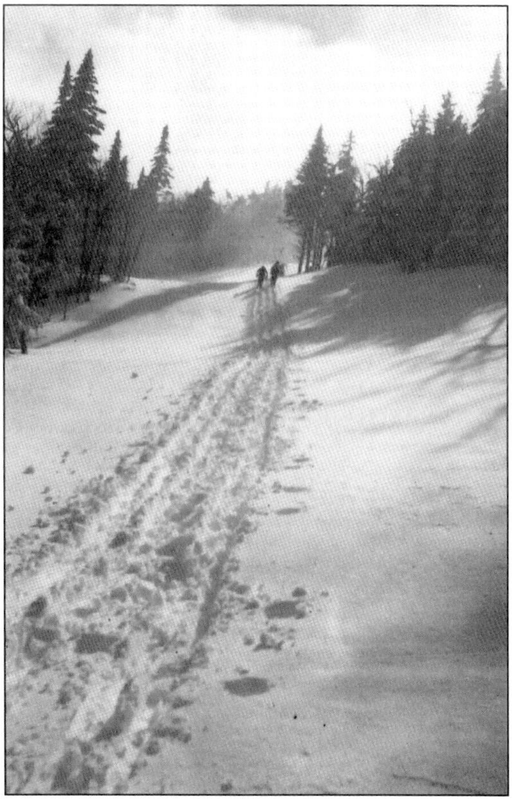

There was also Sugarloaf. As Parkinson tells it, the way to the Bigelow lodge was cut off when Flagstaff Lake was formed by a Central Maine Power Company dam. The Kingfielders, headed by Amos Winter, moved to Sugarloaf for their skiing. There was, indeed, less wind on that mountain than at Bigelow, but there was no trail, as this picture of Sugarloaf in 1950 shows.

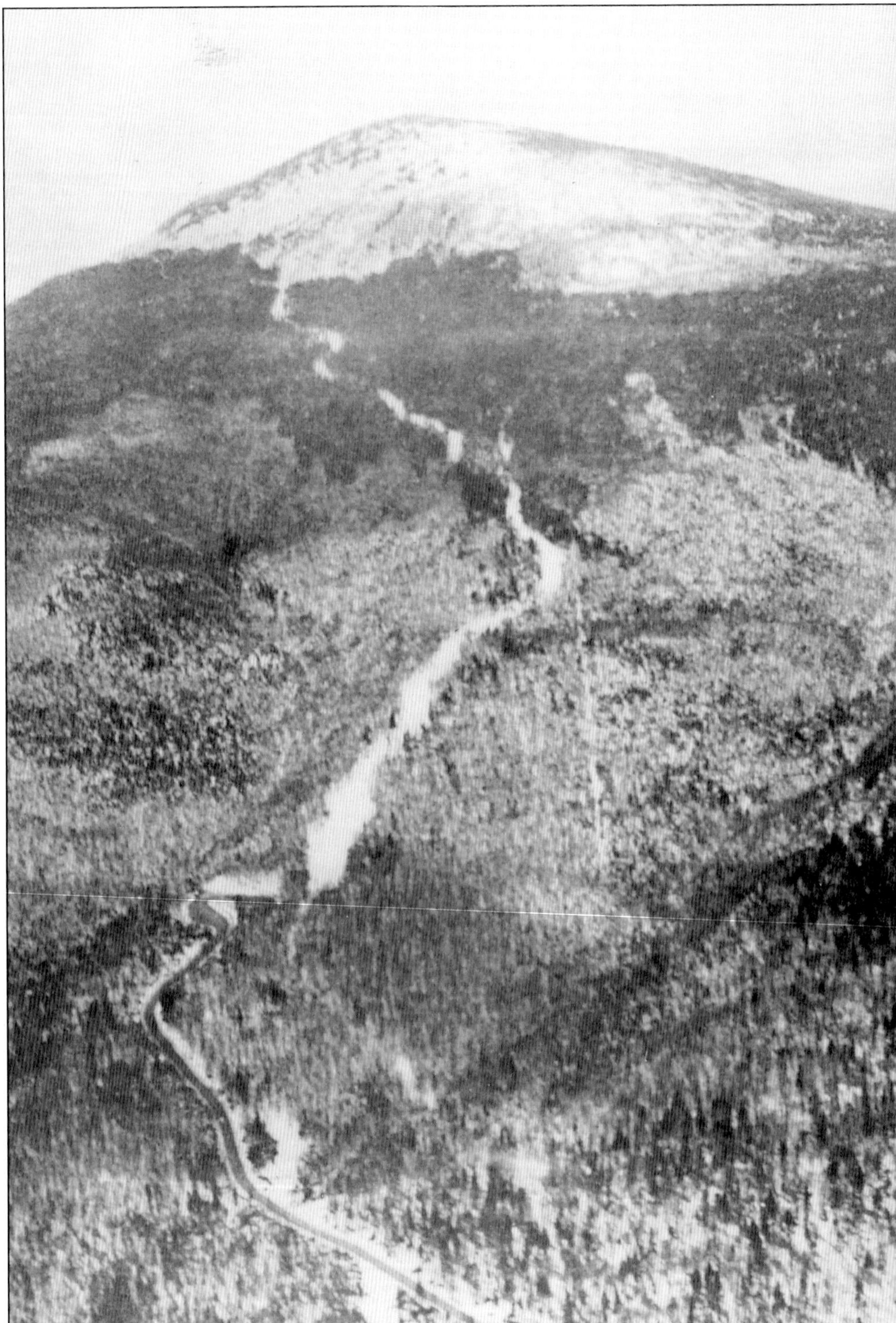

Sugarloaf looms in the winter of 1951, after the first trail, Winter's Way, was cut. The mountain was off and running.

Six

The Winters: Business and Recreation Savvy

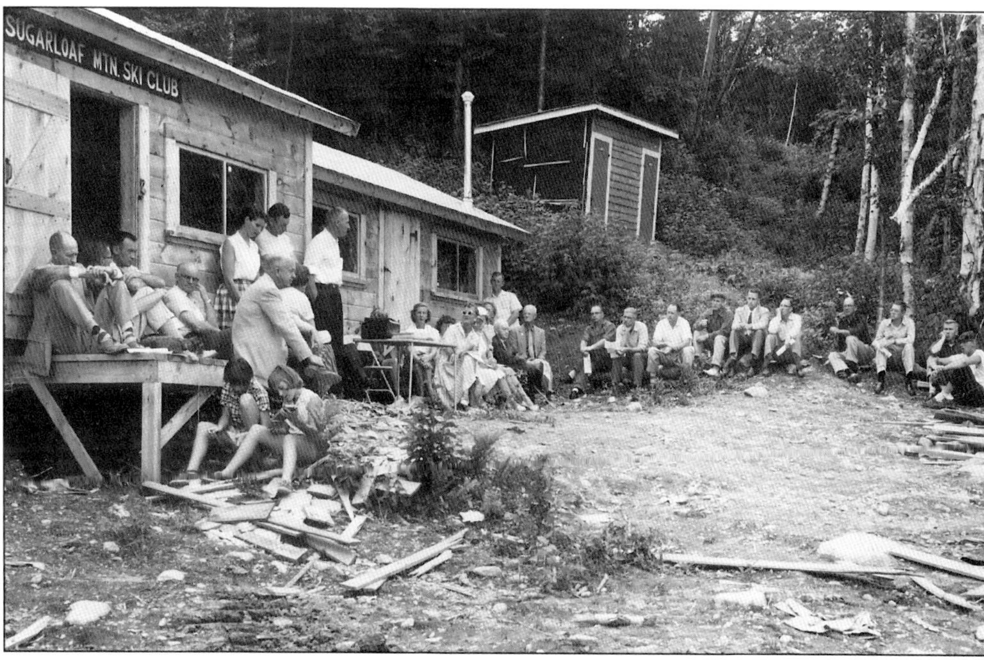

Amos Winter was on his way to becoming a legend. At the dedication of the Sugarloaf Mountain Ski Club's hut in the 1950s (also the first meeting of the newly formed Sugarloaf Mountain Corporation), Amos is fourth from left. Robert N. Bass, with G.H. Bass and Company, a leader in ski boot sales at the time, is seventh from left and third in the standing group. Scott Scully, another leader in the move to Sugarloaf, is fourth from right. Mrs. H. Norton Webber and Mrs. Phoebe Stowell are also in the photo.

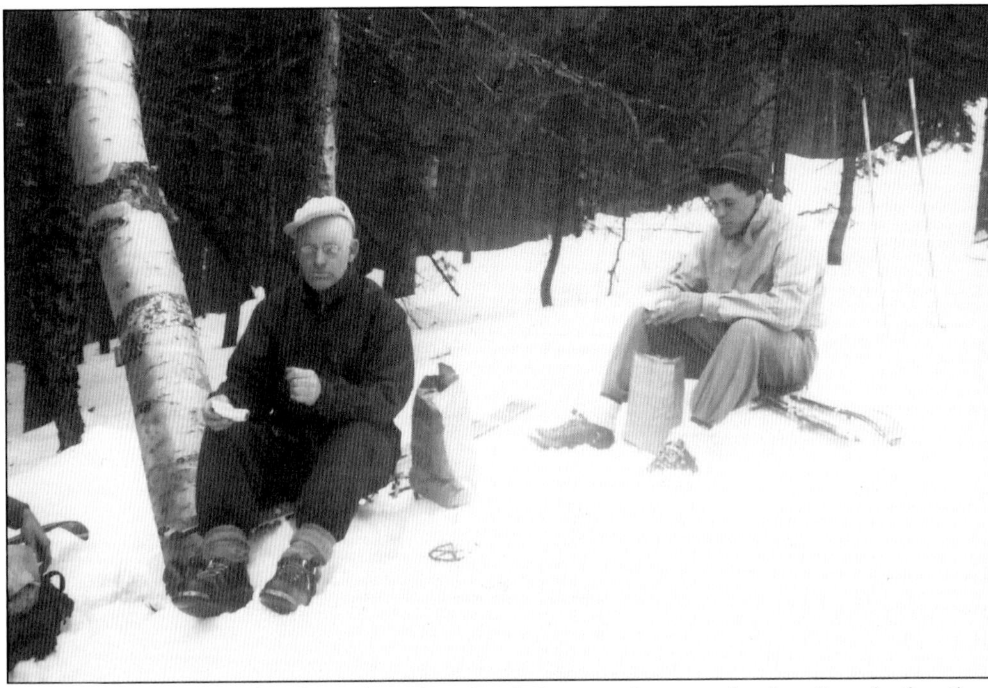

Amos Winter (left) and Stub Taylor take a break from working on the first Sugarloaf trail on April 7, 1951. Amos had promoted Sugarloaf to Robert N. Bass, first president of the Maine Ski Council. The council had been looking for a potentially large ski area to promote skiing in the state. Mt. Blue, the Mahoosics, Grafton Notch, and Old Speck Mountain had all been checked out. Amos pushed for Sugarloaf and won.

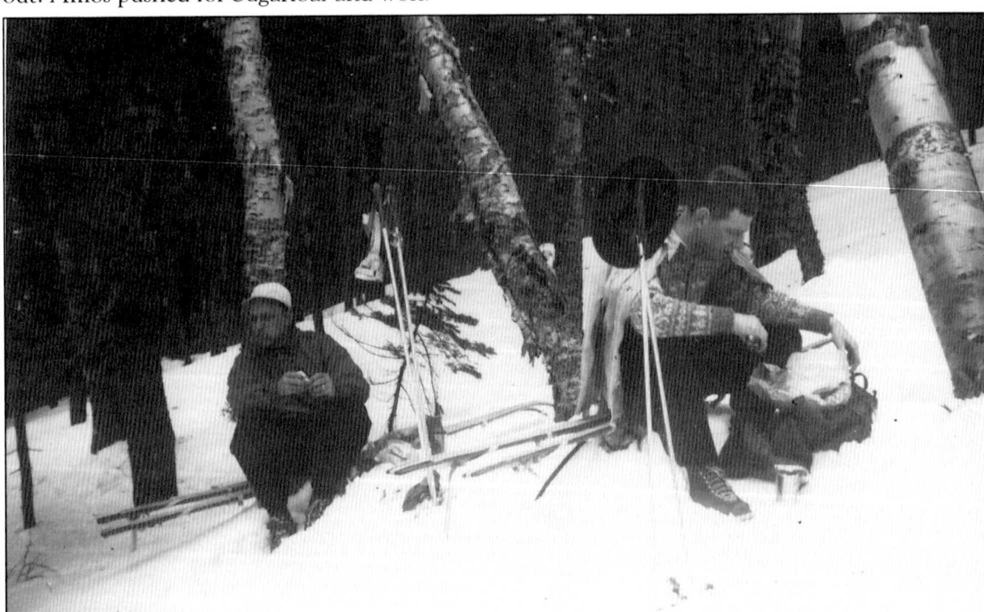

In a photograph also taken on April 7, 1951, and Sidney Thaxter (left) and Fletcher Brown take time off from their trail-breaking efforts to eat. People showed up all that summer and right into the fall of 1951 to help Amos cut the road in from Route 27 and clear out that first trail.

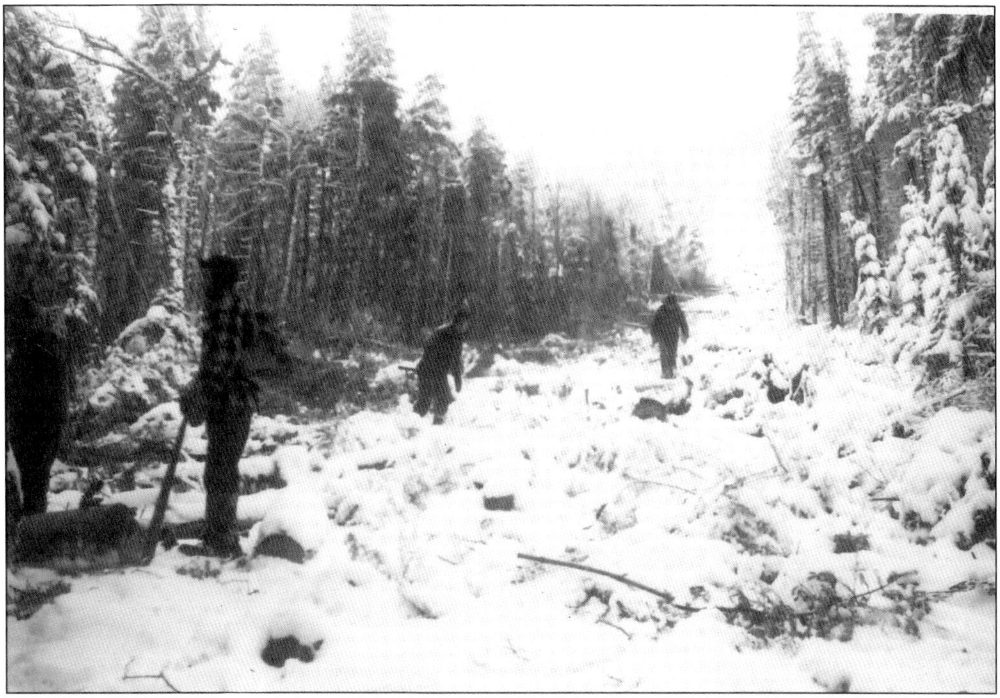

It was tough work that extended nearly to winter. Here it's November 18, 1951, and they're cutting the trail at the top of Winter's Way.

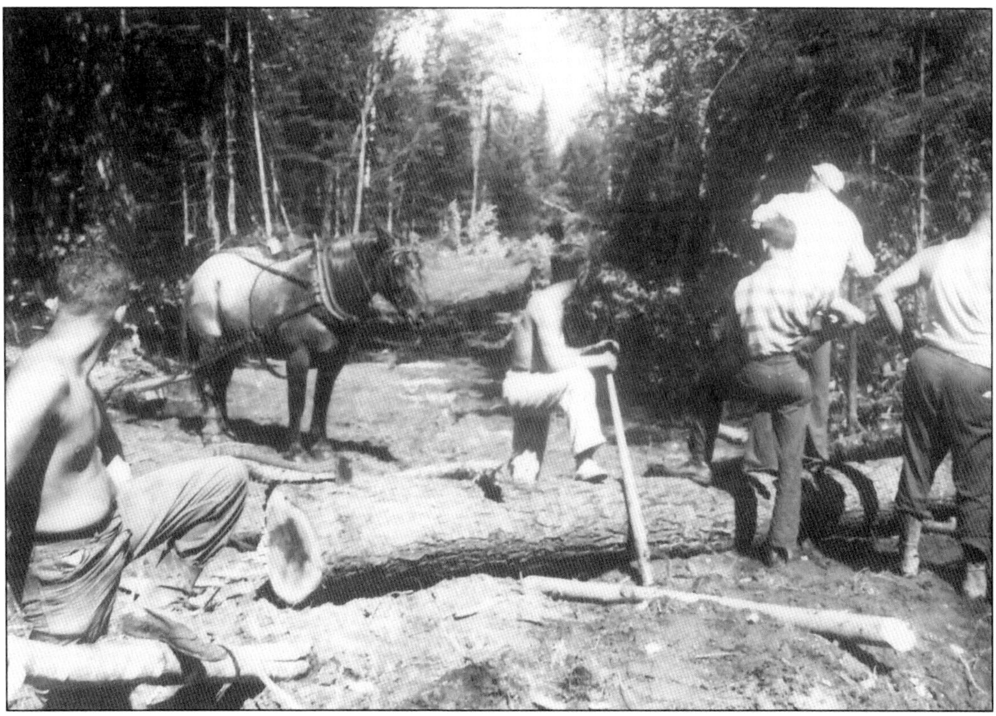

Look at the work! With shirts off in some cases, men work at constructing a bridge on the road from Route 27 to Sugarloaf.

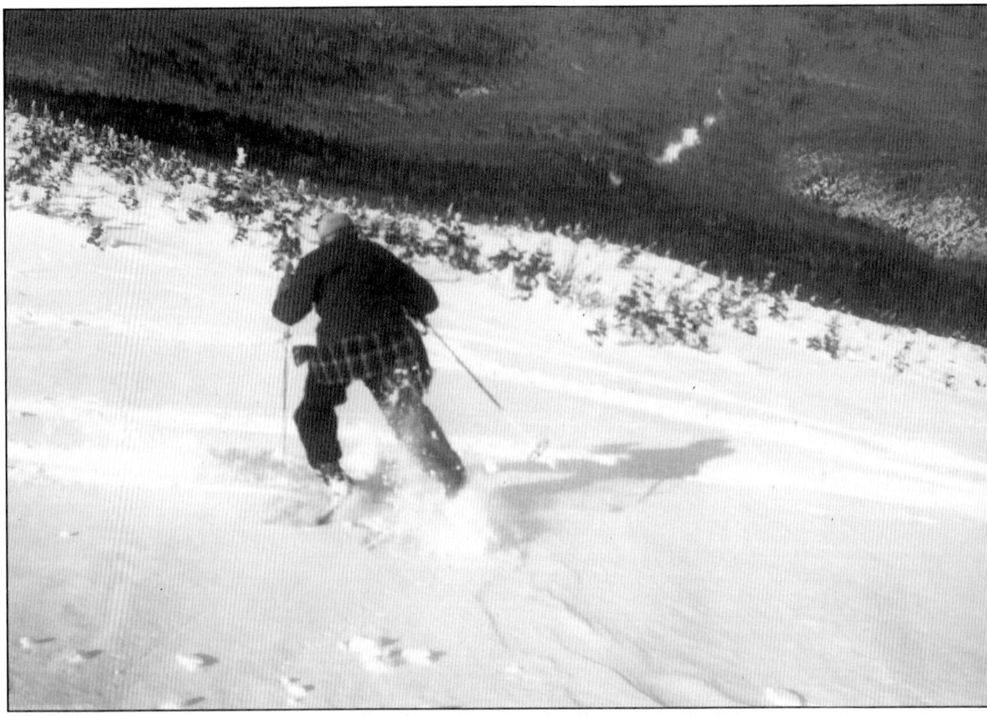

Amos Winter from the rear as he skied in the Sugarloaf snow fields. There were better skiers.

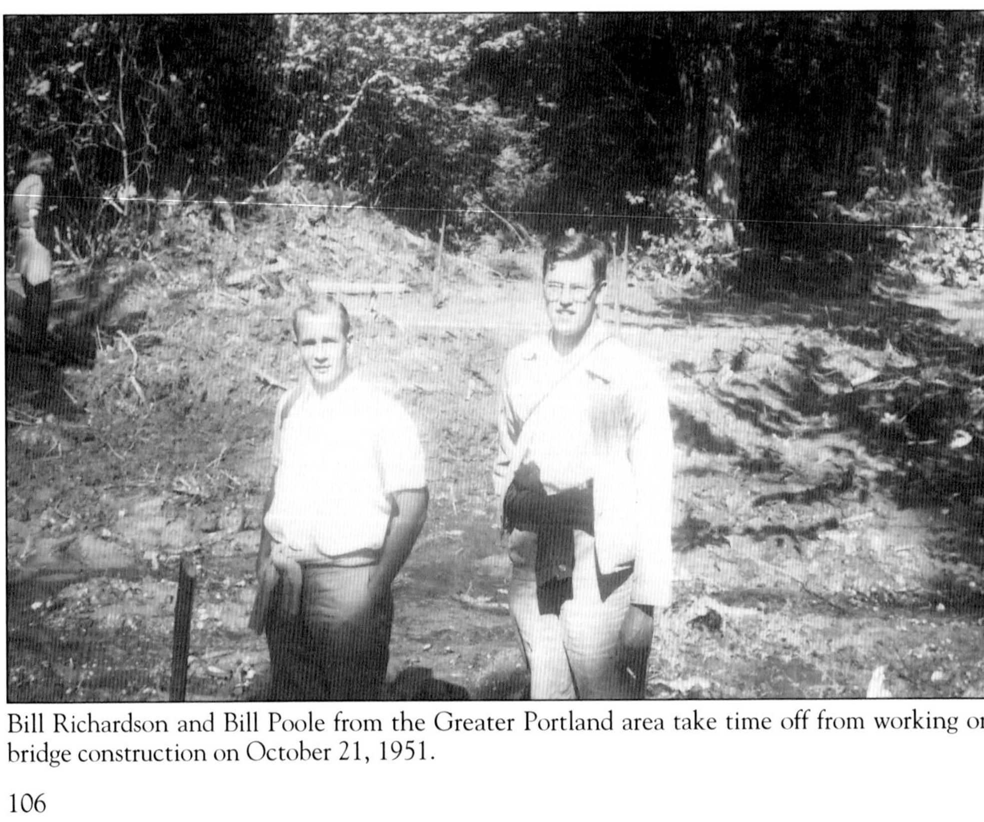

Bill Richardson and Bill Poole from the Greater Portland area take time off from working on bridge construction on October 21, 1951.

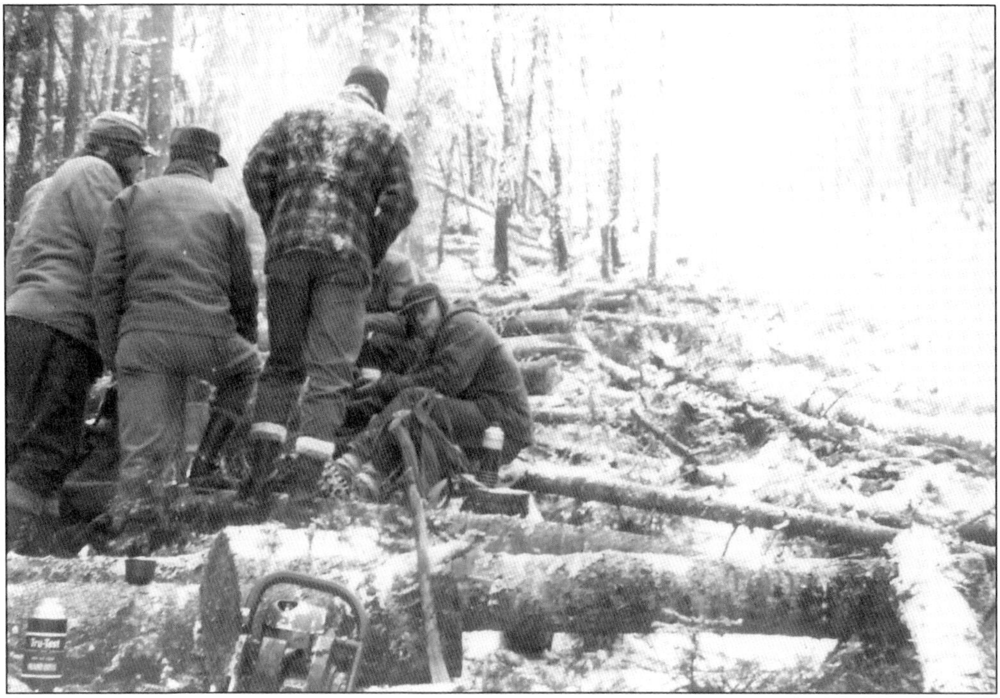

Among the men cutting Winter's Way at Chapman's Corner on November 18, 1951, were Horace Chapman of Bangor, and Amos Winter, Fred Morrison, Stub Taylor, Odlin Thompson, and Louie Hatch, all of Kingfield.

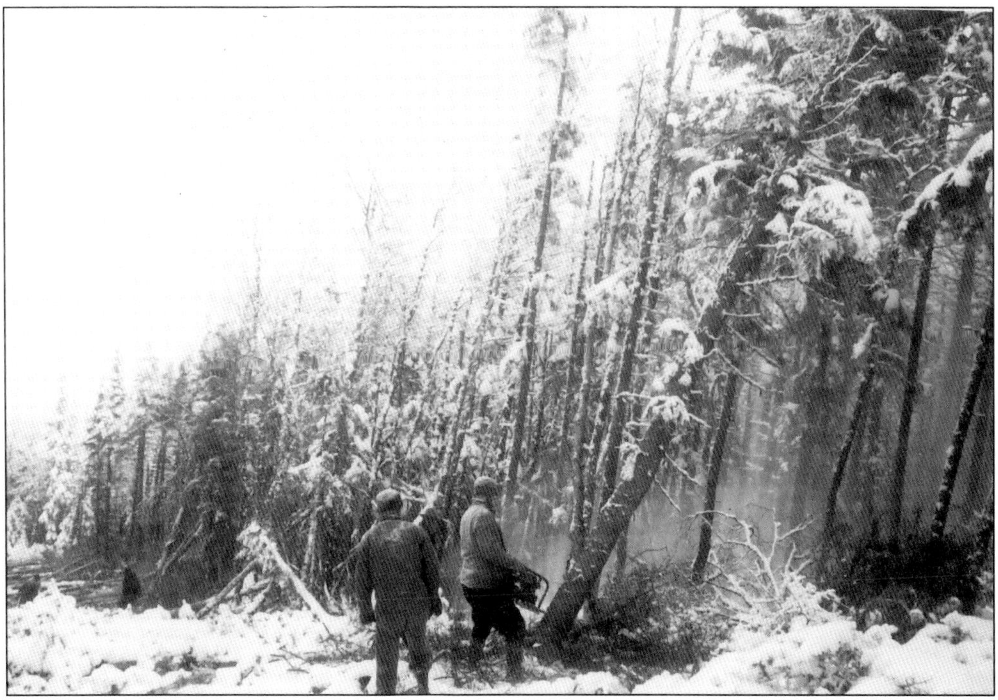

That's how you cut out a ski trail. It's Chapman's Corner again on November 18, 1951.

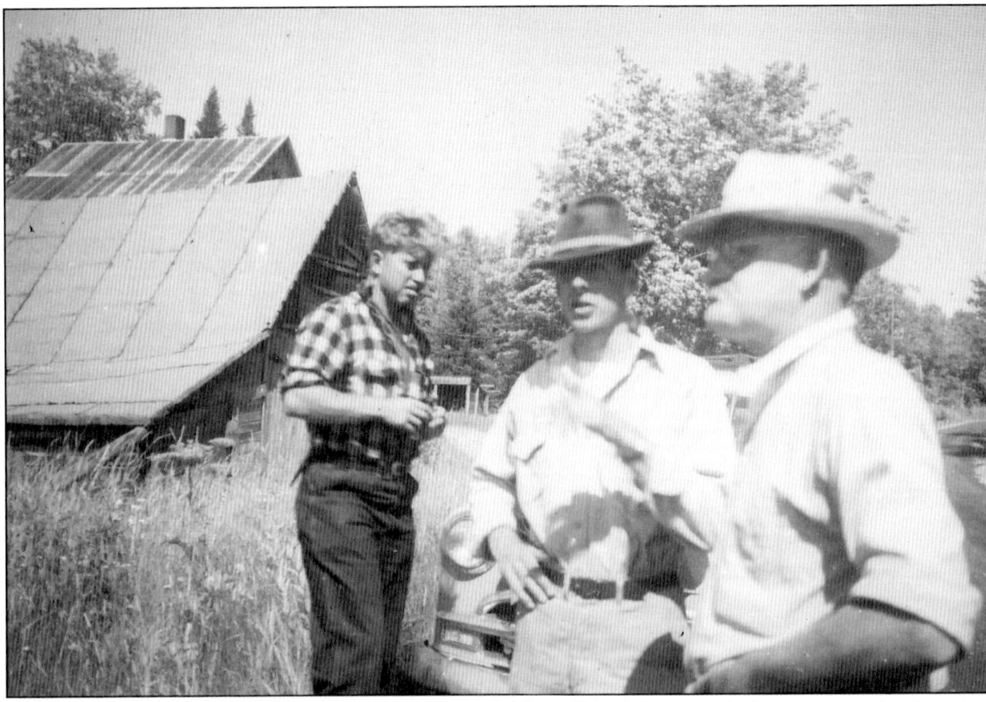

Sel Hannah (left) was called in from Franconia, New Hampshire, to help Amos with planning for the first trail. With him are Fletcher Brown and Amos. The result was Winter's Way, shown below after completion.

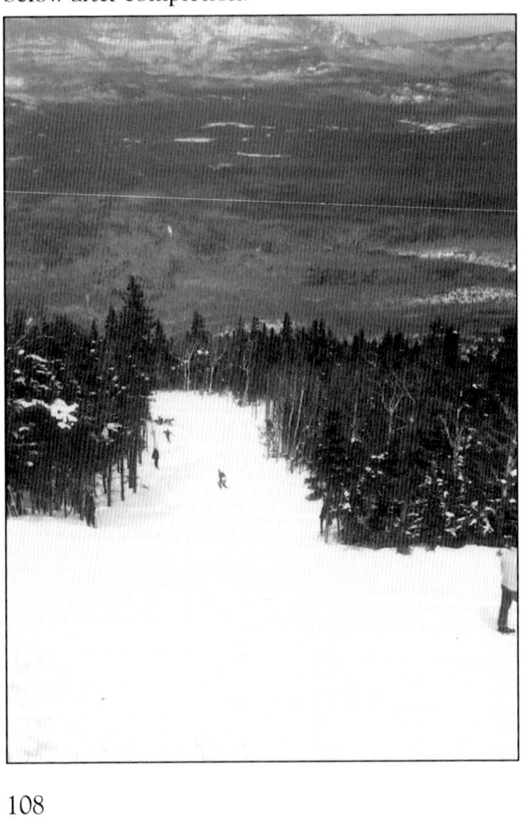

And here are people enjoying the result of the labors on January 13, 1952. This is Mickey Durrell of Kingfield.

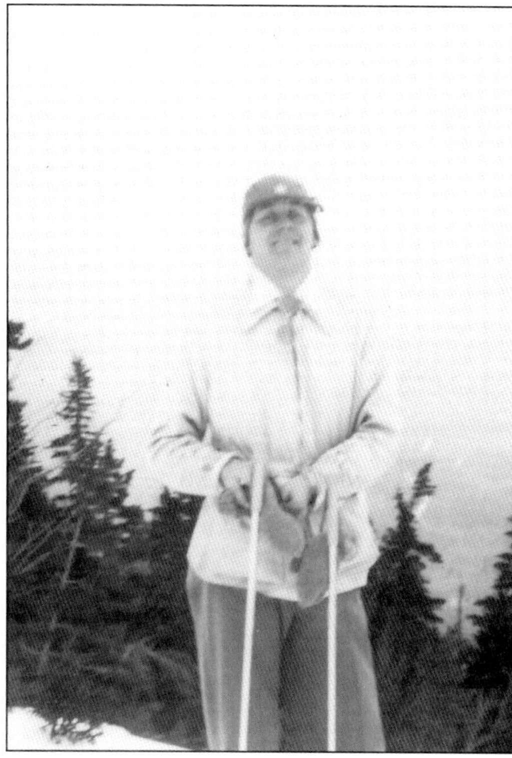

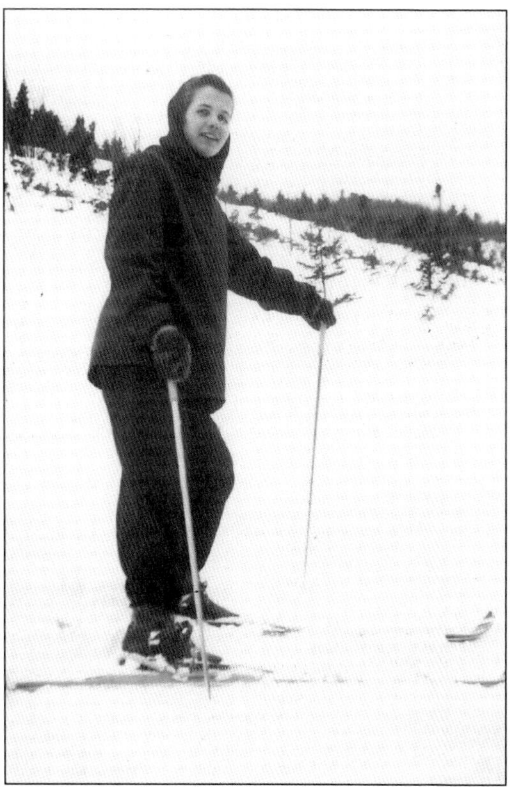

Mary Lou Sprague of Scarborough.

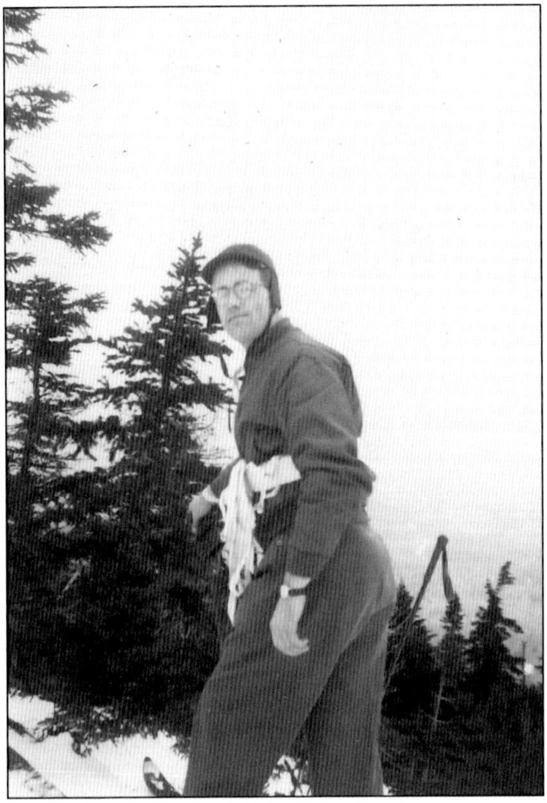

Phineas Sprague, the husband of Mary Lou Sprague.

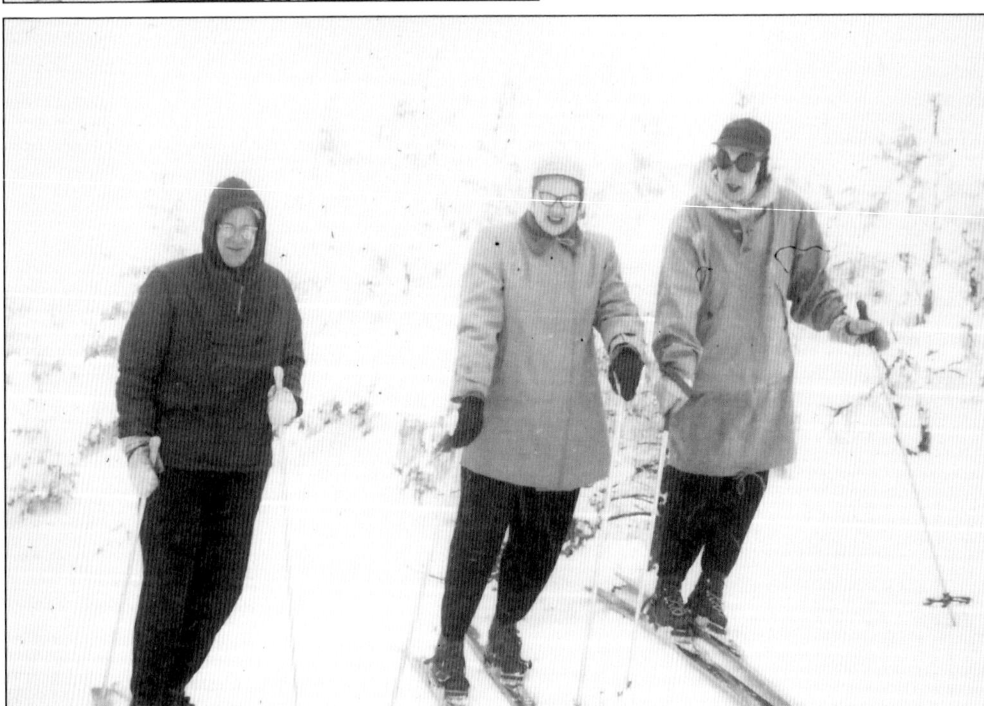

Barry Vroman, Alice Mary Pierce, and Merrill Payson Robbins on skiis.

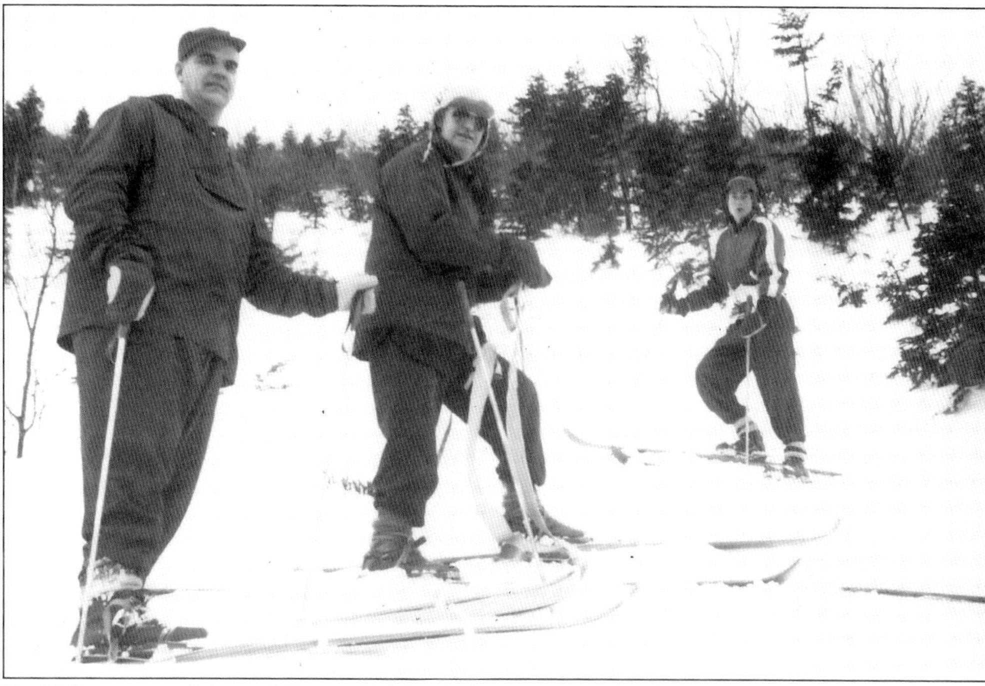

Fred Morrison and Amos Winter with an unknown person.

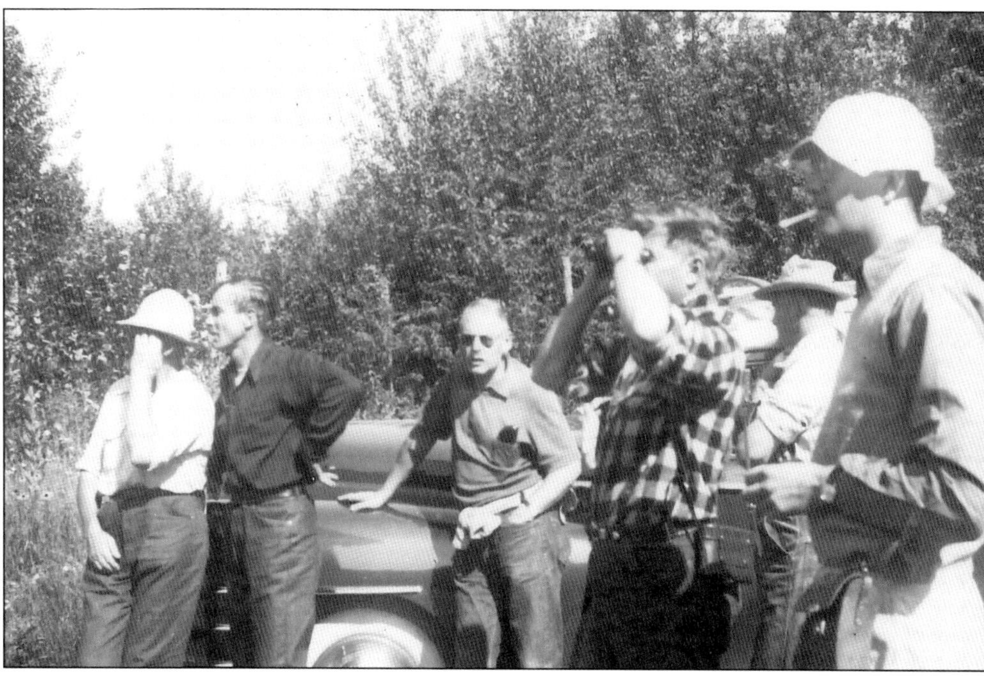

Looking over their handiwork in 1952 are, from left to right, an unidentified person, Wes Marco, Horace Chapman, Sel Hannah, Amos Winter, and Phineas Sprague.

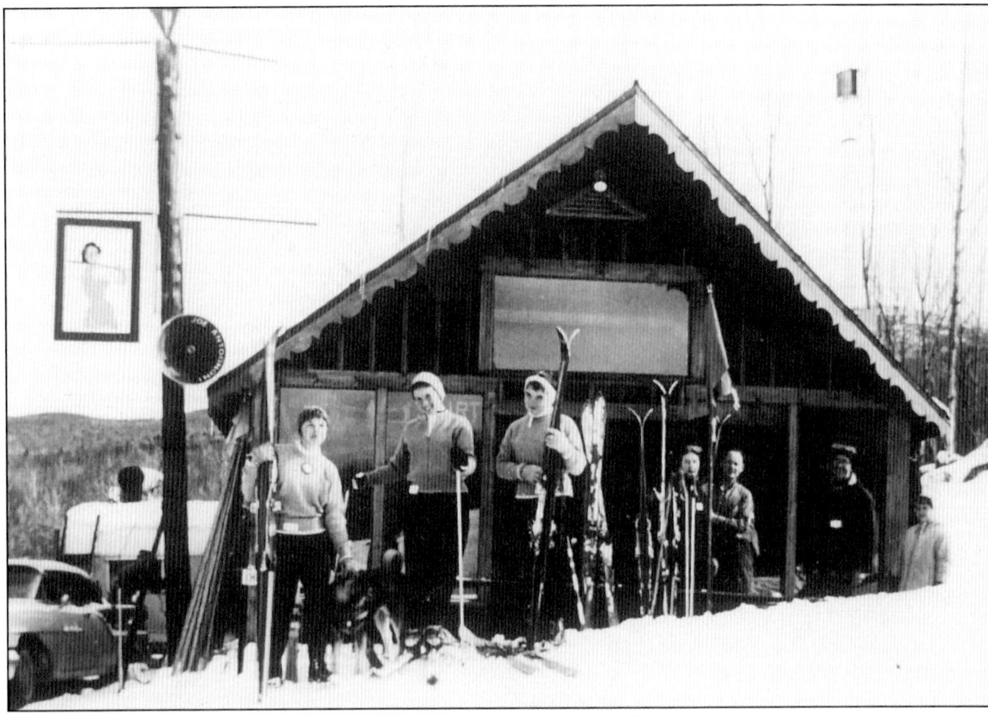

Sugarloaf Ski Area grew and grew. Harvey Boynton's was the second shop on the mountain. The ski shop opened about 1956.

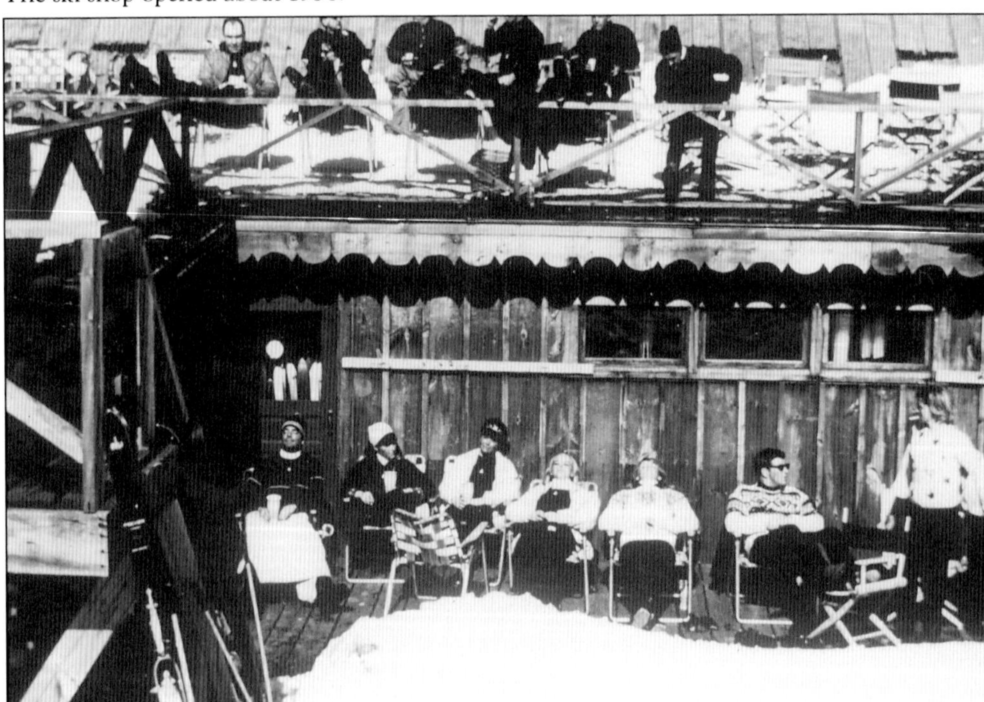

The Beach on top and in front of Harvey Boynton's Ski Shop was where people either cooled off or took the sun.

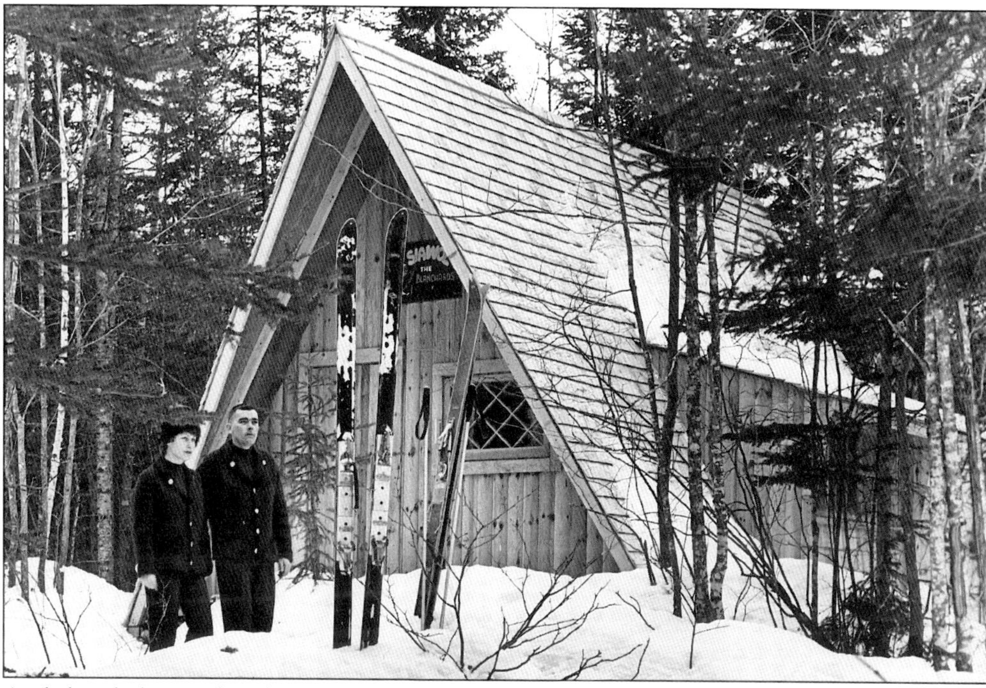

And the chalets and A-frames grew up around Sugarloaf. This is Thatcher "Doc" Blanchard and his wife, Joan, at their A-frame in Carrabassett Village in the late 1950s or early 1960s.

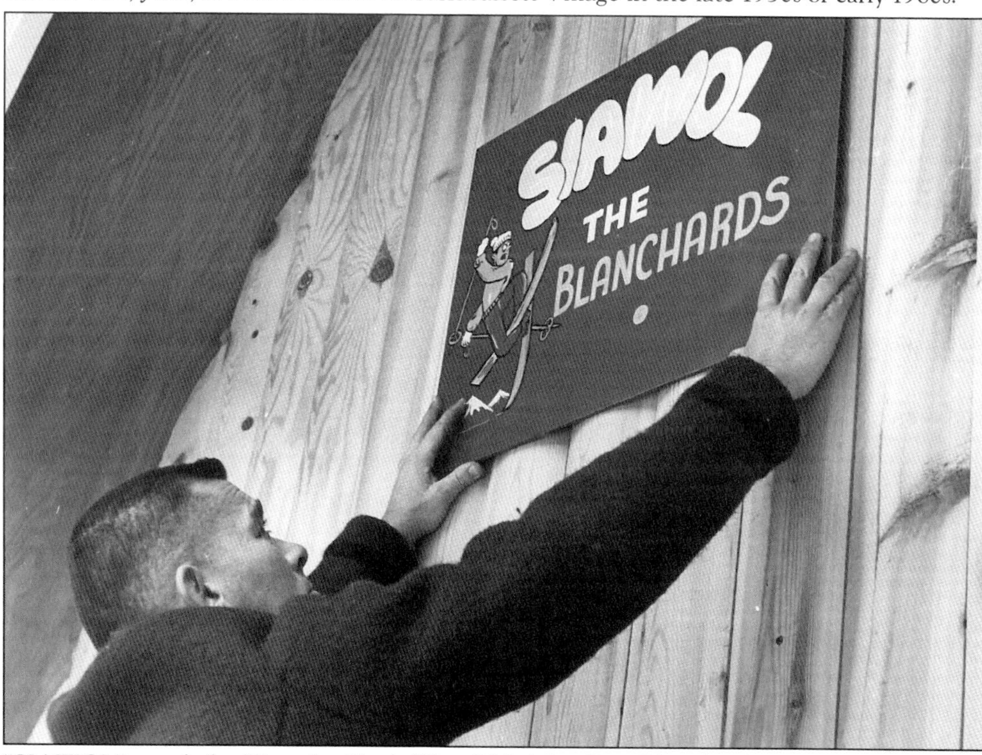

"SIAWOL" stands for "Sugarloaf Is A Way Of Life" as Doc Blanchard puts the sign up in his A-frame.

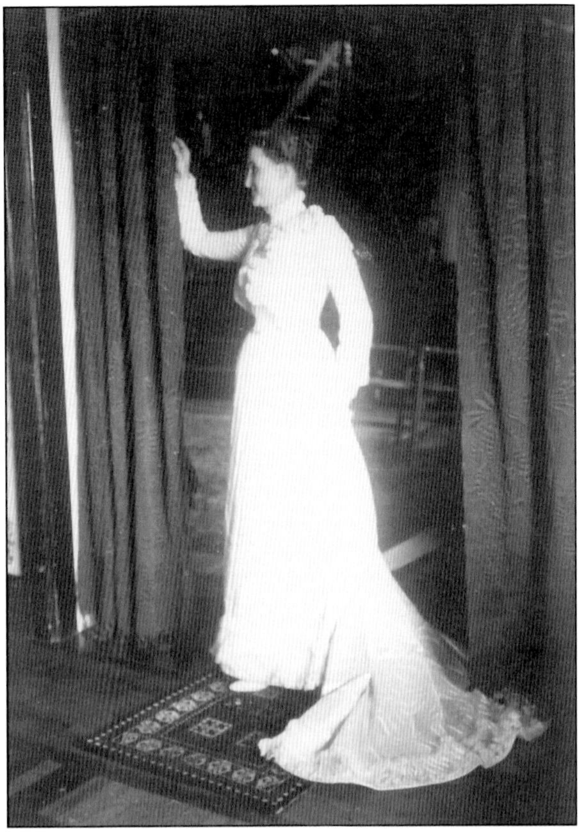

Julia Roesch Winter, second wife of Amos G. Winter and the mother of Amos G. Winter Jr. of Kingfield and Sugarloaf. Parkinson, in his book, says Amos Winter ran Sugarloaf Ski Area as general manager from 1955 to 1966 with "Yankee thriftiness." He may have inherited that from his businessman father and other generations of Winter family who had been in business. But his German mother, who his father met in New York, may have given Amos his love of adventure.

Amos Winter grew up in quite luxurious surroundings. Born in 1901, he grew up in Hillholm, the house his father had built in 1904. It is now the Inn at Winter's Hill, operated by the Winnicks.

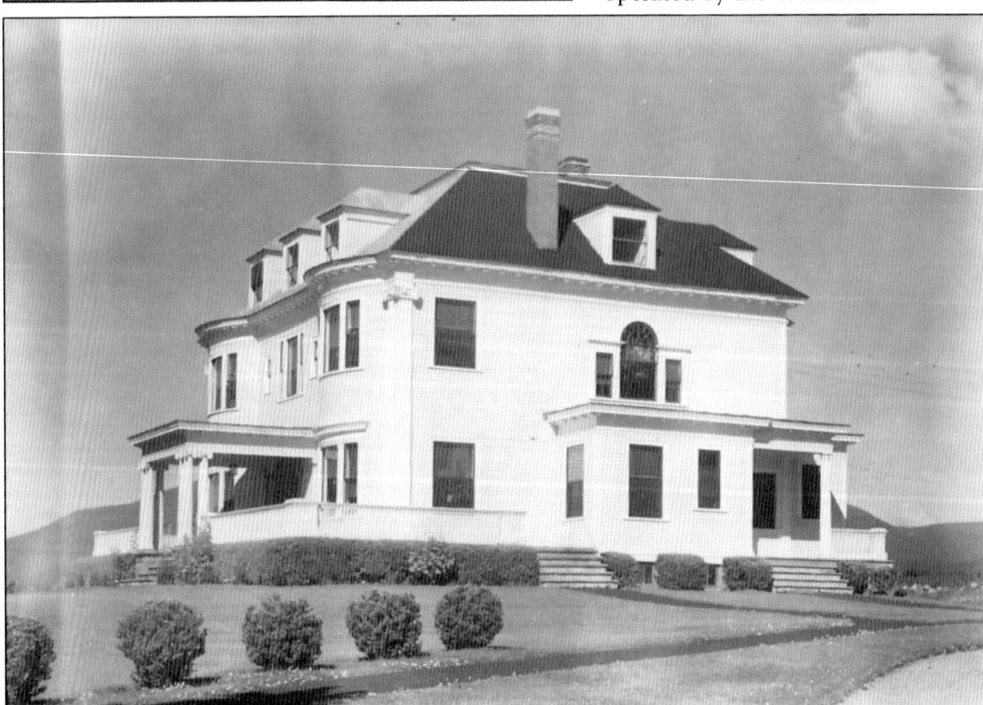

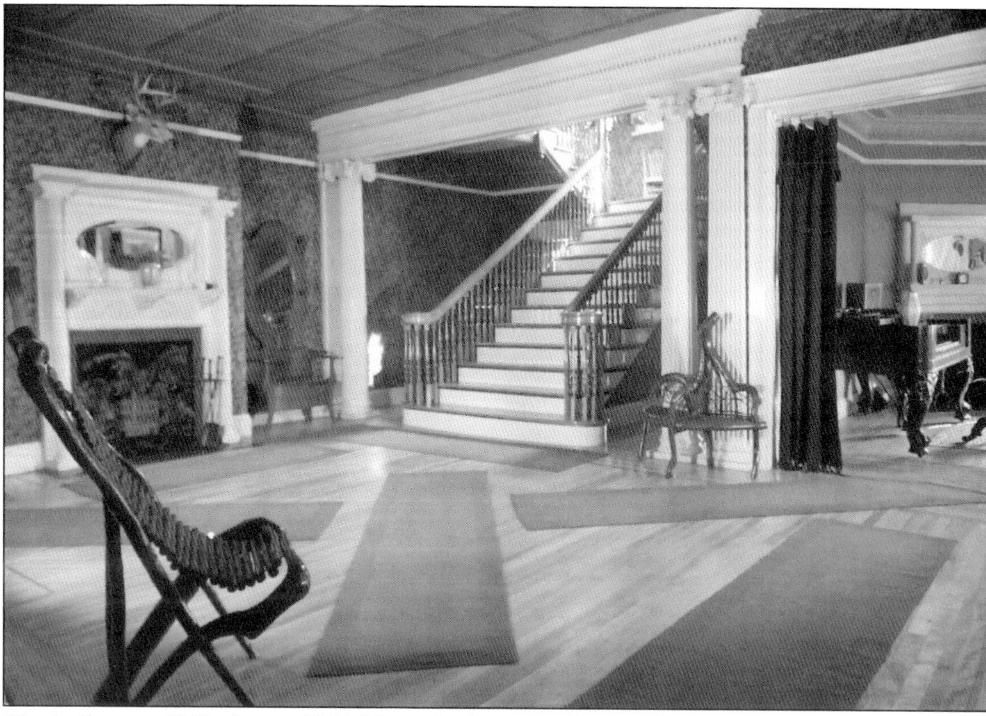

The hallway at Hillholm, *c.* 1906. Note the large fireplace and the beautiful staircase.

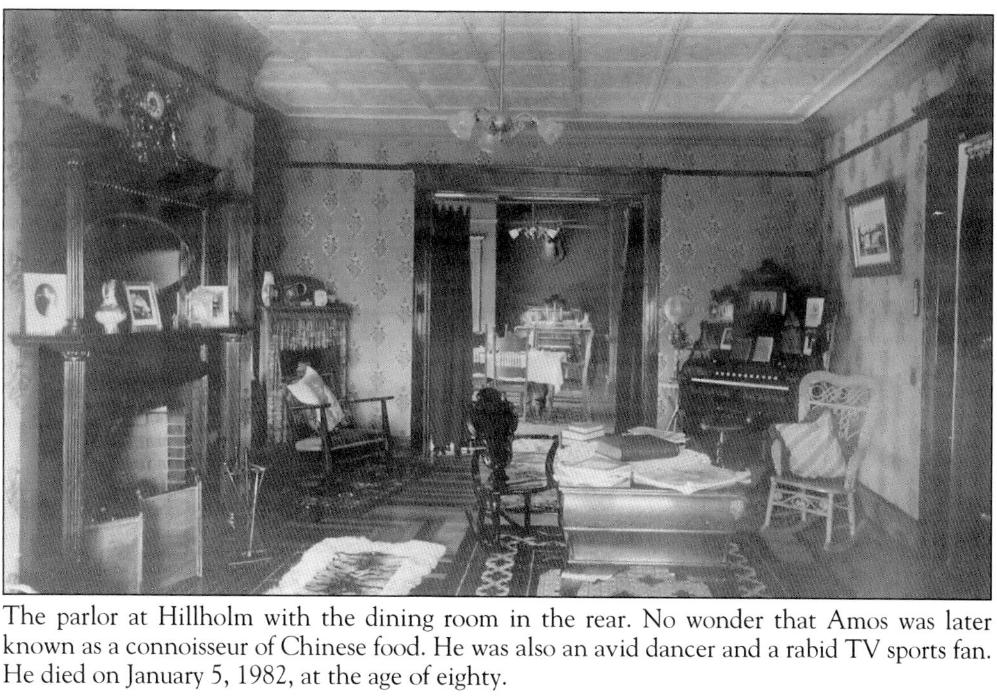

The parlor at Hillholm with the dining room in the rear. No wonder that Amos was later known as a connoisseur of Chinese food. He was also an avid dancer and a rabid TV sports fan. He died on January 5, 1982, at the age of eighty.

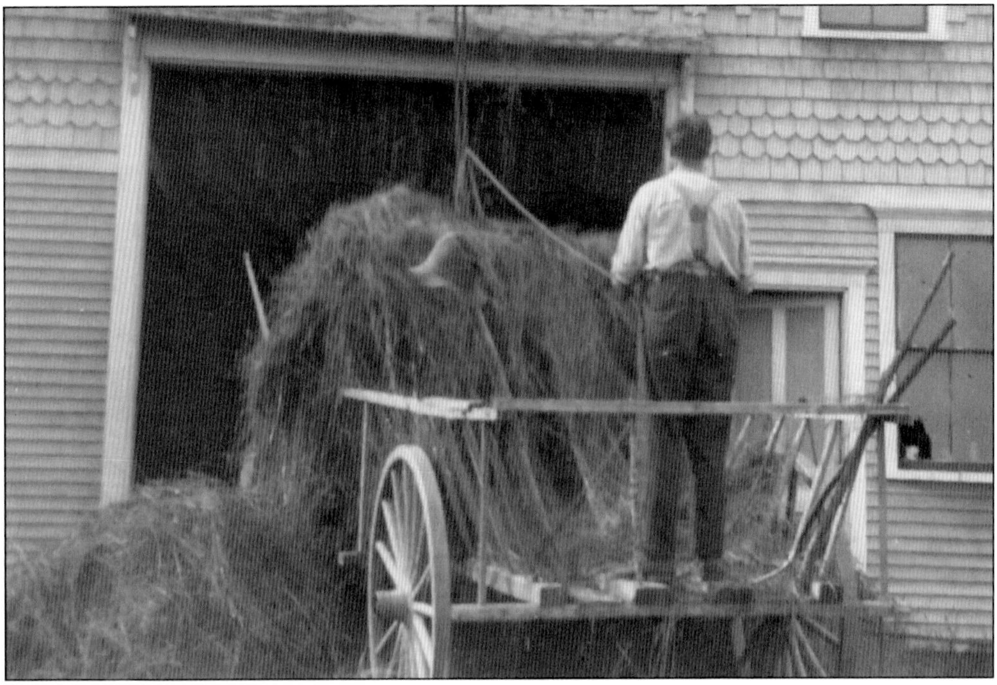

There was another side to Hillholm—work. Here, one of the Winter boys unloads hay into the second story of the big barn by the house. It's about 1920.

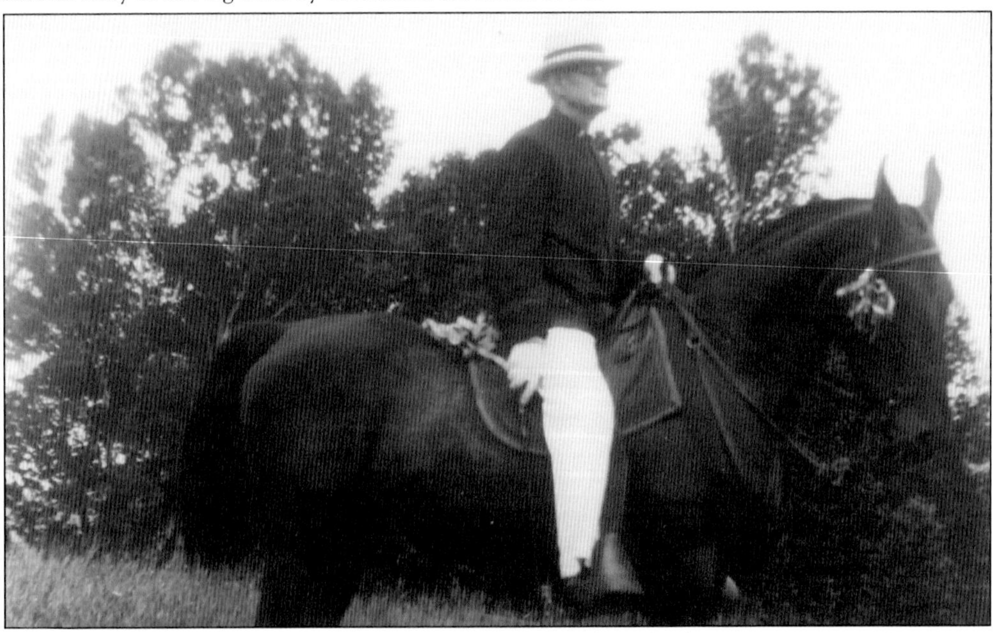

Amos G. Winter Sr., father of the Sugarloaf legend, on horseback, *c.* 1920s. Amos Sr. was no slouch. Returning to Kingfield after graduating from Dirigo Business College, Augusta, in 1883, he received the next year the first trainload of freight that came over the newly arrived narrow-gauge railroad at his store (the rail line ran right to it). The store was then called Station Store and was on Depot Street. Later, the store was known under Winter's name. Note how much he looked like his son.

Amos G. Winter Sr. with one of his sons, probably Wesley, c. late 1900s. Amos Sr. helped organize Kingfield Savings Bank and was its president from June 1895 to February 1914. He was one of the owners and organizers of the Kingfield Water Company and was, for several years, president of Jenkins Bogert Company, a large Kingfield wood products firm.

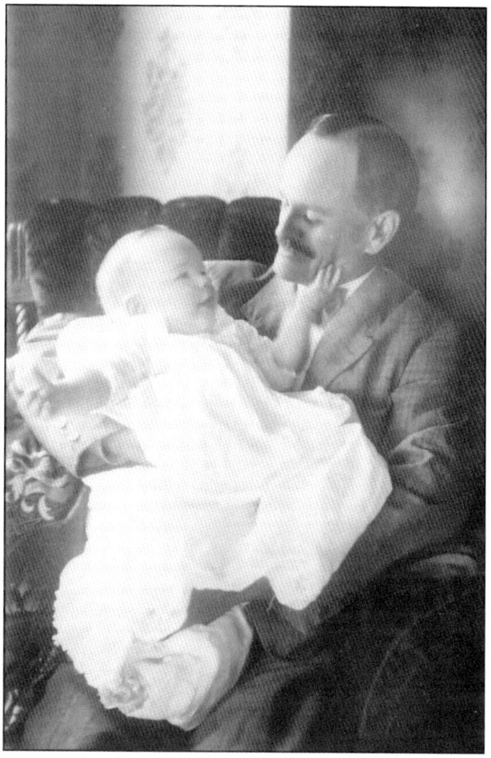

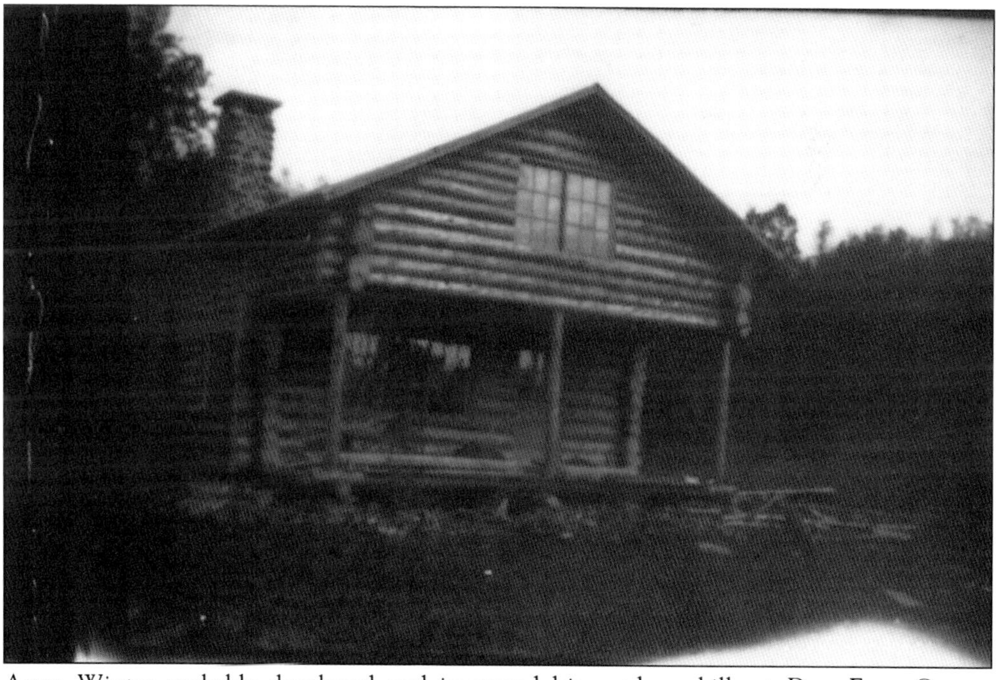

Amos Winter probably developed and improved his outdoor skills at Deer Farm Camps, Kingfield. This is one of the cabins there owned by the Winter family. Amos Winter's half-brother Earland, and Earland's wife, Hilda, owned and operated these camps from 1929 to 1973. Earland had previously been a game warden.

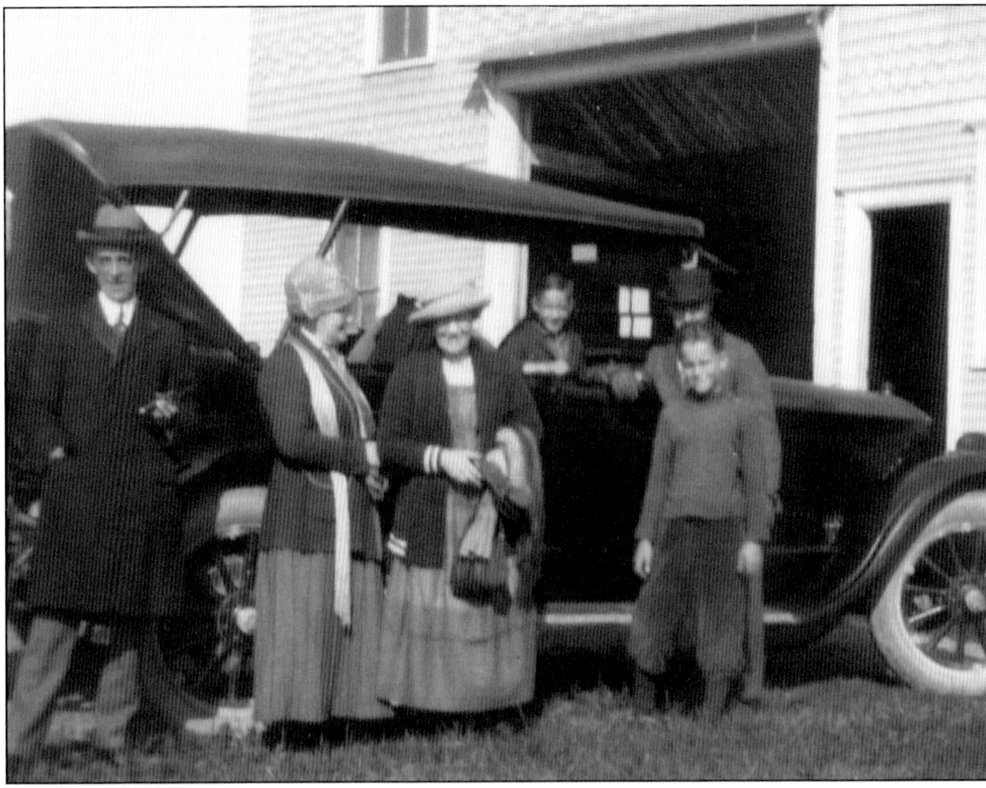

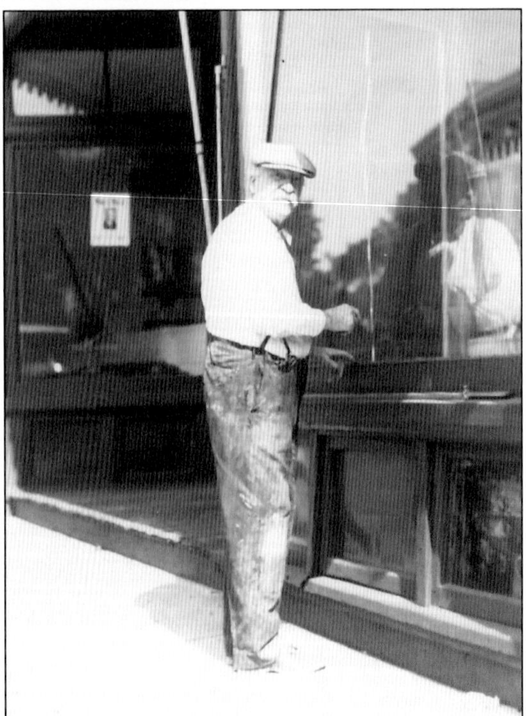

From left to right are Uncle William Duborg, Julia Winter (Amos' mother), Chris Duborg, John Duborg, Amos Winter, and William Winter in front of the Hillholm barn with a touring car. Note Amos' gloves and hat, far different from what he wore at Sugarloaf and in the woods. William, his brother, was a Kingfield selectman for twenty-three years, twenty of those years as chairman. H.G. Winter & Sons was the large lumber products firm in Kingfield. Emil E. Winter Jr. ran an insurance agency on Main Street and had big lumber interests.

Lovella A. Norton is shown here in 1936. He was the wood products expert-contractor-carpenter who actually built Hillholm. Norton eventually established his own wood products company.

Seven

Doers and Shakers

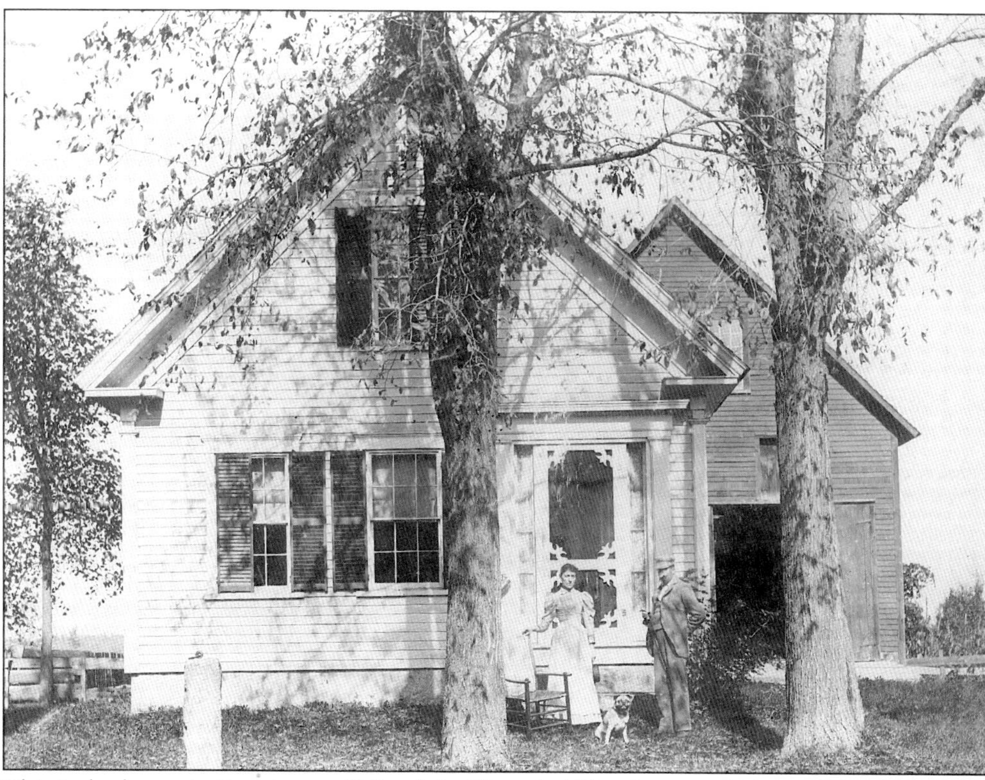

This is the home in Farmington Falls of the Hannibal Hamlin most Mainers don't know. The one they do know was vice president of this country during Abraham Lincoln's first term. This photograph was taken between 1890 and 1906.

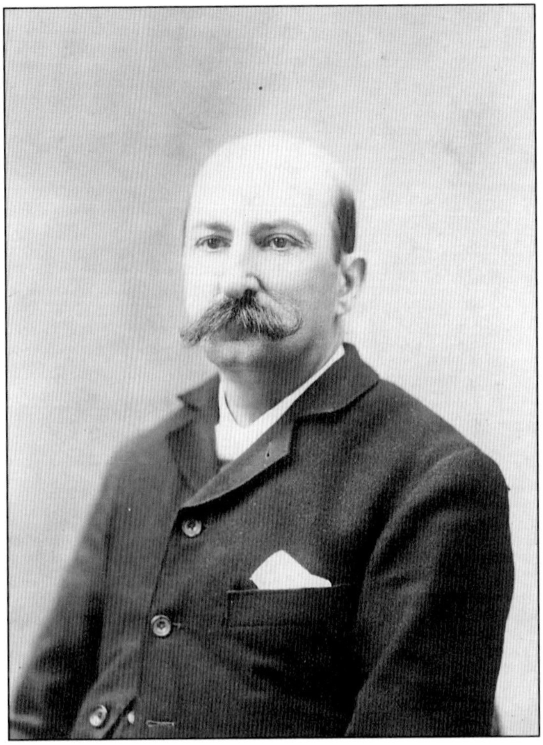

Here is the unknown (relatively) Hannibal Hamlin, who was the Farmington or Farmington Falls postmaster for a time.

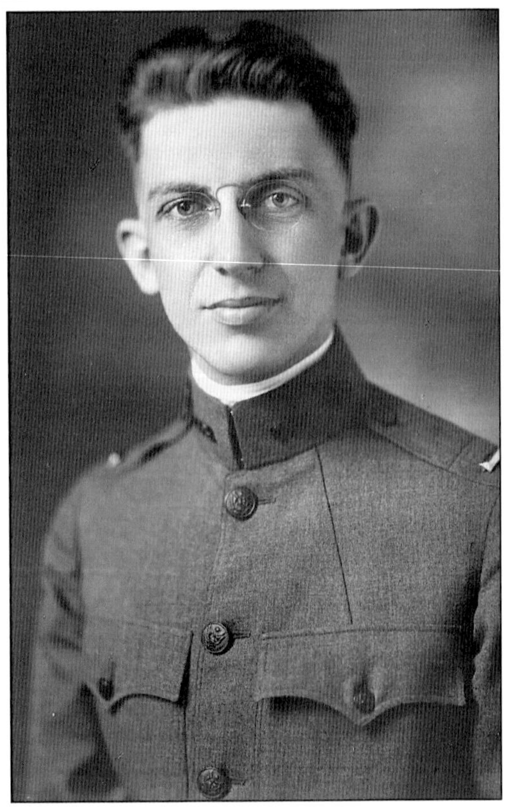

Ben Stinchfield taught French thirty-six years at the Allen-Stevenson School for Boys in New York City but came home summers to Farmington Falls. Much of his summer time and later years were spent in labors for the Nordica Memorial Association, which succeeded in preserving the home of diva Lillian Nordica. He is shown as a first lieutenant in the U.S. Army during World War I. Stinchfield was ninety-two when he died in New York in 1984.

Doris Lake lived on Lake Avenue in Farmington. She died in 1983. The curls are *c.* 1910s. She was the daughter of Minna and Stephen Lake.

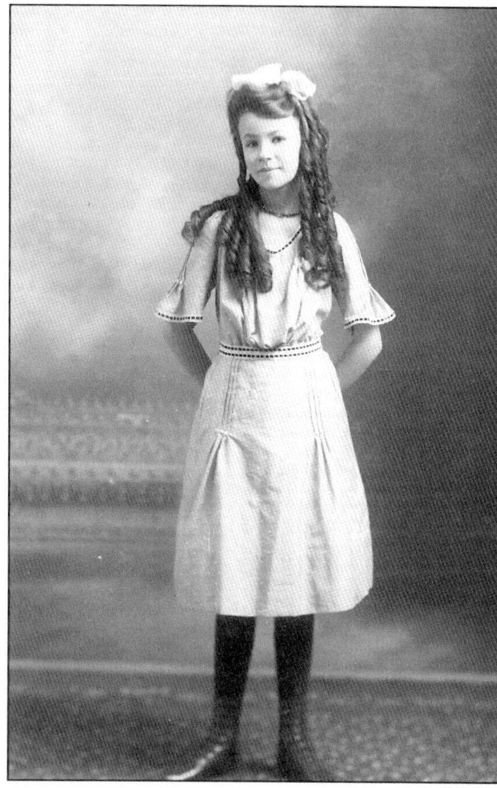

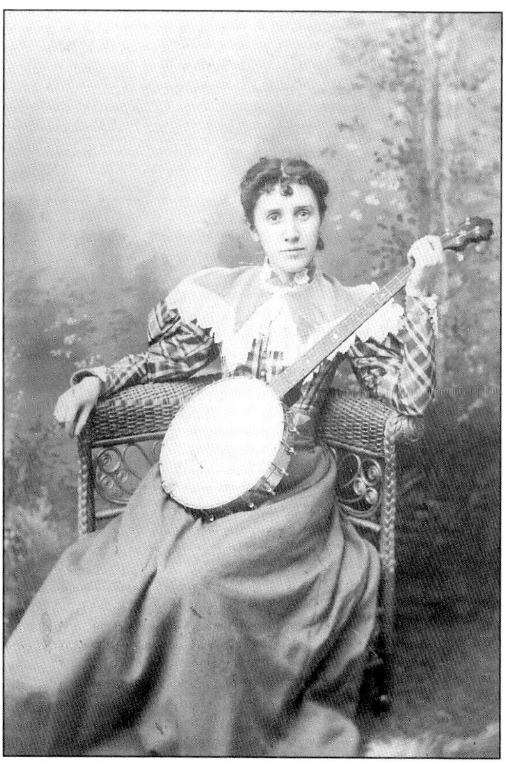

The semi-soulful eyes and banjo (or is it a mandolin?) belong to Margaret Jenkins Avery of Farmington, *c.* 1900s.

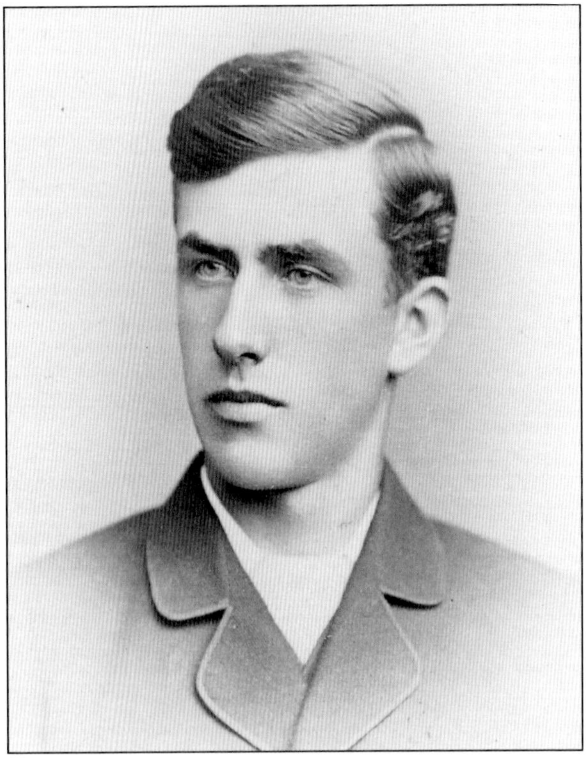

Elmer E. Richards, prominent Farmington attorney, *c.* 1880s. He was also Register of Probate for Franklin County, county attorney, clerk of courts, and president of the First National Bank of Farmington.

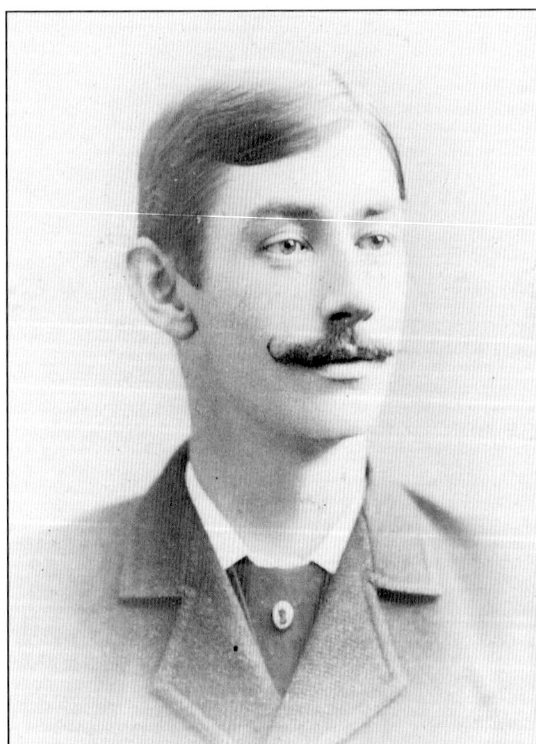

Edmund R. Richards, brother of Elmer. Edmund was, like Elmer, a Bates College graduate. He later became the editor of the *Wood River News-Miner* in Hailey, Idaho.

Floramund E. Voter, born in 1848, was the man most instrumental in organizing the Farmers' Cooperative Telephone Company in Farmington and was its general manager sixteen years and treasurer for twenty years. He was the town clerk at one time, the president of the First Unitarian Society of Farmington, and was the co-owner of Voter and Knowlton and Voter and Weber, insurance agencies, *c.* 1920s.

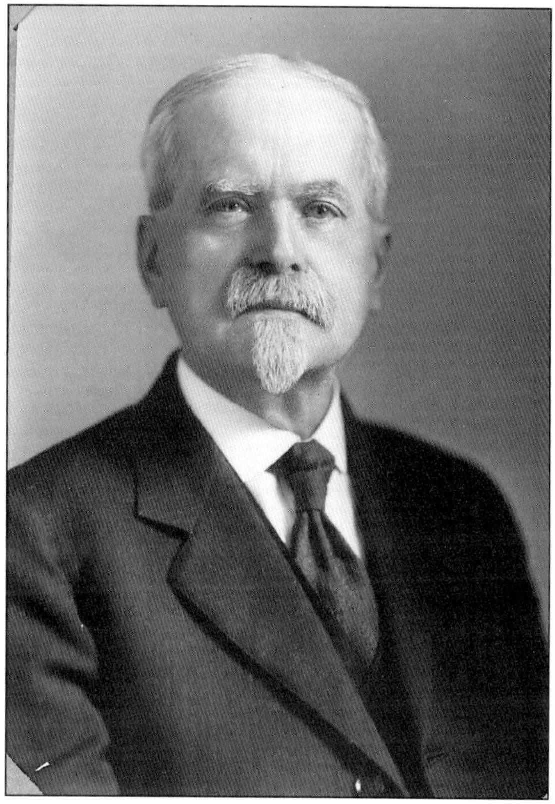

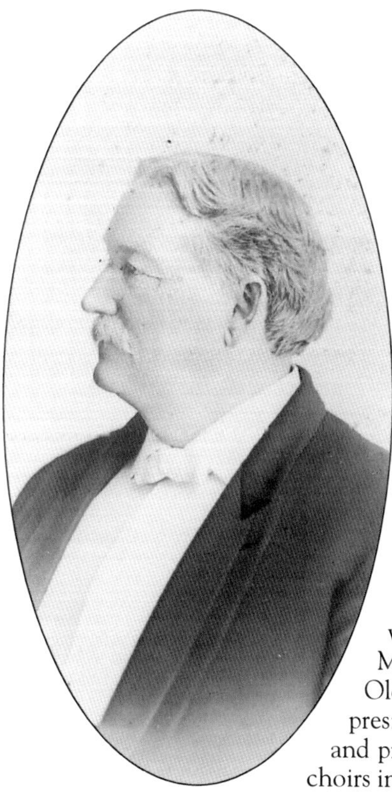

George C. Purington, a Bowdoin College graduate, was principal of Farmington State Normal School from 1883 to 1909, was elected Farmington fire chief at one time, was grand commander of Maine's Grand Commandery Masons, was the Sunday school superintendent at the Old South Congregational Church, was the founder and president of the Farmington Public Library and the founder and president of the Maine Civic League, and was a leader of choirs in addition to playing the flute.

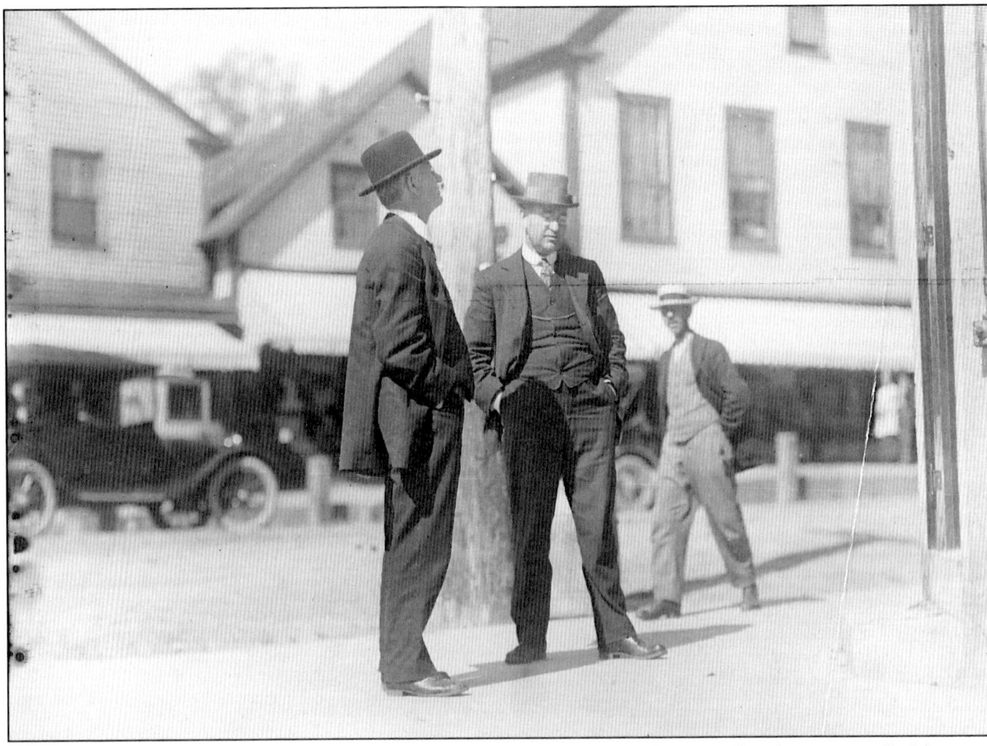

Judge Josiah Thompson (left) was clerk of courts for Franklin County, postmaster during the early 1890s in Farmington, Farmington municipal court judge from 1897 to 1900, and judge of probate from 1900 into the 1920s. He is shown here with W. Raymond Davis, c. early 1920s.

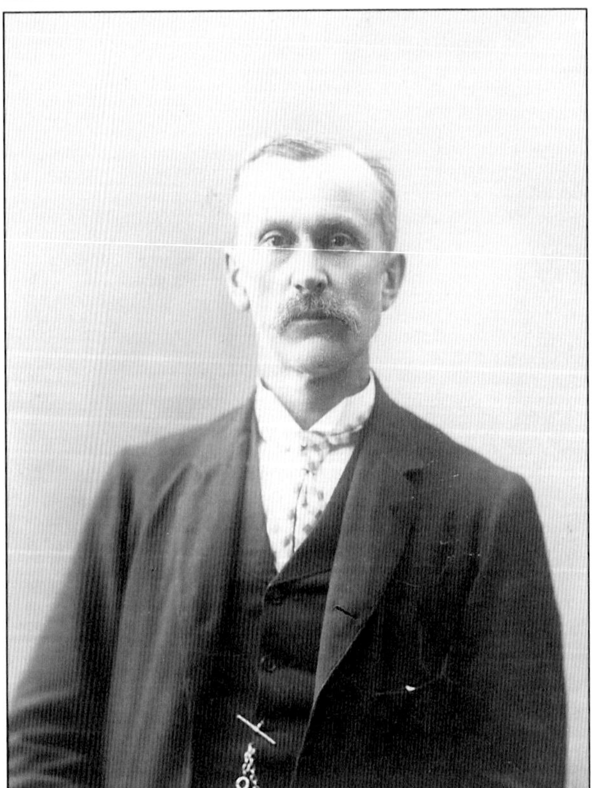

Leonard Atwood of Farmington posed in 1900. He invented the elevator and a patented reel for fishing, and was the owner of a metal products company.

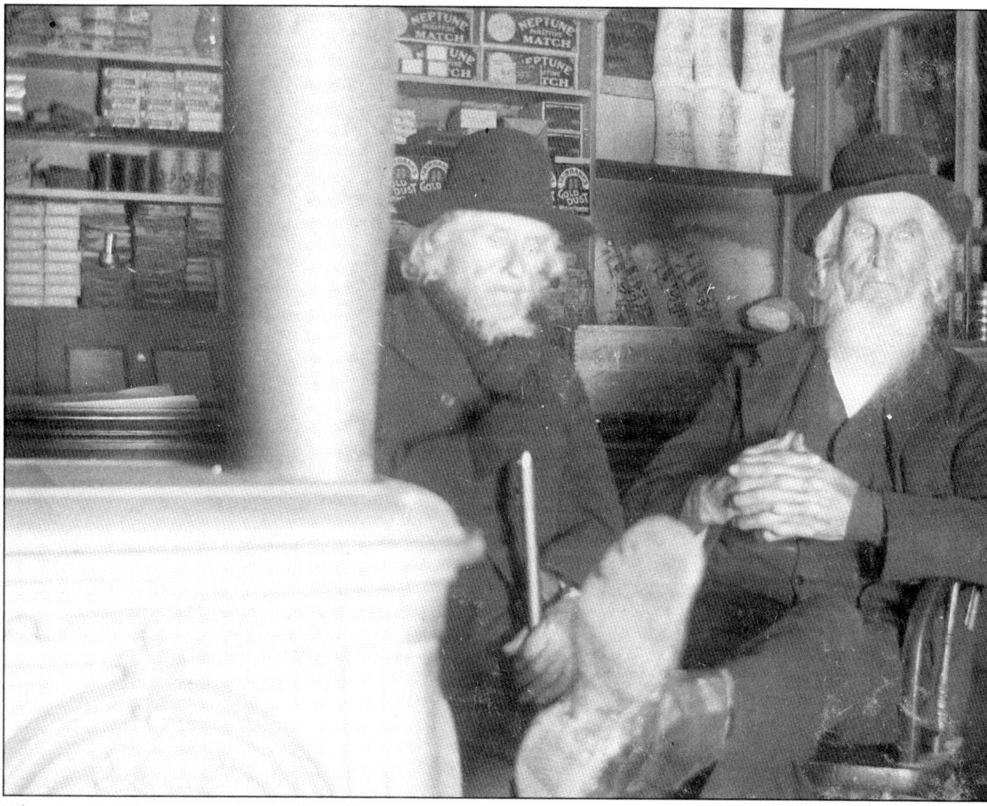

They're liable to grow people old in Farmington. Cathers Drummond (left) was ninety-six years, nine months, and twenty-one days old in 1897. He died on January 19, 1899. With him in a grocery store is John Stewart, only eighty-six.

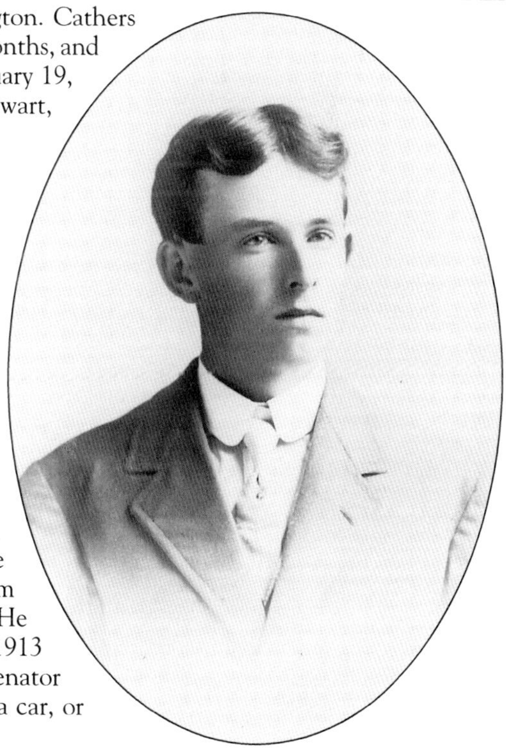

Luther G. Whittier in his 1909 Farmington High School photo. Whittier, who lived until he was ninety-nine, won election to the Maine House of Representatives for the 1965–66 term on his seventh try for a seat as a Democrat. He was in Bowdoin College's famous class of 1913 along with Sumner T. Pike and former U.S. Senator Paul Douglas. Whittier never married, drove a car, or had a telephone.

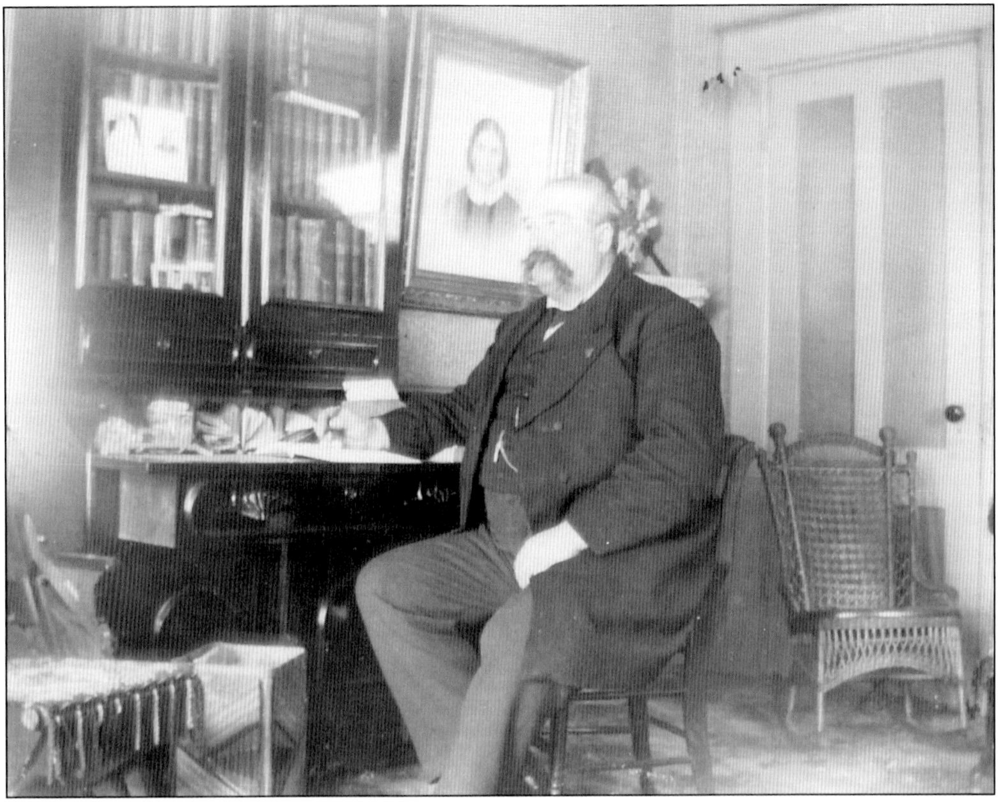

Dr. Alonzo B. Adams of Wilton was chairman of that town's 1903 centennial celebration.

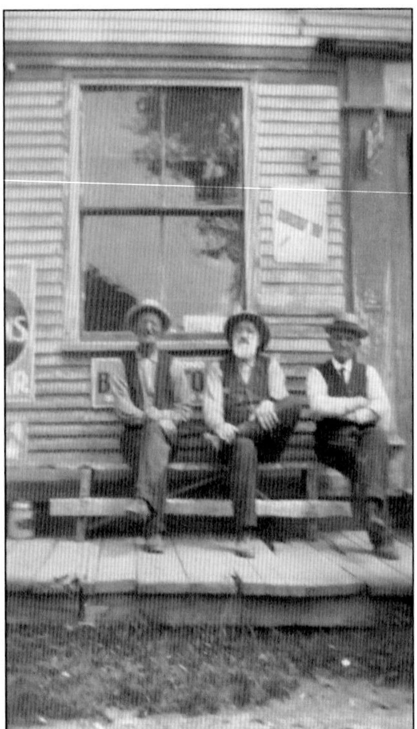

From left to right in front of Whibley's Store, East Wilton, are Oscar Lothrop, C. Naylor Adams, and Charles Whibley, *c.* 1920s. Industry in the area started in East Wilton, but eventually expanding to Wilton.

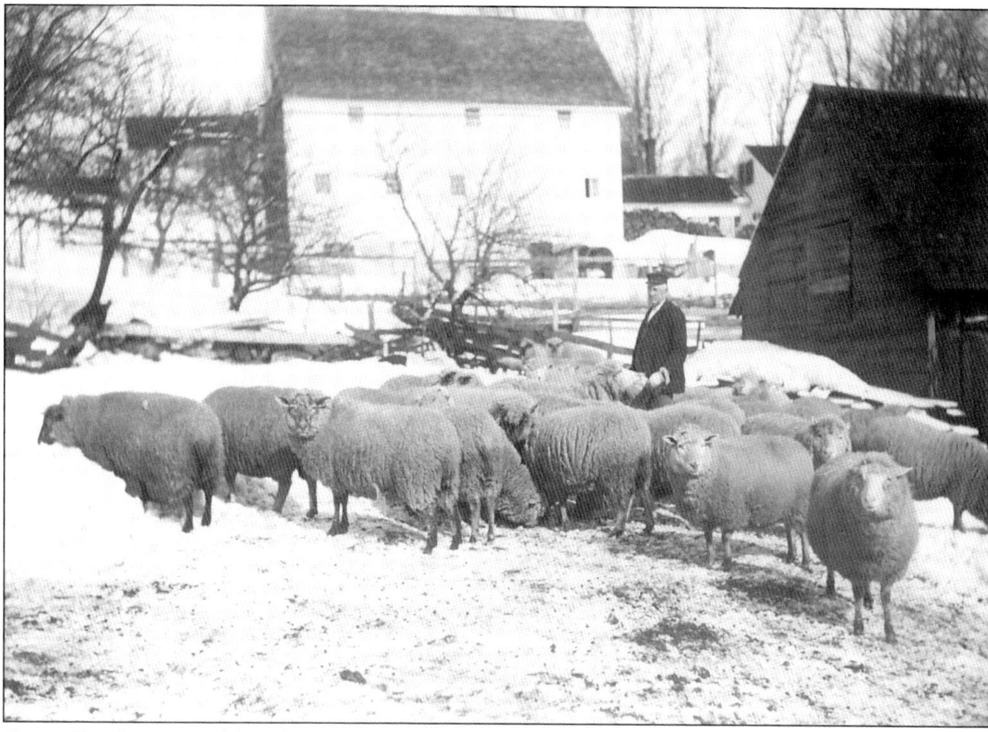

Cyrus Fenderson and his sheep in Wilton, *c.* 1900. In the 1860s, Fenderson led a flourishing band in the town. His home was on High Street.

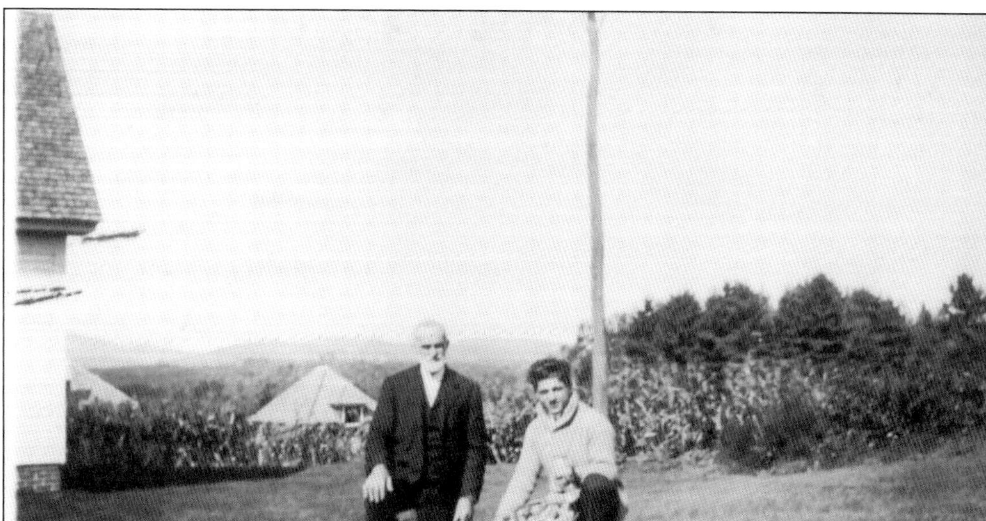

Rawson C. Fuller of Wilton (left) and his grandson, *c.* 1913–14. Fuller, who fought in the Civil War, was born on December 13, 1836, and died on April 6, 1916. He left money to the town of Wilton with the interest to go to repairing and building sidewalks. Fuller lived near the G.H. Bass and Company factory and built a double tenement house on Highland Avenue, Wilton, about 1906.

Acknowledgments

As always, I'd first like to thank Earle Shettleworth, Director of the Maine Historic Preservation Commission, for all his efforts to help. Photographs from Earle provide a base on which I can build themes for the chapters of each book.

Robert N. Bass, former treasurer of G.H. Bass and Company, gave about every kind of assistance possible. He supplied a list of potential sources as well as pictures and information about his family. Stella Breton supplied very useful information and photos of G.H. Bass and Company.

For Wilton, Keith Brann, President of the Wilton Historical Society, and Harold Karkos, who knows as much about the history of that town as anyone, gave great aid. In Farmington, it was Larry Dubord, President of the Farmington Historical Society, and C. Robert Tyler, who, like Harold Karkos, knows as much about his town of Farmington as anyone. Professor Emeritus Gwilym R. Roberts of the University of Maine at Farmington pointed me in the right directions.

Paul Mills and his mother, Katherine, were of huge help on the Mills family as were Peter Mills and Dr. Dora Mills.

For Sugarloaf and Kingfield, Chip Carey pointed me the right way. I owe Chip several so I hope this is to his liking. Donald Taylor of the Sugarloaf Ski Club was of the greatest help. And so was Richard Winnick of the Inn at Winter's Hill, supplying photographs of Amos Winter Sr.

Books on the communities in the Maine State Library were read. Richard Mallett's works on Farmington were especially helpful as was Glenn Parkinson's book on the history of the Maine skiing industry.

Again, I'd like to thank the people at Arcadia, my publisher. Lisa Thompson is my editor and I thank her for her help. The others are Jim Burkinshaw, the executive vice president, Michael Guillory, Aaron Faulkner, Paige Rosella, and Jamie Carter. I guess my flow continues.

Frank H. Sleeper